7/12

Hertfordshire
COUNTY COUNCIL

Community Information

Hertfordshire
COUNTY COUNCIL

Community Information

- 4 MAR 2000

1 1 MAY 2001

2 5 MAY 2001

- 6 NOV 2002

L32a   12\11

Please renew/return this item by the last date shown.

So that your telephone call is charged at local rate, please call the numbers as set out below:

	From Area codes 01923 or 0208:	From the rest of Herts:
Renewals:	01923 471373	01438 737373
Enquiries:	01923 471333	01438 737333
Minicom:	01923 471599	01438 737599

L32b

The Landscape of
the Welsh Marches

The Landscape of
the Welsh Marches

TREVOR ROWLEY

MICHAEL JOSEPH · LONDON

To Linda

First published in Great Britain by Michael Joseph Ltd
27 Wrights Lane, Kensington, London W8
1986

British Library Cataloguing in Publication Data

Rowley, Trevor
The Landscape of the Welsh Marches.
1. Welsh Marches (England and Wales)—History
I. Title
942.4 DA740.B7
ISBN 0-7181-2347-6

Typeset and Printed in Great Britain by
BAS Printers Limited, Over Wallop, Hampshire

Contents

List of Illustrations

Figures

Acknowledgements

Thanks are due to the following for permission to reproduce photographs:
Cambridge Committee for Aerial Photographs: Plates 1, 2, 3, 7, 9, 10, 13, 14, 16, 17, 27, 28, 31, 33, 35, 36, 37, 40, 47, 50, 51, 52, 55, 61, 66
National Monuments Record: Plates 12, 15, 22, 24, 25, 32, 34, 38, 43, 46, 48, 59, 60, 62, 64, 65, 67, 73, 77, 79, 80
Professor Barrie Jones: Plates 6, 8
Richard Muir: Plates 4, 5, 72, 74
Aerofilms: Plates 11, 29, 69
Rowley's House Museum, Shrewsbury: Plate 18
National Museum of Wales: Plates 20, 21

The extract from Poem XXXI from *A Shropshire Lad*, published by Jonathan Cape Ltd, is reproduced by permission of the Society of Authors and the translations from Caratacus are reproduced by kind permission of the translators, Mary Beard and Chloe Chard.

Grateful thanks are also due to Melanie Steiner for producing the finished plans and Shirley Hermon for producing the typescript.

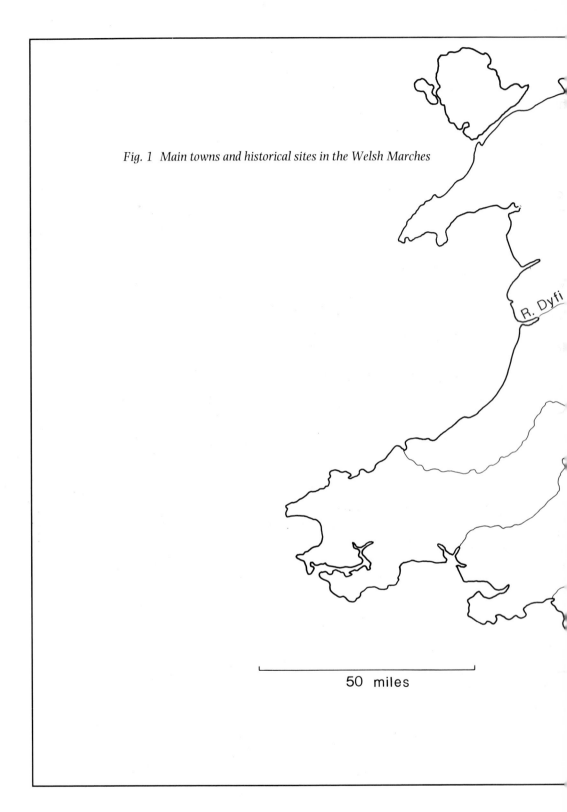

Fig. 1 *Main towns and historical sites in the Welsh Marches*

R. Dyfi

50 miles

Introduction

THE BORDERLAND between England and Wales was first called the Welsh Marches in the decades following the Norman Conquest. They were so named in order to distinguish them from the English land in Norman hands and Welsh land in Welsh hands. The term 'march' comes from the Anglo-Saxon word *mearc*, which simply means boundary. Politically and legally the Marches were distinct from both England and Wales and operated as a separate buffer territory under Norman control. The official recognition of this separate character of the Marches only served to confirm the geographical and historical reality that had been apparent from at least the time of the prehistoric hillforts, which indicate that the Marches formed a border region as early as the Iron Age. It was recognised by the Romans in their attempt to conquer Wales between AD 48 and AD 84, when the Marches formed the north-western boundary of the Roman Empire.

A few centuries later the political domination of the western fringes of Mercia by the Anglo-Saxons culminated in the building of Offa's Dyke. This great earthwork was, as the physical manifestation of the border, to become a symbol of the Marches where the English (and Normans) traded, intermarried and fought with the Welsh.

Although the geographical Marchlands extend from the estuary of the river Dee in the north to the Severn estuary in the south, this book will primarily be concerned with the central Marches – Shropshire and the pre-1974 county of Herefordshire. Both counties take their names from their premier towns which sit on their watery lifelines: Hereford on the gentle Wye and Shrewsbury on the Severn. These two counties, which only assumed their present shapes in 1536 at the time of the Act of Union with Wales, reflect ancient political and cultural territories that can be traced back to before the Roman occupation. The hillforts and castles tell of violence and oppression, while fine churches and elegant market halls tell of peace and prosperity.

The tranquil and largely unbruised Marcher landscape is still essentially rural in character – its towns almost visibly grow out of the surrounding countryside. Agriculture remains the dominant activity, although it is no longer the chief source of employment. Only in recent years has the industrialisation of farming begun to take its toll and to 'sterilise' areas of the Borderland, just as urban development in the 1960s and 1970s succeeded in sterilising many historic town centres, making one indistinguishable from another, in many other parts of the country.

The traditional isolation of the Marchland, however, has largely protected it from the excesses of post-war redevelopment. The 'forgotten' broad belt of countryside, which mainly lies between the river Severn and the Welsh mountains, is thinly populated in comparison with many other parts of Britain; the Industrial Revolution started here, but moved on before inflicting the damage it was to do elsewhere.

It is a nostalgic landscape of deeply engraved leafy lanes and one which over the centuries has inspired many and has produced more than its share of creative artists – William Langland, who came from the Marches (either Ledbury or Cleobury Mortimer) was writing of the Malverns in the fourteenth century. Five centuries later John Masefield, the Poet Laureate, also came from Ledbury. The dramatist William Wycherley (1640–1716) was born at Clive, a few miles to the north of Shrewsbury; while Charles Darwin (1809–82) was actually born in the county town. Wilfred Owen, the First World War poet, was a native of Oswestry, while A. E. Housman (1859–1936), who was originally from Worcestershire, was to produce the most evocative of Welsh Border writing in *A Shropshire Lad* and is now buried under a cherry tree in St Lawrence's churchyard in Ludlow.

The Marches also inspired Mary Webb (1881–1927) to write novels based in the Shropshire countryside, Sir Edward German (1862–1936), author of *Merrie England*, Sir Edward Elgar (1857–1934), and Ralph Vaughan Williams (1872–1958). But it was the nineteenth-century parish priest of Bredwardine, a little village on the Herefordshire Wye, Francis Kilvert, who produced a wonderful diary describing his life and work set in the Border landscape of the 1870s and captured the atmosphere of the region perfectly:

Monnington on Wye   *Tuesday, 6 April 1875*
When I awoke a woodpigeon was crooning from the trees near the house and the early morning sunshine glinted upon the red boles of the gigantic Scotch firs in Monnington Walk. I rose early and went out. The morning was fresh and bright with a slight sunshiny shower flying. Hard by the church porch and on the western side of it I saw what I knew must be the grave of Owen Glendower. And here in the little Herefordshire churchyard within hearing of the rushing of the Wye and close under the shadow of the old grey church the strong wild heart, still now, has rested by the ancient home and roof tree of his kindred since he fell asleep there more than four hundred years ago. It is a quiet peaceful spot.

CHAPTER ONE

The Making of the Marches

THE Welsh Border landscape is one of the most richly varied in the whole of Britain. Its variety consists of plain, upland and mountain, and it is precisely this close juxtaposition of high and low land that has made the region a cultural boundary area for the last two thousand years at least, and a geographical boundary region for far longer. To the north the Cheshire plain gives way abruptly to the Denbigh moors and the Berwyn mountains. In the middle Severn between the river Severn and the river Teme the change is less abrupt, but nonetheless scenically dramatic with the Clee hills, Wenlock Edge and the Stiperstones leading on to the Clun Forest, which forms the eastern edge of the solid Welsh massif. To the south the gentle Herefordshire plain abutts on to the aptly named Black Mountains and the bleak Radnor Forest and further south still the uplands of the Forest of Dean span the southern Wye valley.

1 Lowland meets highland in the Tanat valley in north-western Shropshire

The Marches contain some of the oldest rocks in the world in the form of the Precambrian strata found in the Long Mynd and the Malvern hills. Yet in geological terms the face of much of the Border region is relatively recent, the result of scouring by the Pleistocene ice sheets and the subsequent deposition of their debris, which has given rise to the meres of the Shropshire plain and the gentle lush landscape in the northern part of the Hereford plain.

Because of their diversity the Marches are best divided into smaller distinct geographical regions, running from north to south.

The Cheshire and Shropshire Plains

These plains lie between 250 feet and 350 feet above sea level and consist of a mixture of glacial drift and fluvio-glacial deposits, which in turn have produced soils varying from light sands to heavy loams, in many places obscured on the surface by peat and valley marshes. During the last glaciation, southern Cheshire and northern Shropshire were occupied by two ice sheets, the most significant of which came down from the north by way of the Irish Sea and the Lancashire plain, while the lesser had its source in north Wales. Erratic rocks such as slate, volcanic ash and flint derived from both source-regions are to be found on the plains. On the Shropshire –Cheshire border at Whixall, moss-peat is commercially extracted, giving rise to an obvious conflict between commercial interests and those concerned with the conservation of the natural environment.

In the Ellesmere area there are about three dozen meres and pools of glacial origin. These were formed at the time when the main glaciers were in retreat and large lumps of ice were left behind buried in the glacial debris. As they melted they in turn left behind sizeable depressions which eventually became water-filled lakes. Apart from man-made field ditches most of the meres are fed and drained by slow percolation through the drift on which they lie. This poor drainage, together with associated indifferent soils, has historically limited agricultural activity, but the small lakes, often surrounded by woodland and low glacial hillocks, are most attractive and provide unusual but much frequented lowland beauty spots in a region otherwise better known for its upland scenery. Despite the wide variety of rock types found in this area there is little natural building stone, and the vast majority of buildings are half-timbered or made of brick.

To the north-west, in the region of Oswestry and Wrexham, the geography changes dramatically, with steep sloping hills and valleys heralding the nearby mountains of north Wales. These are made up of carboniferous Ordovician and Silurian rocks which in the area of the Berwyns are reinforced by extensive igneous intrusions. To the south the Shropshire plain gently gives way to the Severn valley, whose own broad flood plain has traditionally provided easy access to the heart of central Wales. It is believed that before the last glaciation the Severn flowed northwards to the Dee or Mersey or eastwards to the Trent. As the ice retreated the material it left behind impeded the river's former course and eventually it re-established itself flowing southwards through a narrow gorge, which glacial meltwater had cut under pressure across the line of Wenlock Edge. Hence below Shrewsbury as far as Buildwas the Severn flows in a wide plain, but it then enters the steep-sided Ironbridge gorge, flowing through it for several miles.

Across the southern central section of the Shropshire plain there is an outcrop of low hills made up mainly of New Red Sandstone (Keuper marls, siltstones and sandstones). Steep-sided sandstone hills such as Grinshill, Hawkestone hill and Haughmond hill contrast dramatically with the rest of the flat Shropshire plain and over the centuries they have provided a valuable source of building stone for places such as Shrewsbury Castle, Shrewsbury Abbey and many local parish churches. Elsewhere on the plain the traditional building material has been timber. However, since the sixteenth century brick has been extensively used and today it, together with Welsh slate, dominates the modest towns and villages. To the east the lower Keuper marl sandy soils give rise to extensive heathland, particularly around Hodnet, to the east of the Tern valley.

The Wealdmoors

The Wealdmoors form a distinctive low-flying sub-region to the east of Shrewsbury, although geologically they are similar to the north Shropshire meres and mosses. They consist of a basin in which peat has accumulated since the disappearance of the Pleistocene ice sheet. In the nineteenth century large-scale drainage operations undertaken by the Duke of Sutherland finally transformed the area and divided it up into large regular arable fields. Today the Wealdmoors present a deceptively tranquil rural landscape, which effectively masks the treacherous and inhospitable reputation this region enjoyed in antiquity, when it was dangerous to stray from the few well-established causeways that crossed the marshes.

The Wrekin and the Shropshire Coalfield

The Shropshire coalfield formed the basis for the only extensive industrial area in the Marches apart from the Forest of Dean. The coalfield extends from Lilleshall in the north-east to Coalbrookdale and Broseley in the south-west and from Wrockwardine in the west to Oakengates in the east, forming a well-defined triangle. It is a relatively small area made up of valleys and escarpments, where settlement and landscape have been heavily influenced by piecemeal mining over the centuries. The ancient volcanic wedge which forms the Wrekin reaching up to over 1000 feet makes up the core of this region. It erupts out of a relatively low-lying area and appears to be higher than it actually is; its highly distinctive hogsback profile makes it a dominant feature and one which has acted as a symbolic landmark for inhabitants of the central Welsh Marches over the centuries. In antiquity the greater part of the area was relatively uninhabited, although close to the Severn which cuts southwards through this area there has always been some sort of settlement on the sand and gravel of the river terraces. The area has always been well wooded, but heath and moorland are found on the spreads of boulder clay and carboniferous deposits. The developing new town of Telford now occupies much of the area but evidence of its important industrial past is contained in the flourishing Ironbridge Gorge Museum.

The Silurian Hills of South Shropshire and Northern Herefordshire

This area displays considerable geographical variety. The most impressive feature is one of the best-known escarpments in Britain – Wenlock Edge, today a wooded scarp running from Much Wenlock in the north-east to Craven Arms in the south-west. This remarkably straight cliff, unbroken for many miles, is formed by an outcrop of a richly fossiliferous Silurian limestone. The Wenlock escarpment, which historically consisted of forest and moorland, barely reaches to 1000 feet yet the heights can be very inhospitable.

Running parallel to this ridge often less than a mile to the east is a similar ridge made up of another sort of limestone known as the Aymestrey. Between the two ridges is a discontinuous hollow, Hope Dale, which passes into Corve Dale, a beautiful broad fertile valley connecting Much Wenlock with Ludlow.

The limestone scarps are often wooded but with bare grey crags. These beds have been (and still are) extensively quarried. The gentler eastern dip slopes, based on the shales, are much more fertile, and are often cultivated almost up to the crest of the scarp. Both in Corve Dale and in Ape Dale there are many small villages built mostly of the yellow-grey local stone, which does not weather well.

Rising eastwards out of Corve Dale is a great stretch of undulating country, with many fields of heavy red soil marking an outcrop of Old Red Sandstone, the underlying rock of a large tract of the central and southern

Marches. Standing out above it are two quite distinctive flat-topped hills
– Brown Clee and Titterstone Clee. The Clees are capped by a layer of resistant
dolerite giving rise to the craggy north-west face which makes their summits
such prominent landmarks in the country around Ludlow.

*2 The river Severn cutting through the Wenlock escarpment in the lower Ironbridge gorge.
In the foreground are the pottery and tile works at Coalport and Jackfield. The large wooded
area on the right is Madeley Wood, beyond which lie Ironbridge and Coalbrookdale*

Where so many rocks are available there is naturally a great diversity of building materials. Yet half-timbered and brick buildings are still abundant, notably in Much Wenlock and in Ludlow, where the red tiles, weathering to a deeper tint than the bricks, provide the dominant colour. Ludlow Castle is built of yellow-grey Silurian stones while in the Onny valley near Horderley the main building material is a local Ordovician sandstone which is quarried in blocks of a variety of shapes and sizes and often has purple and yellow-green stripes running through it.

Over the Herefordshire border one marked area of regional diversity is the vale of Wigmore, a former glacial lake that has left deep deposits of morainic material which are surrounded in a horseshoe pattern by the eroded Bringewood anticline. At one stage the lake overflowed from the lowest part of the encircling hills to create a deeply cut gorge, near the present village of Downton-on-the-Rock. After the ice receded and the glacial lake drained away, the river Teme used this outlet and it became part of the river's circuitous course. There are other striking examples of the effect of glaciation on the local topography in this area, including the gorge of the river Ludd between Sned Wood and Mere valley. These gorges and dry valleys created by short violent rushes of water at the margin of the ice fields have dissected this foothill countryside into quite distinct blocks.

Difficult topography, generally poor soils and the bleakness of the area render the uplands of marginal agricultural value, and cultivation has traditionally been confined to the valley lowlands. Until the seventeenth century much of this area was included in the Forest of Mochtree.

The Shropshire Hills

To the north-west of the Silurian uplands lie what are considered to be the true Shropshire hills. In this area a wide range of rocks create a scene of extraordinary variation where the relation of scenery to geographical structure is probably better displayed than in any other part of Britain. The general lie of the country here runs south-east to north-west. Caer Caradoc erupts steeply from the Stretton valley in a slope broken only by the occasional dark crag, but its eastern face is more irregular, with ribs of exposed rock extending up its flanks. Most of the hill is composed of Precambrian volcanic lavas and ashes. This long narrow hill is cut off by a great fault along its north-western side, a fact which accounts for the smooth face overlooking Church Stretton. In the same alignment are other similar hills, Ragleth to the south-west and the Lawley to the north-east.

Across the narrow faulted trough in which Church Stretton lies is the great bare mass of Long Mynd which, although rising higher than Caradoc, is less impressive in its outlines. On the summit is a smooth-topped plateau which near its borders is deeply cut by narrow V-shaped valleys, of which Cardingmill valley is the best known. Like Caradoc, this plateau area is built up of Precambrian rocks, but because these rocks are softer and have been worn away more, Long Mynd looks smoother than its neighbours.

The country west of Long Mynd brings us to Wales and into scenery characteristic of the principality – between Montgomery and Minsterley there are many irregular peaks and much bleak upland. This country was largely formed by Ordovician rocks of the Welsh type, rather more rugged than the east Shropshire variety, made up chiefly of slates and shales, but also including beds of volcanic ash and lava. The harder beds now stand out as ridges running in a general north-easterly direction, emphasising the prevailing Caledonian 'grain' of the structures. The most pronounced ridge, which lies near the western border of the Long Mynd, is the Stiperstones, which was formed by very hard, light-coloured quartzite, and stands out in bare, tor-like crags, the most dramatic being the imposing landmark known as the Devil's Chair. There are deposits of lead and silver in this area which have been quarried both in antiquity and the recent past.

The Herefordshire Plain

To the south of the Silurian upland is a far gentler landscape, the Hereford plain. These unexpected western lowlands occupy something like 65% of the ancient county of Herefordshire. They extend from the Shropshire border in the north to the Forest of Dean in the south, the Welsh border in the west to the foothills of the Malverns in the east. They are set within a discontinuous frame of hills, and are interrupted by the twin uplands of Dinmore and Wormsley which divide the region into two main sub-regions, the plain of Hereford and the plain of Leominster. The plains are made up almost exclusively of Old Red Sandstone, which here consists of soft beds of red and grey marl. At intervals there are beds of more compact sandstone and cemented limestone which have formed tabular hills such as Wormsley and Dinmore, rising spectacularly from the surrounding lowlands, flat-topped plateaux with steep wooded scarp slopes.

The geomorphological history of these hills emphasises the importance of glacial processes in the development of the Border landscape. At one time the isolated hills formed part of a continuous plateau surface, but erosion has breached the harder beds and bitten deeply into the underlying marls. The results of this process can clearly be seen at Wormsley, a former upland which has been cut into to make three separate hill areas, Merryhill, Credenhill and Nupton hills.

In the extreme south-east of the plain the absence of glacial drift has given the countryside a more mellow appearance, and it has accordingly been traditionally a more prosperous area of arable farming. Ross-on-Wye, with its sandstone buildings, provides a striking contrast to the other largely half-timbered Herefordshire market towns. Eastwards beyond the Wye lies the Forest of Dean which in Herefordshire is represented by the still heavily wooded Penyard hill.

Although generally speaking the flaky local sandstone is not a particularly good building material it has been used extensively, particularly in churches and other public buildings. In this area many of the roofs were covered with a local fossil sandstone until Welsh slates became readily available during the last century. The remarkable Romanesque church at Kilpeck is built of the local sandstone which becomes flaky and pliable as it weathers. Throughout most of Herefordshire timber has traditionally been the main material used in domestic buildings and accounts for the wealth of late and immediately post-medieval farms and manor houses found in this region.

The North-eastern Herefordshire Uplands

The Herefordshire plain is surrounded by uplands. In the north-east are the north-east Herefordshire uplands, or Bromyard plateau, consisting principally of the Dittonian sandstone which forms much of south-eastern Shropshire and north-west Worcestershire. The Herefordshire section is cut off from the main plateau by the river Teme, which forms the basis of the ancient country boundary.

The plateau (500–800 feet) is dissected by narrow valleys, draining to the river Frome. On the plateau soils tend to be shallow and poor, frequently occupied by moorland, but they are deeper in valley areas where streams have cut down into the underlying marls. The landscape owes its appearance partly to the large number of parks found there and partly to the fact that it remains one of the major fruit-growing centres in the Marches.

There is one geological curiosity that has made a small but impressive contribution to the Border landscape – the post-glacial calcareous tufa, or travertine, found in the Teme valley near Shelsley Walsh. This tufa is formed around the outlet of a spring whose waters are charged with a lime solution which leaves a spongy soft deposit, easily worked but none the less relatively durable. It has been used in a number of churches in the county, particularly during the Norman period and most notably in the fine Romanesque church of St Michael, Moccas, on the other side of Herefordshire, where the isolated building stands dramatically remote within a landscaped park.

The Woolhope Dome

To the south-east of Hereford lies the unusual and complex Woolhope dome, a remarkable Silurian outcrop. The core is made up of Llandovery flags, encircled by a ring of Wenlock limestones, and outside this there is a wide deposit of Ludlow rocks. These are fossil-rich rocks forming a complex scarp and vale topography. The dome, a major feature of the Herefordshire land-scape, is very distinctive, consisting of alternating scarps and valleys. Settle-ment is sparse and the area has a heavy woodland cover intermixed with moorland. In antiquity the limestone beds were extensively quarried for building material.

The Malvern Hills

The oldest rocks in Herefordshire, those of Precambrian formation, are largely deeply buried beneath later deposits, exposed only along a narrow tract in the extreme east of the country. These provide a striking natural boundary with the former county of Worcestershire in the form of the Malvern hills. The water table appears as a regular springline at about 600 feet above sea level, corresponding to the limit of cultivation and of historic settlement.

The Malverns rise to just over 1200 feet and their steep slopes are gener-ally used only for rough grazing or woodland. There has been surprisingly little extensive quarrying of the igneous rock on the Herefordshire side of the border. The sharp crest of the Malverns spine is marked by traces of former occupation and by an ancient boundary, the Shire Ditch, created in its present form as a hunting boundary in the Middle Ages, but almost certainly marking a much earlier division.

South Central Herefordshire Uplands (Archenfield)

Moving in a clockwise direction around the hilly frame that encompasses Herefordshire we come to the south central hills. These consist of harder beds of the Old Red Sandstone. They extend from the Wye in the east to the Monnow valley in the west, and are drained to the south-east by several small Monnow tributaries. They rise from just under 100 feet on the Wye to over 600 feet overlooking the Monnow and to 1200 feet on Garway hill. This is not only a geographically distinctive region, but also culturally, as it remained Celtic until the twelfth century, and the vast majority of place-names are Welsh. Reputedly the Welsh and English names of the district,

Erging and Archenfield, are derived from the Roman iron-working settlement of *Ariconium* but as this lies some distance away a few miles to the east of Ross, there must be some doubt about this theory.

Because of the irregular terrain the area has been characterised by a thin scatter of dispersed settlement, largely devoid of nucleated villages. Today it carries a surprisingly thin woodland cover, except in the extreme west overlooking the Monnow and in the slower eastern meanders of the Wye, which have a high concentration of orchards.

The Black Mountain Foothills

Some of the most impressive and 'Welsh' landscape in the Marches is to be found in the deeply dissected upland plateaux which border the Black Mountains. These occupy some hundred square miles of Old Red Sandstone extending into the adjoining pre-1974 counties of Brecon and Monmouth. The geological structure of this region is relatively simple: over much of the area the rocks are horizontal and, because of differing degrees of resistance, erosion has produced a tabular relief. The whole region is slightly tilted to the south-east, so that the highest hills occur on the northern and western fringes. Few summits rise above 1000 feet, and the topography consists of a gently rolling plateau lying between 600 and 1000 feet deeply trenched by the narrow parallel valleys of the Olchon, Escley Brook, Upper Monnow, Dulas and Dore.

These five valleys dominate the human and economic geography of this corner of the Marches. The broadest and most fertile of them is the valley of the Dore, so called because of an adaptation of the Celtic word *dur* meaning water. The Dore stands in the golden valley, whose name stems from a mistranslation of the river's name. The present river is too small for the valley, the bottom of which is up to a mile wide in places; it is therefore probable that during the final glaciation ice extended down the valley as far as Vowchurch and on its retreat created a small temporary lake in the vicinity of Dorstone, and so accounts for the flat marshy appearance of that area today. The presence of glacial deposits as well as downwash for the adjacent slopes makes the Golden Valley live up to its name at least as far as its agricultural prosperity is concerned.

The valleys have naturally monopolised settlement and communication in the region giving it a north-north-west–south-south-east grain; movement from east to west is strictly limited by their deeply engrained courses. One of the consequences is that the upland areas have traditionally been very isolated. Even today, extensive spreads of woodland and rough stone grazing are typical; the density of population is still low and settlements are few and scattered.

The Forest of Dean

The Forest of Dean has an average height of about 650 feet sloping gradually from north to south. The plateau drops away rapidly on all sides and this helps give the region its particular character. It consists of a number of different types of rocks including Old Red Sandstone, which in places incorporates a quartz conglomerate which has often been used as a building material in the past, and which the Romans used for making roads. The conglomerate gives rise to steep-sided hills along the plateau edge. On the inner margin of the outcrop of conglomerate there is a belt of carboniferous limestone containing pockets of haematite which was quarried in antiquity, particularly in the area known as the Scowles.

In the middle of the Forest of Dean basin are the coal measures, the seams varying in thickness from two to five feet. One of the sandstone beds, the Pennant, is particularly thick and resistant to erosion and accordingly underlies much of the high plateau country in the northern part of the forest centred on Ruardean hill. The Pennant sandstone has been extensively used as a local building material.

The area was designated as a special hunting area even before the Norman Conquest, and afterwards became one of the great forests of medieval England, renowned for both its timber and its coal and ironstone mining.

The Lower Wye Valley

Southwards from Ross, the Wye has cut a course through the edge of the Forest of Dean plateau. In the slower section the river flows in a series of large meander loops, each meander loop having a steep river cliff on its outer side and a more gently sloping slip-off slope within the loop. Although this basic form is repeated many times there are significant variations from one meander to the next, due in part to the fact that the river crosses many different types of rock, each of which gives rise to a characteristic valley form. Welsh Bicknor, for instance, is a long spur of shale with a gentle slope down to the flood plain, while at Symond's Yat the river cuts into the carboniferous limestone. These meanders are similar to those of the Dee at Llangollen and are unusual in that meanders are characteristic of rivers winding across broad alluvial plains, and are not usually associated with deep gorges. The Wye swings in big curves, some of them three miles wide, and in several, as in the bend at Symond's Yat, the river almost forms a complete loop.

These meanders are presumed to have started when the Wye flowed over a wide flood plain in an area of low relief. As the sea level fell, probably in several stages, the river was able to cut down its bed, but there had been no time for valley widening and so its meanders became deeply entrenched.

3 A vertical view of one of the river Wye meanders as it cuts its way through the Forest of Dean. Symond's Yat is on the left-hand side at the neck of the meander, and Huntsham Court, where there is evidence of a Roman villa, lies in the middle of the loop

Climate

Climatically the Marches conform largely to the West Midland pattern, with an average precipitation of 27–30 inches a year. However, moving westwards precipitation increases markedly and on the summits of the Black Mountains and the Long Mynd it exceeds 55 inches. There is also a significant shortening in the length of the growing season in the western mountains, so much so that it is claimed that in the Black Mountains there are eleven months of winter and one month of bad weather.

This, then, is the canvas on which man has etched his works over the centuries. The Marches have much land which has been too steep or too wet for fertile agriculture for most of its history. This, together with the remoteness of the region, has meant that it has never been populous. Accordingly it has changed very slowly and man's works once created tend to survive longer here than in most other parts of England.

CHAPTER TWO

Early Man in the Marches

EARLY MAN probably arrived in the area now known as the Welsh Marches anything between half a million and a million years ago. Despite this enormous timespan and the ponderous prehistoric forts that dominate many Marcher hilltops, evidence of early prehistoric man is sparse. The repeated glaciations which did so much to give the Borderland its final physical face removed most evidence of very early man from the landscape. It is true that some of the higher upland areas such as the Black Mountains, Caer Caradoc, the Long Mynd and the Long Mountain would have protruded above the glaciers, but the ice of the final glaciation covered much of the Borderland with a thick deposit, which in the Herefordshire plain was up to 600 feet thick. Immense blankets of glacial moraine were then deposited over most of the areas which would earlier have been occupied by Lower and Middle Palaeolithic (Early and Middle Old Stone Age) man. Although a meagre scattering of hand axes and flint cores have been found on hilly ground above 600 feet, little material of any significance has survived. However, even if we were able to compile the complete archaeological record of the surviving material for this great span of prehistory, it is probable that there would be little of any substance within the modern landscape for us to look at: early man was essentially itinerant, moving across the countryside in small groups in constant pursuit of food.

The Old Stone Age

We do not know when man first appeared on the scene in the Marches. Nevertheless two things are fairly clear: firstly that the geography of the region would have been very different from that of today, and secondly that for many tens of thousands of years man's presence in the region was episodic. Throughout the Old Stone Age man was knitted into the natural environment, he was a hunter-gatherer who responded to the movement of herds of wild animals, which in turn responded to changing seasonal and climatic conditions. Man was a migrant and did not create permanent settlements, nor did he erect monuments either for the living or for the dead, except perhaps of a rudimentary kind. He was in tune with his environment, of which he was an integral part rather than its manager.

Although there were occupants of the Marches before the last glaciation (12,000 BC) the first substantial traces of man in the Borderland dates only from between about 10,000 and 8000 BC. Evidence from this period is largely derived from a few caves found in the carboniferous limestone deposits of southern Herefordshire. The most important of these is King Arthur's Cave which overlooks the Wye landmark of Symond's Yat in southern Herefordshire. The cave is located in a narrow valley between the Dowards leading to the Wye valley, from which there was presumably once a lake or a series of lakes in the Whitchurch/Goodrich area, before the Wye had inscribed its present channel. King Arthur's Cave has two chambers with an entrance about 25 feet wide and is spectacularly situated in woodland about 300 feet above the river Wye. The cave was first excavated in 1871 by the Revd W. S. Symonds, who found the remains of numerous extinct animals, including mammoth, woolly rhinoceros, hyena, bison and cave bear, lying beneath a thick layer of stalagmites. Flint tools found here show that it was occupied both in the Old and Middle Stone Ages. It would appear that to begin with the people lived inside the cave, but later, perhaps as the climate improved, moved to the mouth and ledge, where the ashes of their fires and the bones of the animals they hunted have been found in deposits up to six feet deep. The siting of this cave is remarkably similar to the Old Stone Age caves found in the Cheddar Gorge. Such prominent landmarks and lookouts appear to have been attractive to our earliest settlers, and gorges and narrow valleys with caves would have been particularly important as they would have enabled the movement of herds of animals, such as wild horses, to be carefully monitored and impeded.

Close to King Arthur's Cave there is another cave which is also named after an Arthurian character, Merlin's Cave. Excavations at Merlin's Cave by the Bristol Spelaeological Society have located a possible Old Stone Age flint implement, but any stratification which once existed has been obliterated by later iron ore mining.

As the ice sheets receded the climate improved and more regular hunting and trading patterns evolved. It is possible that after the middle of the eighth millenium BC, with the spread of hazel, pine and oak forests, Mesolithic man was more active in the Marches, but although new finds have recently been made in upland Wales and the West Midlands, the relative absence of evidence from the Borderland is disappointing. The earliest flints found along the Clun–Clee ridgeway, a route which was later much used for trading in the Neolithic and Bronze Age, do however date from the Middle Stone Age (Mesolithic), suggesting an emerging pattern of communication. Scattered finds of the Middle Stone Age have been found elsewhere in the region, but no substantial occupation sites have been located. It has been suggested by Dr Stanford, an archaeologist who has given considerable thought to early man in the Marches, that it may be useful to investigate around the edges of the old glacial lakes at places such as Wigmore, the middle valley of the Teme, along the Church Stretton hills and in the valley of the middle Severn. Such locations would have been favourite places for hunting parties who would have taken wildfowl from the Marches to supplement their diet of venison and wild pig from the forest. In such locations it is possible that there would be deposits of animal and fish bones and shells as well as scatters of flint left behind from flint tool making. It is also possible that hearths and the remains of seasonal dwellings may have survived where conditions are favourable.

The New Stone Age

Even when we move into the New Stone Age (Neolithic) to the period when man began to settle down on a more permanent basis and cultivate the land and breed animals, between about 4000 and 3000 BC, the evidence from the Marches remains scarce. In other parts of Britain the process of settling down to a regime of permanent or semi-permanent agriculture was associated with the construction of substantial stone, or as they are generally known, megalithic monuments. In many parts of the country it was necessary to clear large stones off the ground before cultivation could start. These were then piled up into mounds or banks, and it would appear that some were used to build structures normally associated with burial or ritual practices. The most notable survivals from this period are the chambered tombs, or long barrows. These normally consist of one or more stone compartments which originally contained bodies accompanied by grave goods such as pots and stone tools. The chambers had a capping stone or stones and were covered by an elongated earthen mound. In some instances the mound was surrounded by standing stones, but in many cases these stones have disappeared and in a number of instances the earthen mound has also gone, leaving just the bare stone chambers.

There is a distinctive cluster of such long barrows distributed over the Mendips and the Cotswolds which spills over into south Wales and the Black Mountains; these westerly burials are known as the Severn–Cotswold group of barrows. The most northerly members of this group overlap into Herefordshire, which clearly formed the boundary of a cultural or political territory at one stage during the New Stone Age. The most dramatic surviving example of such a megalithic monument in Herefordshire is Arthur's Stone in Dorstone parish, which, as is often the case, forms the focus for an important group of Neolithic sites. This funerary monument has an irregular polygonal main chamber about 16 feet long covered by an enormous capstone of local limestone and parts of at least two passages or chambers at the north end. There were several stages in the construction of the monument, one of which included what appears to have been the erection of a false entrance. Such false entrances were a common feature of the Severn–Cotswold barrows and appear to have been built in order to deceive tomb robbers, who often ransacked long barrows for their grave goods. Other devices such as side entrances were also adopted in order to protect the burial mounds, and often proved to be effective against not only contemporary and later grave looters, but also early antiquarians who started investigating such monuments from the seventeenth century onwards.

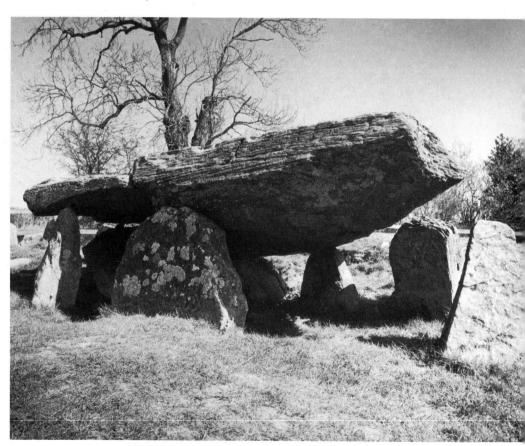

4 *Arthur's Stone in Dorstone parish is the splendid relic of a New Stone Age (Neolithic) burial mound from which the earthen covering has long since disappeared. The bodies, together with simple grave goods, would have been laid out within the central chamber*

At Arthur's Stone, a large blocking stone in the false entrance has some characteristic Neolithic markings inscribed on it known as 'cupmarks'. Originally the monument was probably covered by a long mound, but this has long since disappeared and the interior of the tomb has been pillaged of its skeletons and grave goods. Close by at Cross Lodge Farm there is an intact long barrow which may incorporate another chambered tomb. In the same parish there is a standing stone with Neolithic markings, and in the 1960s traces of a rare contemporary settlement site were excavated nearby. Almost certainly there were originally many more examples of long barrows in the southern Marches, but over the centuries they have been destroyed either to make more room for arable farming or for superstitious reasons, as such monuments were long regarded as the work of the Devil or evil spirits, particularly during the Middle Ages.

Numerous stray finds of Neolithic flint and stone tools have been made, mainly in the southern parts of the Marches, but there have not been enough findings to build up a realistic picture of the society in which they were made. Almost certainly much remains to be found and yet more painstaking fieldwork is needed. Eventually, when evidence hidden in peat bogs or lying on lonely upland wastes has been added to the findings already made, we may be able to paint a picture of life in the Neolithic Marches backed up by a coherent narrative, as full as the story we have of the Cotswolds or Wessex.

One of the problems of writing about the early prehistory of a region where stratified deposits are rare is that there are considerable problems involved in dating those few monuments which do survive. The division between the New Stone Age and the Bronze Age, when metal was first manufactured, is a convenient one when trying to present a continuous story, but when applied to the frail early archaeology of the Marches it can be both frustrating and misleading, as there is no evidence of a clear break. Indeed the practice of erecting megalithic monuments which started during the Stone Age continued well into the Bronze Age, and it is quite impossible to be certain into which chronological pigeon-hole some of the Marcher monuments should be placed. In the foothills below Corndon hill in Chirbury parish (Salop) there are the substantial remains of two stone circles sitting on dry islands in otherwise marshy ground – Hoarstone Circle and Mitchell's Fold. The latter consists of fifteen stones arranged in a circle, the tallest reaching approximately 8 feet. The Hoarstone circle is a little smaller, but originally consisted of thirty-eight stones, most of which are now covered with peat. This area must have been a focus of Neolithic activity, for just across the Welsh border at Hyssington there is the site of an important axe factory based on a local outcrop of picrite, a rock much favoured by early tool manufacturers. The products of this and similar factories much further afield have been found along the length of the Neolithic and Bronze Age trading route known as the Clun–Clee ridgeway.

This routeway extended across south Shropshire from the Kerry hills to the river Severn near Bewdley. Numerous scatters of Neolithic and Bronze Age man have been found along its length in the form of flint and other stone implements and flakes. Dr L. Chitty, who studied the route in detail over a lifetime, believed that it became important as a result of the development of trade in perforated battle-axes and axehammers during the later Neolithic and early Bronze Age. Concentrations of finds close to rivers also indicate that established fording points already formed part of a regular trading system. Along these routes there are a number of places where unusually high concentrations of flint implements were found, and it has been reasonably suggested that such concentrations point to the presence of possible settlement or camp sites. For example, some seventy such sites have been found within a twelve-mile radius of Clunbury – a density which is unparalleled elsewhere in the Marches. Along the north side of the trackway was the most productive locality for flints. George Luff, a schoolmaster from Clun, who began flint-hunting in 1877, recorded that they were 'found in thousands' on the summit of Rock hill, indicating long settlement. He writes:

> The mass of implements upon Rock Hill are found imbedded in the subsoil beneath a growth of gorse, heather and coarse herbage. When the waste lands are brought into cultivation, and this growth is stocked up the plough turns up flints and 'little waggon wheels' (spindlewhorls) and after a shower of rain they may be seen glistening in the sun.

Regrettably, as yet, no accompanying evidence of contemporary buildings has been found in the region to complement the nineteenth-century schoolteacher's findings.

Neolithic dwellings are rare in Britain as a whole and the failure to locate them in the Marches is hardly surprising. None the less there is the evidence of some other structures which were associated with the route – some of them taking the form of embanked earth circles. Most of these monuments have largely been destroyed or severely mutilated, but their former presence has been recorded in a number of places. These include the Grey Stones, near the Welsh Border in western Shropshire, Peny-y-Wern, near Clun, and near the summit of Titterstone Clee, where St John O'Neil excavated an 'Earth Circle' which had a wall of local dolerite (dhu-stone) blocks set in clay, about 3 feet high and 60 feet in diameter. Traces of such circles have been found elsewhere in the Border, normally at high altitude, and it seems possible that some of them are the predecessors of Iron Age hillforts.

Other standing stones in the region could have been erected either during the Neolithic or Bronze Age. Near to Trelleck in Gwent are Harold's Stones, three large standing stones set in a line, with cupmarks carved on them. Another isolated stone, known as the Queen's Stone, stands by the river Wye at Huntsham. This tall megalith (almost 14 feet high) has sharply cut parallel grooves incised on its sides, while yet a further megalith at Michael-church Escley appears to be associated with a Bronze Age barrow cemetery. It is particularly noticeable that the majority of the surviving sites from this period lie in waste areas at a considerable height above sea level. Their survival has been due to the lack of intensive farming activity in such areas over the millennia; quite probably other such monuments were to be found in lowland areas as well, particularly along river valleys, but these have long been destroyed by early farming activities.

Many megalithic monuments have folk-lore stories attached to them.

5 *The lonely standing stones of the megalithic circle at Mitchell's Fold, Chirbury. The site lies on an important prehistoric trackway at the southern end of Stapeley hill*

According to one tradition, for instance, the name of Mitchell's Fold comes from 'fold', meaning a farmyard in Border usage, and Old English *mycel*, big, hence the big yard or big man's yard; and the story goes that a giant used to milk his cow here. An elaboration of this story is that the cow was a magnificent white animal known as the dun cow, which would willingly provide milk sufficient for all comers as long as each person only brought one vessel to be filled. Eventually, however, a malicious witch milked the cow using a sieve and exhausted the apparently endless supply of milk. This resulted in starvation for the poor people who had relied upon the milk, so the witch was turned to stone and the other stones erected in a circle in order to keep her from escaping. Such stories, whose character and events are often interchangeable, are attached to many Marcher monuments. The Devil, or 'Grimm', is often the principal character, and, as we have already seen, others carry names associated with the Arthurian legend and others still are casually attributed to Caesar, Robin Hood or the British folk hero Caradoc (or Caratacus), whose final act of defiance against the invading Roman armies took place somewhere in the Marches.

The surviving landscape evidence for the Bronze Age elsewhere is as incomplete as that of its forerunner, the Neolithic period. Here and there we do find scattered surface hints of a culture period which lasted for more than a thousand years. Over the past decades, however, it has become increasingly clear that the evidence of standing monuments represents only one side of the picture. Just as in the Neolithic period flint scatters hint at a much more significant presence than is demonstrated by the scarce distribution of long barrows, so too in the Bronze Age the accumulating evidence from aerial photography indicates a much fuller landscape than that suggested by a glance at a plan of known surface features. The most important way of discovering buried or 'erased' monuments in the landscape is through what are known as cropmarks.

Cropmarks and Soilmarks

Cropmarks are particularly important in prehistoric and Romano-British studies, but they can also be vital to the understanding of post-Roman landscapes. Cropmarks are features normally only visible from the air, in the form of differential markings in fields carrying a cereal crop. Generally these marks represent either areas where the crop is riper and thus more bleached than the rest of the crop, or where it is less ripe and therefore much greener. Such marks normally indicate the nature of the subsoil, principally its depth and richness and the amount of moisture available. Darker lines may indicate the presence of filled ditches where deep root penetration has led to slow-ripening plants; and lighter lines will reflect wall foundations or roads, where resistance to growth has meant the plants are less luxuriant and will ripen earlier than the main crop. Deep-rooting plants tend to give a clearer picture than shallow-rooting ones. Although grain crops, particularly barley, give the best cropmarks, clover and sugar beet can provide rough indications and differential growth can even be distinguished in pea and bean fields. Archaeological markings in grass are generally only present early in the year, except in severe drought when dried-out areas or parchmarks may appear. Cropmarks result from ditched or buried features whose earthworks have been ploughed out, and as such they represent an erased landscape which nevertheless may have existed in earthwork form not so very long ago.

Recent work using the same groups of sites each year over a period of years has suggested that there are ten to fourteen days in a year, in mid to late July, when the marks are best seen as the crops are ripening. In good years, such as 1959, 1970, 1976 and 1984, as long a period as three weeks may be available, and some marks may even be visible throughout the whole growing period. The character of the subsoil is of great importance: generally the more porous it is the better the chance of cropmarks. Valley or plateau gravel, and Jurassic and carboniferous limestone produce good cropmarks, but sand and sandstone are normally of little use. Sites on clay do not show up at all well, and even on valley gravels patches of clay can effectively mask traces of earlier occupation. All these factors may affect the nature and value of the cropmark features. Only some of the buried features in the ground will show up as cropmarks. Often the most important part of the site can be revealed only by excavation, which involves completely removing the topsoil. For this reason any group of cropmarks can be taken only as an indication of part of what is buried below – in fact, as a clue to the hidden evidence. In the Marches local drift geological conditions have often given rise to natural cropmarks known as frost cracks, and these can often be confused with man-made features.

Since it is often difficult to interpret the shape or arrangement of cropmarks, descriptions of sites are normally based on the shapes of features. Archaeologists therefore tend to speak of 'ring ditches' and 'rectangular enclosures' rather than 'Bronze Age barrows' and 'Romano-British farmsteads', though a detailed knowledge of a region would lead one to expect certain types and forms of site. Occasionally it may be possible to discern a relative chronology of features showing as cropmarks. For instance, it is sometimes possible to identify later medieval buildings built on top of earlier field systems. In normal circumstances, however, archaeological excavation is needed to determine the relationship between overlapping cropmarks.

In recent years many earthwork sites in the Marches have been ploughed for the first time, giving rise to soilmarks. Soilmarks appear after an archaeological earthwork site has been ploughed for the first time, but over the years the marks normally become blurred and disappear as the material from the earthwork is scattered over the field. In some conditions, the soilmarks remain fresh for a considerable time. Soilmarks show up wherever the fill of a ditch is a different colour from that of the surrounding soil; but buildings, banks and ridges will gradually merge with the rest of the field. Deep ploughing will hasten the process. Examining a soilmark occupation site on the ground will often reveal pottery and other artefacts as well as burnt material from hearths, but over the years these too will be dispersed.

Aerial photography has led to the realisation that there is far more evidence of man in the Marches from the Neolithic period onwards than was thought before and that settlement was not, as previously thought, largely restricted to upland areas. Large segments of Britain which have until recently been written off as archaeological deserts are now seen as having carried quite considerable Bronze Age, Iron Age and Romano-British populations. The Severn valley above the Ironbridge Gorge is proving to be particularly rich in archaeological cropmarks, but many of the smaller river valleys are also producing exciting new evidence of early settlement. The work of collecting, plotting and analysing this evidence in the Marchlands is still in its infancy. None the less it is already clear that when this work has been carried out there will have to be a considerable re-evaluation of the extent to which man occupied and managed parts of the Marcher landscape from at least the Bronze Age onwards.

6 *The cropmarkings of a double enclosure at Varchoel Hall. Such enclosures normally represent Iron Age farmsteads which often continued to be occupied during the Roman period and are generally known as 'native settlements'. At the top left-hand corner there is a circular marking known as a ring ditch, which probably represents a ploughed-out Bronze Age burial mound*

The Bronze Age

During the Bronze Age in Britain as a whole the long barrow gave way to the round barrow as the principal funerary monument, and the low conical burial mounds found, for instance, along the line of the ancient track known as the Portway, which follows the spine of the Long Mynd, are the most characteristic monuments of the Bronze Age in the Marches. Again, such mounds tend to be found (or survive best) on high ground, which has led some observers to suggest that they were constructed during a warmer period when the population could have grown crops and lived at higher altitudes than was subsequently possible. The identification of circular crop-marks of Bronze Age burial mound dimensions, known as ring ditches, in the lowlands suggests that this is an over-simplification and that Bronze Age settlements and cemeteries are to be found both on higher ground and in the valleys. A particular problem which is associated with the interpretation of circular burial mounds is that although they are commonly Bronze Age, they appear to have been used from time to time through from the Neolithic Age to the Saxon period. This often makes the dating of such features virtually impossible without excavation. The probable siting of an Anglo-Saxon circular mound is suggested in the place name of Wolferlow, in north-east Herefordshire, which means 'Wulfhere's burial mound'.

At Bromfield a number of such mounds now forming part of Ludlow racecourse and golf club, were neatly landscaped during the nineteenth century when each one had a tree planted at its centre, thereby probably damaging the monuments irrevocably! Excavations in one of them known as the Butt Tump revealed the remains of a teenage child buried with a bronze knife. Four other barrows on the racecourse have been flattened since they were dug in 1884. One of these contained a second burial urn and the contemporary description of the excavation is very interesting, although the techniques used would appal modern archaeologists.

We now come to the fifth and last of the barrows opened at this time (there being another left for future exploration at a distance of about 300 yards from it), which turned out to be one of a most interesting character. It is somewhat larger in diameter than the 'Butt Tump', but not so deep, being only eight feet to the ground level. The work of exploration commenced, as in every other case, by cutting a trench from above. At a depth of two feet only from the top of the mound, to the astonishment of all engaged in the work, an urn containing a quantity of burnt bones was met with. Unfortunately, in consequence of its having been come upon so unexpectedly, it got broken into many pieces by the spade of a workman. The urn, which is of rather crude and ill-burnt pottery, is nevertheless of elegant design, with some attempt at ornamentation round the upper part.

Having carefully removed the urn with all the pieces that could be found, the excavations were continued, when at a depth of about seven feet, a quantity of small flattish stones were come upon, which, as the work proceeded, proved

to be the top stones of a cist. This appears to have been constructed in the following manner: The ground having been scooped out to the depth of a few inches
in an oval form, head and foot stones composed of flat slabs of sandstone, about
fifteen inches square, were placed edgewise at either end, and faced north and
south. Other similar stones, but of smaller size, and also placed edgewise, completed the oval. The interior of this oval space was filled in with small stones,
the under layer of which, and consequently those placed next to the body and
in direct contact with it, upon being turned over, were found to have small portions of bone adhering to them, and there was distinct evidence upon all of their
having been subjected to excessive heat.

On all sides were observed large quantities of wood ashes, which proclaimed
the fact that the crematory process had been carried out in the most complete
manner. The inside measurement of the cist, between the head and foot stones,
was three feet eight inches. It would seem, therefore, that the body, supposing
it to have been that of an adult or fully grown person, must have been placed
in a cramped position, in accordance with the prevailing custom of those early
times.

There are still five upstanding barrows as well as evidence of fourteen
other destroyed barrows in the form of ring ditches nearby. For a short
stretch the A49 close to Ludlow follows their alignment and at the point
at which the modern road swings westwards to cross the river Onny at
Bromfield, they continue northwards suggesting a fording place some half
a mile to the north of the present crossing. Recent excavations close by have
revealed an extensive Bronze Age cemetery with over 130 burials dating
from between 1800 and 900 BC. In the words of the excavator, Dr Stanford,
'Their contents revealed a complexity of burial routine, the significance of
which still escapes our understanding.' However, there is significant evidence of continuity of use of the burial ground and of the marking of graves
with small heaps of earth – miniature barrows perhaps?

The burials at Bromfield form part of an area of intensive occupation
extending over a considerable period of time, with evidence dating from the
Neolithic through to the Anglo-Saxon period. In many respects it is a unique
complex not least because it has produced the only genuine evidence of early,
but Christian, Anglo-Saxon burials in the region. The Bromfield–Stanton
Lacy–Ludlow triangle is one of immense archaeological and historical interest; the concentration of occupation here is sufficient to mark it as a special
area of 'preferred' settlement where, over the centuries and against radically
different economic, social and climatic conditions, it was consistently attractive enough to be used continuously as a settlement and perhaps as a religious area. There is as yet no evidence for Iron Age occupation in the region,
but the presence of a Roman road and marching camp do indicate Roman
interest in the area – especially as there is also an early Christian cemetery
here. The building of a substantial Saxon church at Stanton Lacy, followed

by the post-Norman Conquest development of Ludlow as one of the foremost Marcher towns, highlights the continuing significance of the area.

Fig. 2 Plan showing the continuity of occupation to the north-west of Ludlow

The Bromfield concentration lies at the confluence of two south Shropshire rivers, the Onny and the Corve, and it has been argued that river junctions were particularly important in prehistory. The symbolic significance of such locations was perhaps augmented by more practical considerations, not least the attraction of the lighter alluvial valley soils and the possibility at least of transporting goods by water. A similarly positioned Bronze Age settlement and cemetery has been found to the south of Shrewsbury at Weeping Cross, sited close to the river Severn and the Rea Brook. As with so much early prehistory in the Borderland our understanding is at an elementary stage, but aerial photography is helping us build up a much more substantial picture of Bronze Age occupation and activity in the region.

The Pre-Roman Iron Age

The culmination of Britain's prehistory came during the period which is conventionally known as the Iron Age. The most outstanding monuments in the landscape from this period in the Marches are undoubtedly those massive enclosures marked off by turf-covered ramparts and ditches – the hillforts. Indeed they form the most impressive monuments in the region of any period and are rivalled in their impact only by the medieval castles. In the western parts of Herefordshire and Shropshire it would seem that virtually every hilltop is capped with one of these massive earthwork fortifications.

Generally speaking, most of the Border hillforts are found to the west of the Dee–Severn line, although there are some notable exceptions to the east. We know from Roman sources the names of the tribes that occupied the region at the time of the conquest and there are marked differences in the distribution and size of their forts. In the north, to the west of the Dee estuary, was the territory of the Deceangli, where there are relatively few hillforts, although some of those that do exist are of a considerable size. In particular,

7 The Iron Age hillfort at Credenhill Camp is one of the largest in Britain, its single rampart and ditch enclosing an area of about 70 acres. It lies about four miles to the north-west of Hereford and its central location suggests that it might have been a tribal capital. The recent programme of tree clearance has revealed a number of previously unidentified earthworks in the interior

there are a line of forts commanding gaps on the eastern side of the vale of Clwyd, which include Foel Fenlli (29 acres), Moel Hiraddug (36 acres) and Penycloddiau (64 acres). Among this group there is also the much smaller Moel Y Gaer which has recently been subject to intensive excavation.

To the south, based on the fertile middle Severn valley, lay the territory of the Cornovii, in which there are many hillforts of varying dimensions. These include the massive fort at Old Oswestry, which enclosed only about 20 acres, but which has as many as seven ramparts, and Titterstone Clee, which was one of the most formidable hillforts in Britain until mutilated by quarrying. Further south were the Decangi, whose territory occupied the Herefordshire basin. Here the hillforts were larger, armed with strong ramparts, and more evenly spread. The central position of Credenhill Camp, enclosing over 70 acres, suggests that it may well have been the tribal capital. At the southern end of the Marches in the Dean–Trelleck uplands, were the Silures, whose territory also extended over much of southern Wales. The chief characteristic of the hillforts in this area is the comparatively small area which was enclosed (rarely more than 4 acres), as well as the existence of several ramparts.

It used to be thought that the Iron Age hillforts were built in the century or two before the coming of the Romans as a result of internal quarrels between neighbouring tribes, and that they were strengthened in response to the threat of outside forces. In other words, that they really were forts and that they enjoyed only a brief existence. Investigation over the past twenty years, however, has demonstrated that the Border hillforts had a much longer lifespan. Ffridd Faldwyn, for instance, which sits above the modern town of Montgomery with its castle built by Henry III, has produced evidence of Neolithic occupation, as have a number of other Border hillforts. Indeed, wherever excavation has taken place the evidence points to an early origin for the forts. At the Breidden, Powys, for instance, the earliest feature is a double palisade dated to 975 BC, while at Moel Y Gaer the earliest structures have been dated to 820 BC and excavations at Dinorben in Clwyd have produced evidence from as early as 1170 BC. This is not to say that all the Border forts have such early origins – Croft Ambrey, for instance, appears to have begun life only about 550 BC – but the idea that hillforts arrived on the scene only in the two centuries immediately preceding the Roman conquest has now been truly exploded. Furthermore, there is a body of evidence to suggest that a number of forts had already been abandoned or were in decline before the arrival of the Romans, indicating changing political conditions and possibly some form of social disruption or fragmentation during the later Iron Age.

Not only have ideas about the dating of hillforts changed in recent years, but the interpretation of their function has also altered. Initially their obvious bellicose appearance and location in remote strategic positions led to the belief that they had an exclusively military use, perhaps being occupied only during the periods of unrest. Thus they were given the name 'fort' which itself tended to perpetuate the belief that they were essentially military in character. Excavations at Moel Y Gaer and Croft Ambrey, however, have clearly demonstrated that these forts were not some form of prehistoric barracks, but that they contained many domestic dwellings which in a number of cases had been rebuilt on numerous occasions over the centuries. The identification of buildings regularly aligned along roadways within the forts shows that they could well have been organised in the same way as later villages or towns. In some hillforts there were special areas for keeping cattle or sheep and there were also storage pits for grain. These, together with the evidence of corn-grinding querns, show that the hillforts probably served to store and redistribute agricultural produce. Evidence of forts away from the Marches shows that some of them had specialist areas for craftsmen, and that a very wide range of activities were carried out within the confines of the defences.

It is clear, therefore, that the Marcher hillforts performed a range of functions which almost certainly changed over the years. It is quite true that some of the higher more remote forts appear to have acted largely as defended lookout posts, which quite probably were only occupied in times of unrest or on a seasonal basis, but the majority of those forts lying at between 500 and 1500 feet seem to have offered a range of services to the surrounding countryside in the same way that market towns did in the Middle Ages and after. The largest and most prominent forts also appear to have performed political and administrative functions as well as being the tithe and tax-collecting centres for their region or territory. It is even possible that they were able to monopolise regional trade in certain commodities and thus extract profitable tolls.

Naturally enough today our eye is taken by the massive fortifications, which have often survived because of their inaccessibility and the difficulty of levelling them. Until recently archaeological excavation too has tended to concentrate on hillfort defences and their gateways, which were investigated to provide a chronology for sites. As a result, elaborate histories of hillforts have been constructed often on the basis of very small samples. However, recent research has confirmed that it is essential to investigate the interiors of the forts if we are really to understand them. The fort boundaries, which were often originally in the form of earth banks revetted with stone walls and the associated ditches, performed functions other than that of pure defence, although undoubtedly at times this was of the utmost importance. They could well have acted in the same way as medieval town walls, proclaiming the presence of a more important settlement and acting as a symbol of urban 'status' and privilege. Moreover, they would have provided the means by which goods and produce entering and leaving the fort could be monitored.

Fig. 3 Prehistoric and Romano-British 'native' settlement in the middle Severn valley

When we examine hillforts we are looking at the top of the Iron Age settle-ment hierarchy. What is missing is the great spread of lesser settlements which must have occupied large areas of the countryside, but which over the centuries have been absorbed back into the ground. In recent years aerial photography has added a new dimension to our understanding of the Iron Age. Cropmarkings have demonstrated that numerous prehistoric villages and farmsteads, together with their associated fields and trackways, lie buried beneath the soil of the Borderlands. Such Iron Age evidence is particularly common on the lighter soils of the terraces of the major river systems and on glacial sands and gravels, but they have also been identified in other areas. It is clear that we must now imagine that considerable parts of the lowland Border region were managed and farmed in the centuries preceeding

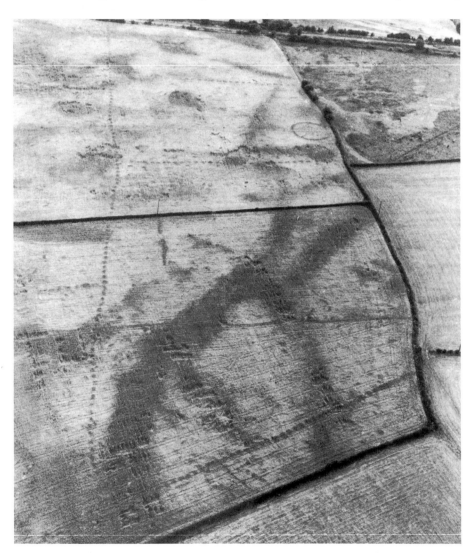

8 Cropmarkings of Bronze Age or Iron Age field boundaries near to Llandysilio (Four Crosses) in the Vyrnwy valley, a little way to the west of Offa's Dyke. The boundaries are demarcated by lines of closely set pits, known as pit alignments. The regular modern field is a product of nineteenth-century parliamentary enclosure

the Romans. What is more, unlike the hillforts, many of these settlements appear to have survived virtually unaltered into the Romano-British period.

The vast majority of lowland sites have been located in the valleys of the Severn, the Wye and the Teme. In those areas the most common Iron Age feature is the cropmark enclosure. In Shropshire, for instance, some 330 of these have been located. The majority of sites are rectangular, marked out by a simple single ditch enclosing, typically, about an acre. Interior features are rarely visible, but gaps or entrances in the enclosure ditch can frequently be identified. In some cases the enclosures are surrounded by a double ditch while others have attached compounds. In certain rare cases, there is a complicated pattern of ditches which seems to mirror the elaborate hillfort pattern. More often, however, enclosures appear in isolation, although occasionally there is a complex of cropmarkings that suggests either repeated rebuilding or possibly the existence of a more complicated village structure.

Although evidence of field systems is relatively rare (some forty examples have been found in Shropshire) a number of them clearly relate to nearby settlement enclosures. The earliest field systems appear to consist of small, irregular fields which were very closely knit together. Sometimes these were within a larger, well-defined enclosure, as at Muckleton and Shawbury Heath; while other systems show fields divided by pit alignments and ditches, for example near Stanton Upon Hine Heath. Here the pit alignments run as parallel lines, perhaps delineating a trackway, with ditches running laterally off this to divide the land into small fields. Often these small fields are overlaid with a pattern of parallel ditches forming roughly rectangular fields; this 'brick wall' type of pattern was occasionally interspersed with trackways. Preliminary excavations of a site at Four Crosses, Powys, has shown features, including pit alignments, that date back to the late Bronze Age. If the same holds true of other areas in the Marches then perhaps there were several phases of field creation with the more regular fields dating from the late Iron Age or Romano-British periods. In the case of Shawbury, there are two settlement sites which border a Roman road, both showing field systems of the 'brick wall' type on aerial photographs.

The pattern of Iron Age cropmarkings in the Marches is far less complicated than that found in, for instance, the upper Thames valley and the comparative simplicity of this pattern might suggest that many of the farmsteads were contemporaneous, associated with a period of colonisation similar to that which took place during the early Middle Ages. Alternatively there could have been a major agrarian reorganisation, perhaps associated with an expansionary phase of the hillforts. Much work remains to be done on the identification and investigation of these traces of early settlement and agriculture, but we should not forget when viewing the splendours of the hillforts that there is a submerged Bronze and Iron Age landscape beneath our feet.

Sites to Visit

Arthur's Stone, Dorstone, Hereford

The ancient monument known as Arthur's Stone is situated at 1000 feet above sea level on Merbach hill at the head of the Golden Valley. The monument gives its name to the extensive parish of Dorstone in which it lies, and until the mid nineteenth century was the gathering place for village celebrations. Arthur's Stone consists of an elongated polygonal chamber built of sandstone with its long axis north-north-west to south-south-east, approached by a passage to the north-north-west of it which is set on an east–west axis. Between the passage and chamber, and bridging over the different orientations of the two parts of the monument, is a smaller ante-chamber or passage consisting of two great stones. The main chamber is roofed over by one large capstone (now broken in two) and consists at present of nine low wallstones. To the south of the chamber are two isolated stones set in the ground whose relation to the chamber is not clear. There are very distinct remains of the barrow around the chamber but they are not clear enough to reconstruct the shape of the mound.

Dorstone village is itself of considerable interest. It lies 400 feet below Arthur's Stone, and has a medieval castle at one end and a medieval church at the other. In between is a triangular market place typical of many dormant medieval Marcher boroughs; however, it has no market hall, only a market cross. Dorstone was attacked and severely damaged by Owen Glendower in 1404, but before that Richard de Brito, one of the assassins of Thomas à Becket, came here and founded a chapel in the church, probably after returning from completing his penance in the Holy Land. Dorstone was also for a time the terminus of the Golden Valley Railway which opened from Pontrilas in 1881 before it was extended to Hay. The line finally closed in 1957 leaving behind Dorstone as one of the several forlorn abandoned railway stations of western Herefordshire.

Caer Caradoc (Gaer Ditches)

In the uplands of southern Shropshire is perhaps the densest concentration of hillforts in the region. Caer Caradoc, a few miles to the south of Clun, lies at the centre of the cluster and is one of the finest, with commanding views in all directions. On the south-east side is a single rampart, ditch and counterscarp; on both sides there are extensive and deep internal quarry ditches which are thought to have been possible hut platforms. Such internal quarries are a common feature of Marcher hillforts and can be clearly identified on aerial photographs. The entrances at the east and west are inturned and the western one may have had guard chambers attached. Outside the easily accessible west entrance is an additional defence in the form of a bank and ditch which lie across the direct approach. Opposite, on the northern side of the entrance, the outer bank rises up higher than elsewhere, as though to complement the hornwork, forming a platform from which missiles could be hurled. Rabbits have dug into the banks and here and there have revealed sections of the massive stone walls which originally made up the exterior face of the fortification and today serve as a reminder of the energy and resources that went into the building of these abandoned early 'towns'.

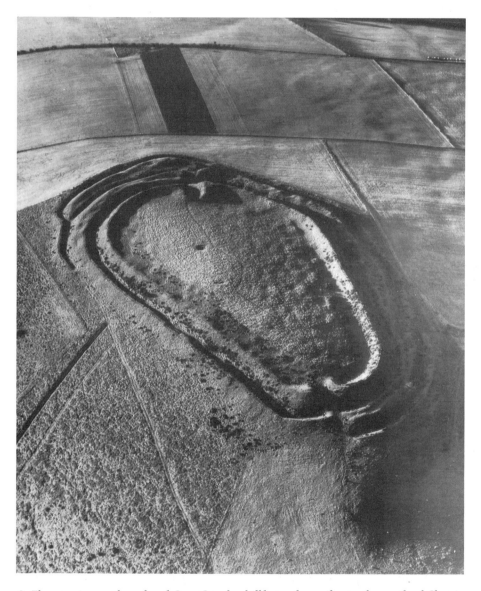

9 *The massive earthworks of Caer Caradoc hillfort a few miles to the south of Clun in Shropshire. The fort is named after the legendary British hero Caratacus whose last stand against the Romans was made somewhere in the Welsh Marches*

We know little of the history of Caer Caradoc apart from its association with the legendary British tribal leader Caratacus, whose name is attached to several Border hillforts where he was believed to have made his final stand against the Romans. Caratacus was a Belgic prince based in the south-east of England. Soon after the initial phase of Roman conquest in AD 43–8 Caratacus established himself as a leader of the Welsh tribes against Rome and from Wales he carried out raids into Roman-held territory. At this stage the Roman frontier which had been established by Aulus Plautius ran between the Humber and the lower Severn. Ostorius Scapula moved his army westwards towards the Severn to search out and bring Caratacus to battle, who in the meantime had moved from southern to central Wales. Caratacus's last stand was in AD 50 when the Roman legions were forced to make a frontal assault. Tacitus describes the geography of the site of Caratacus's last stand as follows:

> He chose a place for the battle where the entrances and exits were to our dis-advantage, but favourable to his own troops. On one side there was a pre-cipitously steep gradient, and where there were gentler approach routes he piled up stones to form a kind of embankment. There was also a river of uncertain depth flowing past and here bands of fighters were stationed to provide defences.

Although the Romans won the battle the British tribesmen melted away into the woods. Caratacus, despite escaping and fleeing to the Brigantes of north Britain, was eventually captured and sent back to Rome in triumph where the Emperor Claudius spared his life. The brief topographical descriptions provided by Tacitus are insufficient to locate the site of Caratacus's last stand with any precision – indeed the description would fit any one of thirty or forty border hillforts. Some three carry Caratacus's name (in the form of Caradoc) but there is no further evidence to substantiate any of these locations. Nevertheless one feels that if such an event did take place nowhere could have provided a more appropriate setting for such a valiant scene than the remote beautiful site of Caer Caradoc.

Herefordshire Beacon (British Camp) and Midsummer Hill Camp, Malvern Hills

The Herefordshire Beacon is one of the finest examples of a contour fort in Britain, with its ramparts and ditches clinging to the distinctive shape of the Malvern hills. The highest point of the hill is crowned by a medieval castle mound known as the Citadel, which has been dated to the twelfth century. Around the base of this mound was the earliest Iron Age fort, an enclosure of about 10 acres with entrances at the north-east and south-west. The little fort was enlarged to over 30 acres through the construction of the massive ramparts and ditch with counterscarp that surround the site today. Much of the material for the main defence came from a quarry which can be clearly identified in the form of an irregular ditch around most of the southern part of the fort. Of the four entrances, that at the north has been damaged by the modern footpath, but the southern gateway is approached by what might be a contemporary zig-zag pathway. Under the right circumstances, in low light or under a thin covering of snow, traces of terracing and small hut circles can be identified and it has been estimated that the total population of the fort at its height was between 1500 and 2000 people. A little to the south-east of the camp is Clutter's Cave, which has produced no obvious prehistoric evidence although it is tempting to think that there should be. Shire Ditch, which runs from the southern tip of the fort, appears to have been constructed as a hunting or county boundary in the thirteenth century although it may represent the rebuilding of an earlier territorial boundary.

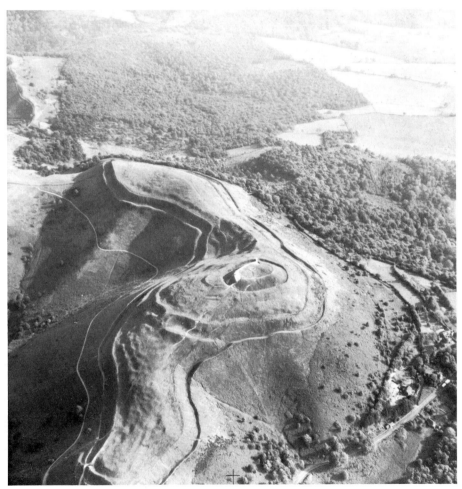

10 The massive fortifications of the hillfort referred to as the Herefordshire Beacon which clings to the southern summit of the Malvern hills. In the centre is a probable medieval castle known as the Citadel

Some way to the south lies Midsummer Hill Camp, which consists of two hilltops enclosed by a bank and ditch containing an area of about 40 acres. This fort is an irregular shape with a long narrow spur jutting out to the south and an oval area to the north-west. Its rampart is stone-faced and there are traces of shallow internal quarry ditches. At the north-west is an entrance which was originally inturned and there is another at the south-west. Excavation of the latter has shown that it was rebuilt on numerous occasions, with guard chambers made of both wood and stone. Hollows in the interior suggest there were about 250 huts, and those which have been excavated appear to have been rectangular in shape. The buildings seem to have been laid out in a regular plan with streets between them. Radio-carbon dating suggests that occupation of the fort began about 400 BC and possibly ended when it was burnt down by Ostorius Scapula when he attacked the Decangi in AD 48. There is a low rectangular mound on the eastern side of the fort which is probably a pillow mound, an artificial rabbit warren dating from medieval times.

Croft Ambrey

Excavations on another Herefordshire site, Croft Ambrey, have graphically illustrated the story of that site. The excavator, Dr Stanford, has shown that there had been a sequence of wooden buildings there which were repeatedly rebuilt and some twenty successive gate posts set up before they were finally dug out at the time of the Roman conquest. Croft Ambrey appears to have been disarmed and abandoned in AD 50 when Ostorius Scapula pursued his campaign in the Marches against Caratacus. Even after the site was abandoned it was probably used as a sanctuary, and Stanford concludes that the British population 'survived and returned to worship outside their ancient stronghold'.

The excavations at Croft Ambrey are some of the most important pre-historic excavations in Britain. The investigation not only made it possible to identify, for the first time, a new 'culture' in western England, but also provided more reliable chronology than had previously been available.

The fort occupies a long narrow hill, with a very abrupt scarp on the north, and gentler, though still steep, slopes on the other sides. In about 550 BC, a small rampart and ditch were built on the summit of the hill, to protect an enclosure of about 7 acres. The interior was closely set with small 'four-post' buildings regularly spaced along streets. This house pattern continued with little change throughout the six centuries of the hillfort's life. The gateway in this phase was a simple double portal, formed by three large posts, which was rebuilt several times. No pottery, and very few relics of any kind, survive from the occupation of this earlier fort.

About 390 BC a new and massive rampart was built, following a line mostly outside the old one. Although large, it was of simple design, with a single bank and ditch and the crest carrying a timber palisade, and this rampart style remained unaltered for almost three centuries. There were, however, changes in the design of the gateways during that time: the gate passage was lengthened and a pair of rectangular guard rooms provided; sandstone, brought from the foot of the hill, was used for the lower courses of walling. This phase lasted until about 260 BC when the system of guard rooms was abandoned. In the last phase the gateway arrangements were similar, except that a bridge was added across the passage in front of the gate. To this period, also, can be attributed the second bank and ditch formed outside the main bank. There were no further alterations, and the effective occupation of the hillfort ended with the arrival of the Romans in AD 48.

Outside the main enclosure there is an annexe of about 15 acres. No evidence of dense occupation has been found, but the annexe does contain a remarkable sacred site, which in its earlier phases consisted of a levelled terrace cut into the hillside. The religious ceremonies, whatever they may have been, left much charcoal, ash and burned bone, and many fragments of broken pottery, the latest dating from about 300 BC.

The occupants of the first enclosure lived in little rectangular huts. Some similar buildings were used as storehouses or granaries – we know this because some carbonised grain has been found there. The buildings were regularly set out in streets and they had been repeatedly rebuilt on the same site, sometimes as many as six times. This barrack-like settlement differs so radically from the haphazard round house pattern usually to be found in this country that Dr Stanford believes that the Croft Ambrey settlers must have come from outside Britain, although Croft Ambrey itself was probably the work of descendants of the original invaders. This is certainly not a universally held view.

Another interesting result of this work is the evidence for the development of an extensive trade system. In the early phases there is hardly any pottery, but in later phases it becomes plentiful, coming from potters working in the Malvern hills region eighteen miles away; nevertheless the discovery of a large proportion of pot sherds which have been repaired using iron rivets suggest that even these supplies arrived infrequently.

Mitchell's Fold, Chirbury, Salop

This stone circle stands on level ground on the ancient ridgeway which follows the axis of Stapeley hill. The position is an exposed one with very extensive views both to east and west over the Severn valley and the Welsh hills. A hard stone called picrite is found here and was exploited in the early Bronze Age for the manufacture of axe hammers.

Fourteen stones remain giving the circle a diameter somewhere between 85 and 90 feet. Possibly there are only thirteen stones since some of the low pieces in the eastern sector may be natural, and much of the site is buried and overgrown. The stones are very irregularly spaced: each sector has wide gaps in it, suggesting that many stones have been moved. Four stones or stumps which form a group on the east side are separated by distances varying between about 4 and about 8 feet, a range which makes it difficult to estimate the original number of stones in the circle, although some think it may be as many as thirty. Of the stones now standing, the tallest is 6 feet high, but all the others are much less than this (up to 3 feet), and some are only stumps. The circle does not appear to have changed much since 1754, when the antiquarian William Stukeley made a drawing of it showing fourteen stones in exactly the same positions as they are today.

There is a local tradition that a nearby tenant farmer removed one of the stones from Mitchell's Fold intending to use it as a step for a cowshed, but was so alarmed by a violent thunderstorm in the night that he returned it the next day. There is another local tradition, that a dolmen (standing stone) stood at the centre. About 80 yards to the south-east is a much-weathered cubical block (also apparently shown in the Stukeley drawing) which stands on a small cairn. This is the so-called 'altar'. A second cairn, much ruined, lies just north-west of this.

Mitchell's Fold has been known by a variety of names in the past : Stukeley calls it Midgel's Fold, or the Druids Temple, before relating the story of the cow which provided the endless supply of milk. An alternative ending to the legend has been provided by some folklore historians. According to this tradition, after the witch had milked the cow dry it went to Warwickshire where it turned into the Wild Dun Cow which was killed by Guy, Earl of Warwick, on Dun's More Heath between Coventry and Rugby. This tradition contradicts the story associated with the Cow Stone or the Dead Cow Stone which lies on the west side of the ridgeway close to Mitchell's Fold.

There are a number of other sites with related folklore stories, many of which lie a little to the west in Wales. Among these are the Speckled Cow's Crib in Powys and the Hag's Milking Fold, also in Powys. The legend of the Dun Cow at Mitchell's Fold appears to have been current by the later Middle Ages. There are numerous hotels, inns and public houses bearing the name Dun Cow in Shropshire, Warwickshire and County Durham. Not far from Mitchell's Fold, at Middleton, in Chirbury church, which was consecrated on Christmas Day 1842, there is a carved capital illustrating the folklore of Mitchell's Fold. The sculptor incorporated into his design a sequence of three events : firstly the village folk queueing to obtain their pails or jugs filled with milk, secondly the witch milking the cow into her sieve, and thirdly the construction of the stone circle.

However quaint such legends may seem to us in the late twentieth century Mitchell's Fold in its remote and wild part of the Marches still has an eerie atmosphere, particularly in the depths of winter.

Old Oswestry (Yr Hen Ddinas)
Forts were a feature of the lowland landscape as well as the hills. Old Oswestry fort, for instance, crowned the summit of a low clay glacial hill

on the western edge of the Shropshire plain. With its multiple ramparts it ranks among the largest of the forts within the territory of the Cornovii and rivals the Wrekin in its claim to be the focus of power in their Iron Age territory. Since it is a site under the guardianship of the English Heritage Commission it deserves to be better known.

However, it was covered by trees until the beginning of this century, which probably explains why it has received relatively little attention.

The site, which lies on a minor road about a mile to the north-east of the modern town of Oswestry, was described by the famous Border archaeologist Sir Cyril Fox as 'the outstanding work of early Iron Age type in the Marches of Wales'. It covers some 40 acres and appears to have undergone many vicissitudes. It was excavated by Professor Varley in 1939, but unfortunately there is no final report on his findings.

11 *Old Oswestry hillfort occupies a relatively low lying position, but its defences present a formidable obstacle to attack. The purpose of the hollows on the right-hand side of the photograph has yet to be identified. The suburbs of modern Oswestry spread out along the railway line towards the foot of the fort*

The earliest settlement, of timber-built round houses, was unfortified. Subsequently it was deserted for some time, and the remains became covered with turf. Next, the hilltop was enclosed by a rampart about 10 feet thick, with a stone revetment on both sides and an accompanying ditch, plus a second rampart and ditch. The ditches and their associated ramparts were some 30 feet apart, possibly to allow for the instability of the hill slopes, which are built of glacial gravel. The dwellings during this phase were also round, but made of stone.

In the next phase the innermost bank was enlarged, partly burying one of the huts, and two more similarly spaced banks and ditches were built (making a total of four around most of the circuit) and at the same time the entrance was inturned.

The final stage of the evolution of the defences saw the construction of a pair of very large banks around the base of the hill, enclosing and partly burying the earlier works. These ramparts also used the unstable glacial material but this time reinforced with layers of clay, and boulders were used to form the outer edges. During this final phase the internal dwellings were still round, but one at least had two rooms, and they were massively built with thick stone walls reinforced with upright posts.

At the western entrance there are a series of deep hollows, called annexes by archaeologists, which are preceded by a pair of outer banks. Despite their striking appearance it is not at all clear what use they served. They cannot have served as cattle enclosures, as some observers have suggested, for they have no entrances. In very wet conditions they do hold water and it is possible that they were used as cisterns, but if so they are unique in their size and situation. It may be that they were designed solely to protect and define the very long entrance passage, and that the spaces within served no practical purpose but were not worth the labour involved in refilling them.

During the Roman period the fort appears to have been deserted, though a few scraps of Roman pottery have been found in the ditch silting. However, Old Oswestry has long been put forward as one of those sites where occupation was resumed at the end of the Roman era. There is evidence for Dark Age use in the form of some crude pottery which was interpreted by the excavator, Varley, as Anglo-Saxon. The traditional name of the place was Caer Ogyrfan, the 'fort of Gogyrfan' (Gogyrfan the father of Guinevere); but in view of the revised interpretation of the pottery as Iron Age oven linings, one must now regretfully abandon the romantic vision of King Arthur riding through the ruins of the great west entrance to visit his future in-laws. No firm evidence for reoccupation exists although in view of the important historical role played by Oswestry in the emergence of Anglo-Saxon domination in this part of England it would seem probable from circumstantial evidence that the site was resettled. Added to this, in the eighth century the fort was incorporated into the line of Wat's Dyke. Recent work by Professor Barrie Jones in the area has shown that the stronghold was surrounded by a substantial number of native farming settlements. These farmsteads must have been producing an agricultural surplus sufficient to support such a massive hillfort and its inhabitants.

The Romans in the Welsh Marches

ALTHOUGH THE Roman presence in Britain lasted for almost four centuries, relatively little above-ground evidence survives from their occupation in the Welsh Marches. However, although standing Roman buildings and Roman earthworks are rare, there is a considerable amount of evidence hidden below the ground. Apart from the archaeological record, evidence of the Romans is to be found hidden away in place names, the most obvious being Chester itself. Chester derives from the Old English word *caester* which was the Saxon adaptation of the Latin *castra*, meaning fort; *caester* was regularly and somewhat indiscriminately applied by the Anglo-Saxons to settlements which were believed to have had Romano-British associations.

12 In the centre of the photograph are the cropmarks of a first-century Roman fort lying on the eastern bank of the river Severn. Such forts were built of turf and timber, but followed the regular 'playing-card' shape of later stone-built forts

Other indications of former Roman occupation come in the street patterns of some towns and villages, in the alignment of modern roads which follow their Roman predecessors, and occasionally in the form of isolated pieces of standing masonry, as at Caerleon and Wroxeter.

Fig. 4 The network of Roman military forts in the Marches and central Wales (after Webster)

Conventionally the onset of the Roman occupation of Britain saw the beginning of written history. We know the names of the principal commanders involved in the conquest of the country and of the tribes they fought, even the names of some of the native leaders, and the dates of main rebellions. But the story of the Romans in the Marches, although a crucial one, is far from complete and the historical and archaeological records are, not for the only time, at variance with each other.

One of the most important battles of the conquest, known as the 'last stand of Caratacus', took place in or close to the Marches. The circumstances and location of the battle are described by Tacitus in some detail:

> The Romans now moved against the Silures, whose natural spirit was reinforced by their faith in the prowess of Caratacus, whose many battles against the Romans . . . had raised him to a position of pre-eminence amongst the other British chieftains. Since his strength lay not in military superiority but in the tactical advantages to be gained from knowing difficult terrain, he transferred the scene of the conflict to the territory of the Ordovices. He recruited from those who dreaded the establishment of the Roman peace and staked his fate on one last confrontation. He chose a place for the battle where the entrances and exits were to our disadvantage but favourable to his own troops. On one side there was a precipitously steep gradient, and where there were gentler approach routes he piled up stones to form a kind of embankment. There was also a river of uncertain depth flowing past and here bands of fighters were stationed to provide defence.

Antiquarians of past generations, in their attempts to identify this famous site, have been more inspired by local patriotism than a close study of the words of Tacitus, and there are many hills which bear the name Caer Caradoc – none of which precisely fit the qualifications given by the historian. Firstly, it must be in Ordovician territory and by a river with a difficult crossing. This implies a sizeable river and the most likely one is the Severn. Earlier antiquarians have always chosen a hillfort, but only a rampart of stones is mentioned as defending the steep slope and this at one point only; the rest of the hill rose sheer. So the site could be one of a number of hills close to the Severn in its upper stretches, probably in the narrow valley below Caersws. The most likely hills would be those above Newtown, since this is where the old east–west trackway meets the Severn, which is the route that would probably have been followed by the Roman army.

Tacitus then goes on to describe how the Roman commander Ostorius Scapula led his troops to victory, forcing the British to retreat into the Welsh mountains, and capturing Caratacus and his family. As a result of this resistance, however, Caratacus's fame spread beyond his own island and was acclaimed as it filtered through the neighbouring provinces as far as Italy. According to Tacitus, Caratacus was subsequently taken to Rome, where, after being displayed before the Emperor Claudius and having made an eloquent speech, he and his family were given the freedom to live out their lives in Rome. How much of the Caratacus story is historical fact and how much legend is impossible to say; it is clear, however, that he captured the popular imagination both of the Romans and of the British and later on of the English. His role as a legendary folk hero is therefore a major one.

The process of subduing the British continued even after Caratacus had been defeated. We know, for example, that a legionary base was established at Wroxeter in the sixties AD, but that within twenty years it had been abandoned and had been replaced by more permanent western military bases at Chester and Caerleon. These two major centres held legions containing about 5000 men each and formed the corner-stones of the Roman defensive system in the west. They controlled movements out of Wales along the northern and southern coastal plains and additionally were sited close to tidal water, which helped in the supply of the necessary stores required for their own garrisons and those of the outlying auxiliary forts.

Elsewhere a network of forts was set up to cover Wales, the most easterly lying of which ran along the Welsh Marches at places such as Usk, Abergavenny and at Jaylane, which lies just to the west of Leintwardine. Subsequently a more permanent fort was established at Leintwardine indicating that all was not necessarily peaceful either in the Marches or throughout Wales. Eventually, towards the end of the Roman period, attention switched to the northern Marches where defences were refortified against potential attacks from across the Irish Sea and from northern Britain. The historical record is, however, for the most part as silent on these developments as it is about the civilian conditions that prevailed throughout the Marches.

One of the great enigmas of the Roman period in the Borderland is the size and apparent affluence of the Roman town at Wroxeter (*Viroconium Cornoviorum*). It was a substantial town with the fourth largest circuit of town walls in the whole of Roman Britain, enclosing an area of about 180 acres, but unlike towns of similar size it does not seem to have had the subsidiary network of villas which operated around places such as Cirencester. Indeed evidence of Roman villas is rare in this part of the Borderland, and although there may well be many sites yet to be discovered, the Roman rural infrastructure hardly appears to have been strong enough to support a town of the size and apparent prosperity of Wroxeter. Instead of the normal pattern of villa estates, the area around the city is dotted with native British farmsteads, survivals from the Iron Age where the lifestyle appears to have changed little following the Roman conquest. Perhaps the most obvious change for the British was in their use of mass-produced Roman pottery and utensils as opposed to the locally made products they had previously made do with. It is therefore clear that we are dealing with a pattern of settlement and a Romano-British agricultural regime that is somewhat different from that operating in southern and central England, and possibly one in which the vestiges of military control were stronger than in the remainder of the Civil Zone of Roman Britain. Whatever the reason, the full story of the Roman occupation of the Borderland remains to be discovered.

Fig. 5 A plan of Roman Wroxeter based largely on aerial photographic evidence. The street layout and the foundations of a considerable number of buildings are visible within the town's defences. The defended area covered approximately 180 acres (after D. Wilson)

Roman Camps

For a few decades in the middle of the first century AD the Marches formed the western boundary of the Roman Empire, with massive legionary forts at Chester, Wroxeter and Caerwent as well as a series of lesser forts and marching posts, many of which enjoyed only a short active life. For the most part these rectangular structures, which were originally built principally of turf and timber, are buried underneath later Roman deposits, or, as in the case of a number of marching camps at Wroxeter, have been ploughed out and are now identifiable only as cropmarks. However, Caerwent (*Venta Silurum*) was refortified with a substantial stone wall in the middle years of the third century AD, providing us with the most substantial surviving military structure in the Borderland.

At Chester, the playing-card shape of the Roman fort is still etched out in the town plan. In the region of the cathedral and streets such as Bridge Street, Eastgate Street and Hall Street the roads follow lines originally marked out as part of the internal communication pattern of a Roman fort. The Chester fortress called *Deva* after the Celtic name for the Dee, which meant 'goddess', lay on the north bank of the river where it flowed around the end of a low sandstone plateau. It was a site well placed to serve both north Wales and north-western England. The lines of the eastern and northern walls of the fortress were later re-used for the medieval walls, parts of which can still be identified. A section of the Roman quay survives below the medieval wall some 600 feet away from the fortress, although the line of the Roman river course is now completely filled up. The earliest activity at Chester appears to have been when turf and timber defences were built in the late seventies AD. Early in the second century AD a stone wall was added to the front of the rampart and stone gate towers were built. The plan of this stone fortress carefully followed that of its wooden predecessor. Excavations within this fort have so far revealed second-century barracks, granaries and workshops as well as a substantial *principia* (headquarters building). Additionally there was an intramural bath building with a *palaestra* (covered exercise hall). Outside to the east of the fortress was an amphitheatre originally built in wood and later reconstructed in stone.

Unlike the majority of lowland military sites Chester does not appear to have attracted a substantial civilian population. However, just to the south along Watling Street at Heronbridge, there was a small manufacturing settlement with stores and workshops and tile and pottery producing centres nearby. The other major fortress, *Isca*, at Caerleon, was named like Chester after the river on which it stood, located on a spur of higher ground in the valley of the tidal Usk. The defences, enclosing some 70 acres, were originally constructed in the late seventies of clay, turf and timber, but by the end of the first century the conversion of the fortress to stone was well underway. A stone wall was inserted in front of the rampart, and within the fort there

13 The centre of modern Chester around the cathedral. The twentieth-century street plan owes much to its Roman predecessor

were barracks and the other usual military buildings; to the west there was an amphitheatre, substantial remains of which survive today. The amphitheatre seems to have lain within a walled annexe which accommodated a parade ground and bath buildings, one of which lies beneath the medieval castle bailey. Outside the annexe walls there was a civilian settlement which contained the *mansio* (official guest house), which dates from the mid second century. Inscriptions mentioning Diana and the Mythriad have been found indicating that there were temples dedicated to these deities in the vicinity.

An even more unusual survival can be seen at Leintwardine on the Shropshire/Herefordshire border where the village high street mirrors the *via principalis* (principal road) of the Roman fort and civilian settlement and where traces of ditches and ramparts can still be identified around the village. The fort at Leintwardine village was built sometime after the nearby fort at Bucton had been demolished. It was constructed on rising ground to the north of the River Teme and there was a small annexe containing a bathhouse between the fort and the river. It would appear from such military evidence that Leintwardine functioned as a supply depot for the central Marches, held perhaps by a single unit of about 500 men.

The chancel of the parish church which sits on the eastern line of the defences is substantially higher than the nave because it was built over the defensive rampart. At Leintwardine the Roman road known as Watling Street West crosses the river Teme, and this crossing clearly formed the focus for a number of military and civilian settlements. Close to Leintwardine is another unusual Roman survival in the Iron Age hillfort at Brandon Camp where cropmarks of an apparently Roman military nature have recently been identified within the boundaries of the hillfort ramparts, alongside the more usual Iron Age ring ditches and enclosures. The Roman re-use for military purposes of prehistoric hillforts is not unknown, the best example being the Roman fort which lies within the massive hillfort at Hod Hill, Dorset, but such examples from Marcher hillforts are rare.

14 Brandon Camp, an Iron Age hillfort to the south of Leintwardine. In addition to the prehistoric cropmarks visible inside the fort, there are some faint rectilinear markings which appear to represent Roman military buildings. This suggests the fort, which lies in an area of intense Roman military activity, was garrisoned probably during the early phases of the occupation

There appears to have been a fort, similar to that at Leintwardine, at Forden Gaer, near Montgomery, where there was one of the most important Roman stations in mid Wales. This lay on the traditional political watershed, later to be marked by Offa's Dyke, on a ford at the point where the river Severn turns due west to run into central Wales. The fort, which is about 7 acres in size, is still identifiable on the ground through earthworks marking the former defences, but it is best seen from the air when its conventional playing-card shape can be clearly appreciated. Forden Gaer was probably founded during the early stages of the Roman attack on Wales, but the main period of military activity here was somewhat later (AD 85–125), when it lay on the arterial road that gave access to central and northern Wales from Wroxeter and Chester.

Roman Towns

Most of the Marcher towns had clear military origins changing to a civilian role only as the theatre of conflict moved decisively northwards and westwards. With the exception of Wroxeter, they were relatively small, serving as administrative and commercial centres for the local rural population.

The Roman towns of the Borderland did not survive long into the post-Roman period. With the eventual collapse of Roman administration sometime in the fifth or sixth centuries, the urban tradition appears to have died out completely. The advanced level of Roman technology had meant that Romano-British towns could be sited in lowland areas and defended, if need be, by massive man-made walls and ditches. But this situation did not last very long after Roman control had ceased, and when urban life began to revive three or four centuries later sites were chosen with completely different criteria in mind. One of these abandoned Romano-British towns provides us with the most substantial surviving segment of civil Roman masonry in the whole of Britain – Wroxeter, *Viroconium Cornoviorum*, which was a city built on a flat glacial plateau overlooking the Severn. It was originally established as a military base from which the conquest of Wales could take place, but was developed as a civil town after the western command was transferred to Chester in about AD 78. The town became the capital of the British tribe the Cornovii, whose original headquarters appears to have been in the hillfort on top of the nearby Wrekin.

An inscription from over the entrance to the forum was erected about AD 130 in honour of the Emperor Hadrian by the *Civitas Cornoviorum*. When the forum gateway collapsed the inscription was smashed into fragments, but it has been restored and is housed in Rowley's House Museum in Shrewsbury; there is also a replica on display in the site museum. The visible buildings at Wroxeter represent part of a large bath house complex from the middle of the town, with the famous upstanding masonry known as the Old Work forming the gateway between the baths and the exercise area. It is one of the few substantial pieces of civilian Roman building that has survived in Britain, as in most towns where there was later medieval occupation the walls have been dismantled and the stone re-used elsewhere. The Old Work has the appearance of the skeleton of a great brooding primeval beast, and although now it is seen completely out of its original context, it gives us some idea of the size and scale of the original Roman city. Outside the bath area the main lines of the street plan and associated buildings have been identified from parchmarks on aerial photographs.

15 *A photograph of the Old Work and bathhouse at Wroxeter, taken earlier this century. A considerable amount of excavation and restoration has taken place since then, but the picture captures the atmosphere of an abandoned Roman city, the fourth largest in Roman Britain*

There is a long history of excavation at Wroxeter which goes back to the Middle Ages. The earliest recorded digging here was in 1292 when four men were brought to court for having 'dug by night at Wroxeter in search of treasure', but it was reported that they found nothing. The Roman city has provided a ready source of worked stone over the centuries for farmers and road builders. The great civil engineer Thomas Telford noted that the site of the city was distinguished by 'a blacker or richer soil or mold than the adjacent fields and the stone foundations of ancient buildings at no great depth under the surface of the ground are manifest in long continued drought, so that when the occupiers of the land need any stone for building they mark the scorched parts and after the harvest dig out what serves their purpose'. This is one of the earliest references to parchmarks, features which in recent years have been widely used by archaeologists to identify stony sites from the air. Among his many other claims to fame Telford was one of the first people to have undertaken archaeological excavations at Wroxeter and claimed that he was the first to identify the baths here. After some small pillars and a paved floor had been found, Telford 'caused the place to be cleared to a considerable extent and thus brought to light a set of Roman baths'.

It used to be thought on the basis of rather slender archaeological evidence that Wroxeter suffered a violent end, possibly at the hands of unruly mercenaries, but recent extensive excavations have demonstrated that after the Roman buildings had collapsed or been dismantled, substantial structures were built on top of the rubble. As yet the precise date of these buildings and their implications is uncertain. Additionally the tombstone of a late fifth-century Irish chieftain has been found within the defences, indicating that *Viroconium* was active during the sub-Roman migration period. Nevertheless by the middle of the sixth century *Viroconium* appears to have been finally abandoned and left to generations of stone robbers who used the crumbling buildings as a convenient quarry. The present parish church of the small hamlet of Wroxeter contains substantial amounts of re-used Roman masonry and the pillars flanking the gateway to the churchyard are appropriately and poignantly formed by Roman pillars. When urban life revived in Shropshire in the Saxon period a naturally defended loop in the Severn at Shrewsbury some five miles to the north-west of Wroxeter was eventually chosen in preference to the flat Severn terrace site as the centre of commerce.

In Herefordshire the Roman town of *Magnis* at Kenchester presents something of an enigma. It lies on a gravel terrace in the Wye valley a few miles to the west of Hereford, just below the extensive Iron Age fort at Credenhill. Nothing survives above ground but the unusual hexagonal shape of the defences, a little like that of a distorted kite in plan, and they can still be traced in field boundaries enclosing an area of about 22 acres. The pattern of roadways and internal divisions has been identified from cropmarkings. William Stukeley, visiting the site in 1721, identified its gateway and recorded that Kenchester

> was a palays of Offas, as sum say.
>
> Peaces of the walles and turrets, yet appere *prope fundamenta* and more should have appeared if the people of the town and other therabout had not in tymes paste pulled down muche and myked out the best for these buildings. Of late one Mr Brainton buylding a place at Stretton a myle from Kenchester dyd fetch much tayled stone there towards his buildings.

Subsequently there have been a number of excavations which have indicated that the massive defences, which are over six feet thick, were rebuilt on at least three occasions between AD 150 and 350 and that within the walls there are substantial buildings including some with mosaic pavements.

16 Aerial view of the Roman town of Kenchester. Much of the interior road system shows up in the form of parchmarks and the shape of the town defences is demarcated by the modern field boundaries

Among the 'excavators' were a 'party of gentlemen' from Hereford, who dug here in the 1840s with Dean Merewether, an early excavator of the great prehistoric tumulus at Silbury hill in Wiltshire. When Professor Richard Atkinson was excavating the heart of the mound in the 1960s he came across an urn which had been deposited by the Dean to mark his earlier abortive search for a 'golden horseman' at the core of the great mound. The precise nature and function of the settlement at Kenchester is still not entirely clear: it seems to fall into the category of a small town although some authorities have suggested that it was little more than a village. The presence of bastions added to the defences would, however, put it in the very rare category of a fortified village. There is, however, no evidence to suggest that Kenchester was ever a regional capital and it is commonly assumed that the whole of Herefordshire was governed from Cirencester as part of the administrative canton of the Dobunni. Like Wroxeter, in the post-Roman period it was abandoned and its successor was at Hereford on a crossing of the river Wye some six miles to the east. The font in the nearby church is of re-used Roman masonry and farm buildings in the vicinity use stones from *Magnis*. Its place name, however, was incorporated into the Saxon tribal name of the Magonsaetan who occupied much of Herefordshire and southern Shropshire in the post-Roman period.

A number of other small-sized towns appear to have existed at places such as Whitchurch (*Mediolanum*) in Shropshire and *Ariconium* close to Ross-on-Wye in Herefordshire. At *Mediolanum* a military fort was build in the first century AD on the road running from *Viroconium* to the legionary base at Chester. Later a small civil settlement grew up here. The modern high street follows the line of the original Roman road and the basic street plan reflects that of the Roman town. At *Ariconium* extensive evidence of iron working has been found and it has been suggested that the Roman complex here may have extended over as much as 250 acres comprising a posting station, villa estate and industrial site. *Ariconium* was included in a Roman road gazeteer, the *Antonine Itinerary*, and the survival of its name for the district of Erging or Archenfield which lies to the west of the Wye shows that it was a settlement of some significance. Early Roman material has been located here and it is possible that it was occupied in the pre-Roman Iron Age. The persistence of a dialect word 'scowles', a Celtic term to describe the muddled overgrown holes and hillocks of ancient iron-ore workings, suggests a very long history of industry in the region. Not far away at Whitchurch another industrial site of Roman iron processing was uncovered in the 1950s. Excavation here has revealed a number of iron workings dating from the fifteenth and sixteenth centuries as well as the Roman period. It is clear that the Romans had considerable interest in the mineral resources of the Borderland. Five pigs of lead inscribed with the name of the Emperor Hadrian have been found near the Stiperstones and a hoard of thirty Roman denarii was discovered in a copper mine on Llanymynech hill.

One of the most exciting of the Roman industrial sites in the Marches is at Linley Hall, where the West Onny river emerges from the hill country between the Stiperstones and Corndon hill. The Roman interest in this district is undoubted because of the lead pigs mentioned above. The Linley Hall site has an area of some 12 acres and the muddled earthworks here appear to cover a major Roman industrial plant certainly associated with the lead working and possibly silver mining as well. Elsewhere extensive mining in the eighteenth and nineteenth centuries at Shelve and Snailbeach have removed or obscured all evidence of Roman occupation. It has also been suggested that industrial remains found at a group of three Roman marching camps at Brompton may have been connected with silver working.

It is difficult to assess just how deeply Romanised the Welsh Borderland became. Apart from the towns and evidence of mineral working, there is relatively little evidence of Roman rural settlement. Villas are rare although not unknown, and there are undoubtedly a number of others awaiting discovery. Far more common are the 'native' Romano-British settlement sites, which have been located by aerial photography largely on river gravel spreads. Although very few of these have yet been excavated they do appear to represent the continuation of Iron Age settlements into the Roman period. So far little is known about the make-up of such settlements, but they are probably the predecessors of later medieval villages.

Roman Roads

Part of the Roman road system has been preserved in the pattern of modern communications. The eventual movement of the political and commercial centre from *Viroconium* to Shrewsbury in the post-Roman period, however, brought a subtle adaptation of the original network. Watling Street, which linked Wroxeter with Redhill (*Uxacona*), Pencridge (*Pennocrucium*) and eventually London, has been preserved in the line of the A5. A minor detour from the Roman road at Overley hill forms part of Telford's improvements to the London/Holyhead road early in the nineteenth century. The ancient road alignment is nevertheless preserved in parish boundaries. West of Shrewsbury the Roman road joining *Viroconium* to the massive fort at *Lavobrinta* (Fordengaer) is preserved as a secondary road only as far as Westbury. The Roman road then proceded westwards along Long Mountain, the line now being marked for two miles by Westbury parish boundary; the modern road, however, follows the river Ray southwards implying that during the Roman period the marshy Ray valley did not provide convenient access into central Wales. Along the Roman road travelled the consignments of minerals which the Romans extracted from the central Welsh hills as soon as they had established themselves at Wroxeter. The road from *Viro-*

conium to *Mediolanum* is preserved in short stretches as a modern road, but it can be identified from field boundaries and cropmarks. The road running southwards from *Viroconium* to Leintwardine is easily identifiable on the ground running southwards through the always important Church Stretton gap, and there is a remarkable stretch of Roman road between Craven Arms and Leintwardine which stands out very clearly in aerial photographs, and which also goes under the name of Watling Street.

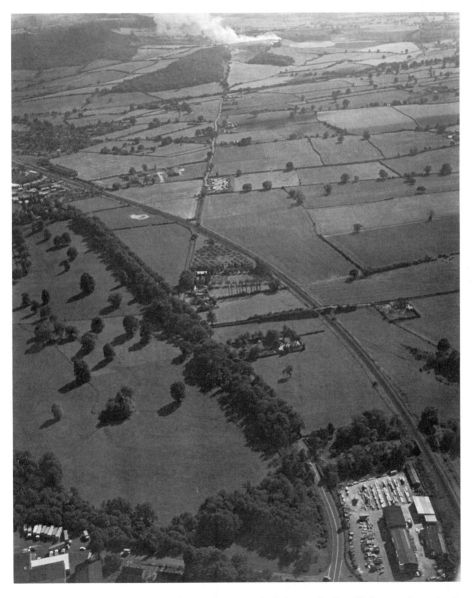

17   *A Roman road in the region of Eardisley, Herefordshire, which still plays an important role in the shaping of the modern landscape*

In eastern Shropshire the line of the road running from *Pennocrucium* to *Mediolanum* can be traced in the modern road pattern. A stretch of this road which crosses the flood plain of the river Tern to the south of Market Drayton has been known as the Longford since at least the thirteenth century. The name Pave or Pavement Lane, found in Woodcut parish near Newport and elsewhere in the Marches, may also refer back to former Roman roads. There are also a considerable number of villages in the Marches which incorporate the name Stretton (Old English, *straet-ton* – literally, street village), indicating settlement by or along a Roman road. The preservation of Roman roads both as parish boundaries and as incorporated into later road systems indicates that there was a substantial degree of at least passive survival of the Roman communication pattern into the Saxon period.

Places to Visit

Wroxeter (Viroconium)

Wroxeter lies five miles to the south-east of Shrewsbury. The most obvious feature is the Old Work which has miraculously survived generations of stone-robbers and over 1800 years of Marcher weather. It was originally part of the south wall of a large aisled building which occupied all the area between the site museum and the rest of the site which formed an exercise hall (*palaestra*) for the baths. About AD 350 it collapsed and in the building rubble several timber structures, some very large, have been identified by recent excavation. Philip Barker, who has dug this part of the site, has suggested that the buildings were occupied into the fifth and sixth centuries. The rest of the exposed site belongs to the public baths, most of which have been exposed since the middle of the nineteenth century, meaning that the detailed history of the development cannot be recovered. The *piscina*, or swimming bath, however, has only recently been excavated. The baths were erected after AD 150 and many of the visible walls belong to this period, but below there was an earlier civic building which appears never to have been finished.

The bath house was entered through the double doors leading from the exercise area which partially filled the present gap in the middle of the Old Work. On the underside of this gap can be seen the two rounded impressions left by the relieving arches, now disappeared, which lay above the lintels of the two doors. The bath complex itself consists of the normal range of rooms including the *frigidarium* (cold plunge baths) and *tepidarium* (moist heat) and *caldarium* (hot). On either side of the latter are recesses for hot baths where there are small tile columns known as *pilae* which form part of the hypercaust system. The small swimming bath, *piscina*, has an apse at each end, an unusual feature of Roman baths, and is the only visible example of a Roman *piscina* in Britain apart from the great bath at Bath. The excavated evidence suggests that in fact it was never completed.

On the other side of the road from the bath house complex is a long line of column stumps which formed part of the portico of the eastern side of the forum. The whole of the latter was excavated in the 1920s but only this part has been left exposed, providing an impressive but tantalising hint of the former splendour of civic Wroxeter. The remainder of the site is presently under farmland and represents one of the most important archaeological reservoirs anywhere in Britain. Its location here on the western fringes of England has protected it from too much serious damage in recent years but the opportunity it represents for fully understanding the nature of the Romano-British town has yet to be completely grasped. In addition to a small museum on the site at Wroxeter, much excavated material from the Roman town is on display in Rowley's House Museum in Shrewsbury.

18 *The forum inscription from Wroxeter. Excavations at Wroxeter in the 1920s produced one of the largest and finest inscriptions from Roman Britain, recording the erection of the building by the* Civitas Cornoviorum *(the Cornovii tribe) under the Emperor Hadrian in* AD *130. The original is in Rowley's House Museum, but there is a copy in the little museum on the site at Wroxeter*

It is not surprising that the Romans paused once they reached the river Severn at Wroxeter: just a few miles to the west are the lowering hills of the Welsh massif, a region which although the Romans conquered they never seriously occupied. Today it is an evocative site in its isolation but for the Romans it must have represented the most westerly edge of the civilised world, rather like *Volubilis* in Morocco represented the last serious outpost of civilisation before the Atlas mountains and the Sahara desert.

The other monument to visit at Wroxeter is the now redundant church of St Andrew which is worth seeing for the massive re-used Roman masonry which makes up the northern wall of the nave, as at nearby Atcham. The pillars of the churchyard are also made up of re-used Roman pillars. One wonders what lies below the floor surface, sited as the church is within the defences of the former Roman city.

19 *The gateway of the churchyard of St Andrew's, Wroxeter, with its evocative use of Roman columns. The church, which lies within the defences of the former Roman city, has a considerable amount of re-used Roman masonry in its walls*

Caerleon (Isca)

Caerleon, which means the 'city of the legion', was the home of the second Augustian legion and is situated four miles to the north-east of Newport. The fortress here was established by Frontinus in AD 74/75. There was reconstruction of the area in the third century, but before the beginning of the fourth century the fortress was no longer garrisoned, part of the legion having been transferred to Richborough in Kent. Regular excavations since 1926 have provided many details of the layout of the 50-acre fortress but only one small portion in the west corner is visible today.

The interior of the fortress was occupied by rows of barrack blocks, originally sixty-four in all, arranged in pairs facing each other. The church of Caerleon overlies part of the headquarters and thus roughly marks the central point of the Roman fortification.

20 Aerial view of Caerleon showing the outline of the Roman fortification and the amphitheatre on the left-hand side

21 Excavations in progress at the amphitheatre at Caerleon in the late 1920s. The work was carried out by Sir Mortimer Wheeler, then director of the National Museum of Wales

The outstanding Roman monument at Caerleon, however, is the amphitheatre dug by Sir Mortimer Wheeler in 1926/7, which is still the only completely excavated one of its sort in Britain. It was constructed in AD 80 and appears to have been primarily used for military exercises and displays, although no doubt blood sports and gladiatorial combats were staged here too. There were various modifications in the middle of the second and at the beginning of the third centuries until it was finally abandoned when the garrison left. Long before Wheeler's excavation the amphitheatre was known locally as King Arthur's Round Table. Geoffrey of Monmouth in his *History of the Kings of Britain* (1136) linked the Arthurian legend with Caerleon, much of which must have still been standing to a considerable height in the early Middle Ages. Next to the little museum which was originally founded by the Caerleon Antiquarians in 1850 is the parish church dedicated to a sixth-century saint, Cattwg (Cattock) of Llancarfan.

Chester (Deva)

Unlike Wroxeter the Roman *Deva* is largely built over. With the outstanding exceptions of the north wall and the amphitheatre, its surviving remains are in the form of isolated fragments scattered throughout the modern city. The first major fortress was built here around AD 76–8. The initial garrison, as shown by tombstones, was the second Adiutrix legion, but this was replaced in AD 87 or later by the twentieth Valeria Victrix which then remained at Chester throughout the Roman occupation. Rebuilding in stone started at the beginning of the second century, first of the defences and then of the internal buildings. The defences were rebuilt on a larger scale during the early fourth century. The final withdrawal of the garrison occurred about 380. To the north of the east gate is a fine portion of Roman fortress wall. King Charles Tower stands on the Roman north-east corner and from here to the north gate runs an amazing section of well-preserved Roman wall standing to a height of 15 feet and missing only its wall walk.

Elsewhere in the town can be traced the remains of the Roman street pattern as well as a considerable range of other fragmentary Roman building, including the *sacellum*, where the legionary standards were kept, the *principia*, and the bath house. However, the most interesting monument in Roman Chester is the amphitheatre, which is now open to the public. Only the north half is visible, the remainder lying buried under a convent. Excavations have shown that the original timber amphitheatre was replaced at the end of the first century by a stone one. Adjoining the entrance on the left was a small room which was used as a shrine to Nemesis, the goddess of fate. The arena floor shows traces of repair in about AD 300 after a long period of disuse. There are two other extramural monuments of intrinsic interest: part of the Roman quay wall, situated on the racecourse opposite the end of Black Friars, and a much-weathered figure of Minerva in the public garden called Edgars Field, to the south of the river. The Grosvenor

Museum in Grosvenor Street contains one of the finest displays of Roman military material and sculpture in Britain.

Caerwent (Venta Silurum)

One of the most impressive sites in the whole of Roman Britain, Caerwent was the market town of the Silures tribe. It covered only 44 acres but had all the usual buildings, forum, basilica, temple and baths, expected of a tribal capital.

Caerwent was a frontier town founded at the end of the first century which may have originated as a yet unlocated fort, but despite its apparently military layout the site displays most of the characteristics of a Romano-British town. The main street, which is in fact part of the road from Gloucester to Caerleon, crosses the settlement between opposite gates. In the middle of the town the forum and basilica were the dominant features; however, because of the relatively small size of the town these structures are modest in size compared to those at Wroxeter. Other public buildings included a bath house complex to the south of the forum and a temple to the east. There was another sub-circular temple just outside the eastern wall of the town. A large building just inside the town's southern gate is believed to be a *mansio*, the official guesthouse and inn, and consists of some twenty rooms arranged around three sides of a courtyard. To the north of the forum there is the base of a structure which may have been an amphitheatre. In addition to the public buildings there were a number of large courtyard houses which were splendidly furnished with mosaic floors and fitted out with a high level of plumbing; perhaps these were occupied by the former tribal leaders. The remaining areas of the town appear to have been occupied by shopkeepers and craftsmen.

The defences at Caerwent, which form by far the most spectacular surviving remnant of Roman occupation here, started in the form of an earthen rampart erected sometime after AD 130, possibly in reaction to increasing local unrest following the removal of many troops from south Wales. In the second half of the third century a massive stone wall was inserted at the front of the rampart. This was 10 feet wide at the base and stood over 16 feet high in places. Later on, sometime after AD 350, a series of bastions, probably intended for housing catapults, was added as a precaution during deteriorating political conditions.

The greater part of the Roman town now lies under fields and orchards. However, there is still much to see: in addition to the massive Roman walls, there are the foundations of a number of the houses and there are also the remains of a Romano-Celtic temple. In the church porch are two Roman inscribed stones, one of which records Paulinus who, having commanded the second Augustan legion at Caerleon, went on to become the governor of two Roman provinces in Gaul, Narbonne and Lyon. The parish church is now dedicated to St Stephen, whose saints day is identical to that of the festival of St Tathan, a fifth-century Irish missionary. It therefore seems probable that an earlier church was dedicated to the Irish saint, who reputedly founded a monastic school at Caerwent. In the south-east corner of the Roman town is a mound which may have been a small Norman castle or motte which utilised the surviving Roman walls as part of its defences. It was probably one of the castles thrown up by William Fitz Osbern, Earl of Hereford, during the initial stages of the Norman Conquest of Wales in about 1070.

CHAPTER FOUR

The Dark Ages – The Post-Roman Hiatus

The Roman Legacy

The centuries following the end of the Roman administration are traditionally known as the Dark Ages, and represent one of the most fascinating yet tantalising periods in Borderland history. They are fascinating because it was during this time that the characteristically subtle balance between English and Welsh developed; and it was also when many places acquired the Anglo-Saxon names by which we now know them. They are tantalising because of the absence of firm evidence, either documentary or archaeological, with which to build up a clear picture. And so any historical account of the period must remain sketchy and tentative. Legends from the early part of this period are common, involving larger-than-life figures such as Ambrosius Aurelianus and King Arthur and a collection of early saints.

It is clear that the Romanisation of the Borderland was very patchy, with villas and Roman settlements concentrated in the areas around the major towns, notably in the Wye valley around Kenchester and the Severn valley around Wroxeter. Elsewhere, particularly in the hilly areas, there is little evidence of Roman activity and occupation apart from mining and it seems probable that throughout the Roman era the inhabitants of these regions lived a life very similar to that of their Iron Age forebears. For example, it is almost certain that Latin had made little progress as a vernacular language and that British (or Celtic) was still spoken by the vast majority of people in the Borderland in the fifth century. Roman place-name survivals in the Marches are surprisingly rare. Only the names of major settlements appear to have survived, and even then in a severely modified form. As I have already mentioned, the Roman *Magnis* (Kenchester) appears to survive in the tribal name of the Magonsaetan and possibly in the place name Maunde, while the largest settlement of them all, *Viroconium*, has influenced the form of several local place names, including Wroxeter itself, Wrockwardine and the Wrekin, which the place-name historian Margaret Gelling considers may have carried the Romano-British name *Viriconio* even before it was applied to the town. The Romano-British names which many smaller settlements must have carried have disappeared, possibly through a process of distortion which has rendered them unrecognisable, or more likely because they were dropped in favour of British, and later Anglo-Saxon, names. This is reflected in the fact that many places such as Shrewsbury, *Amwithig*, Wenlock, *LlanMeilen*, and Leominster, *Llanllieni*, carried both English and Welsh (British) place names well into the Middle Ages. This does seem to suggest the survival of the British language over quite considerable areas.

Early Christianity

One legacy the Romans may have left in the Marches was Christianity. It is true that Romano-British Christianity was essentially urbanised, and that the main focus of the Christian church in the late Roman period was most likely Wroxeter, which probably had its own bishop. The collapse of the Roman cities may not, however, have resulted in the complete disappearance of Christianity. One clue to the survival of British Christianity is in the place name Eccles, which comes from the early Welsh *egles* – church, which implies that Christianity must have preceded the Anglo-Saxon language here. Eccleston, near Chester, and Eccleshall in Staffordshire both incorporate the distinctive *eccles* element, and both lie within the former territory of the Cornovii. Further south, in Herefordshire, are Eccleswall and Eccles Green, whose names may also represent communities of British Christians who survived the general breakdown of Roman life in the Marches. The question of sub-Roman Christian continuity is, however, an extremely awkward one, made all the more difficult to unravel by the arrival of a new wave of Christianity in the sixth and seventh centuries.

This revival of Christianity was stimulated not from its traditional sources in Continental Europe, where contacts had been more or less totally severed by the advance of the pagan Anglo-Saxons in eastern England, but from the Celtic west and from the Mediterranean. From the mid fifth century onwards contact between the Celtic west and the Mediterranean world was re-established in trade routes along which spiritual ideas appear to have travelled as freely as commercial traffic. Christianity expressed itself through monasticism and led to the 'Age of the Saints' which marked the golden age of Celtic piety and devotion in the south-west, in Wales, and to a lesser degree in the Marches.

Church dedications can provide valuable hints about the degree of British survival. It is true that during the early Middle Ages many churches originally belonging to Celtic saints were rededicated to saints fashionable with the Normans, but there was considerable opposition to this process and the proposed Roman saints' names were frequently rejected locally. A compromise was often made by rededicating the church to the Virgin or to St Michael and All Angels. This normally resulted in a renaming of the village as well, and so on the Herefordshire/Monmouth border there are some Llanfihangels and Michaelchurches, and a dozen or more Llanfairs (dedicated to the Virgin): there are at least 150 such dedications altogether in Wales and the Border counties. Here and there are clues to earlier dedications. The most notable of these is Dubricius or Dyfrig, who died in the early sixth century, one of the earliest and most important saints of south Wales. Reputedly he was born at Madley, the son of Pepin, king of Erging (Archenfield) near Hereford, and went on to found churches at *Ariconium*, Hentland, Whitchurch, Madley and Moccas. As with all such early saints his life is shrouded in mystery, and Geoffrey of Monmouth would even have us believe that he crowned Arthur king of Britain at Caerwent. More probably he is said to have consecrated Bishop Sampson, the chief saint of Brittany. Dedications to other Celtic saints include Dewy (or David) at Dewchurch and Kilpeck, and St Beuno at Llanveynoe where there is an early Christian memorial stone. Sellack, near Ross, was anciently known as *Llan Sulluc*, called after St Tysylio who was born at Pengwern and passed through Herefordshire on his way to south Wales and then on to Brittany.

22 Crucifixion carved on panel from St Beuno and St Peter's church, Llanveynoe. Although it is probably ninth- or tenth-century, it has been suggested that it may be Dark Age in origin

23 Inscribed lintel of the ruined church of St John the Baptist at Llanwarne in Archenfield, Herefordshire. The script is mid-Saxon and appears to continue a tradition of early Celtic Christian inscriptions

Following in the wake of Anglo-Saxon political success and conversion to Christianity we find church dedications to early Saxon saints, some of which may have replaced existing Celtic dedications and many of which in their turn also disappeared after the Norman Conquest. While the majority of surviving Celtic dedications are found in Herefordshire and the southern Marches, most of the early Saxon dedications came from Shropshire and the northern Marches. I have already mentioned St Mildburg (d. 715) at Much Wenlock, whose shrine became an early pilgrimage centre, and St Oswald (d. 642) at Oswestry. It has been suggested that the place name Cressage (Old English, Christ's Oak) was a reference to a prominent tree at which the gospel was preached. Such preaching places were common during the mid Saxon period and often provided the location for later parish churches. Significantly the ancient church at Cressage was dedicated to the Celtic St Sampson. Appropriately enough another early dedication is found at Wroxeter, where the church is named after St Andrew, one of the most popular saints with early Christian Anglo-Saxons. Close by, on the river Severn, is a unique dedication to St Eata (d. 686), a companion of St Aidan and Bishop of Hexham. In Hereford there were also dedications to St Owen, a sixth-century Breton saint who came to England with St Cadfan, and St Guthlac, a late seventh-century Mercian hermit saint.

24 The parish church of St Eata at Atcham, just upstream from Wroxeter. St Eata was a seventh-century saint and churches dedicated to him are singularly rare. Although parts of the building were constructed during the Middle Ages, the large blocks of stone used in the nave were originally from the Roman town

Among the slightly later Marcher saints of this period was Alkmund (d. *c.* 800), who was originally entombed at Lilleshall, which became an important cult centre before his body was translated to Derby. One of the most important of the Border saints was Aethelbert, King of the East Angles. He was venerated as a martyr because of his murder by King Offa of Mercia, whose daughter Aelfthryth he was visiting at Sutton Walls with a view to marriage. He was assassinated there on 20 May 794 and his body was placed in the river Lugg at Marden and later translated to Hereford, where the cathedral is dedicated to him. During the Middle Ages Hereford became a pilgrimage centre, reputedly second only to Canterbury in England.

Sub-Roman Survival

Let us now turn our attention to the political story of the Marches during the post-Roman era. The nature of the evidence is so fragmentary that it allows a number of widely differing interpretations. There is little overall agreement over dates or the role played by the personalities involved. There is not even any absolute concensus about the date when Roman troops were withdrawn from the Marches. During the last part of the fourth century it appears that conditions in the region were deteriorating fast and that most of the troops were being redeployed in response to attacks, principally from the north, from the Picts and the Irish. Under the Emperor Theodosius (379–95) posts were given to district officers known as *praefecti*, on the understanding that they ruled their districts as petty kings and passed their titles and responsibilities on to their heirs. It is probable that Maximus, who had been an officer serving under Theodosius the Great, subsequently established such an organisation in Wales using either Irish settlers or the existing Celtic tribes as an army. Various attacks seem to have been repulsed by General Flavius Stilicho during the last years of the fourth century. Stilicho was a colourful personality, a Vandal by birth, but married to Theodosius' niece, Serena. The court poet Claudian reports that Stilicho and his troops were taken away from Britain in about 402 and implies in some lines he wrote that the removal of the legion that curbed 'the savage Irish and [read] the marks tattooed on the bodies of dying Picts' was responsible for allowing these barbarians into the region.

During the confused events of the following years we hear of the rise of Vortigern, which is not a personal name but a title such as 'the high chief'. There are various stories and legends concerning Vortigern's attempt to maintain the kingdom, but it is enough to say that according to tradition one of Vortigern's sons, Brittu, became the ruler of the kingdom of Powys, a territory which incorporated both north Wales and much of the northern central Marches. It is believed that the name Powys is derived from *pagenses* – 'the people of the countryside'. It has been suggested that this was a period of relative peace in the Marches and there are strong indications that places such as *Viroconium* still continued to be occupied in one way or another. Evidence for this comes from recent excavations by the archaeologist Philip Barker, showing substantial post-Roman buildings sited on the top of collapsed Roman buildings and revealing attempts to prop up and restore existing buildings. At Wroxeter considerable efforts were made to strip the tile linings off the city's drains, perhaps in order to repair the roofs of surviving buildings at a time when many of the traditional Romano-British building materials had ceased to be produced.

One of the most intriguing aspects of the Borderland during this period is the virtual absence of metal and ceramic artefacts, pottery, and coins – trinkets which all ceased to be used. Utensils appear to have been made from friable materials such as wood, leather and basketry which normally leave no evidence for the modern archaeologist to study. One exception to this was found, however, at Wroxeter in 1967, a much-used stone with the following funerary inscription:

CUNORIX
MACUS MA
QVI COLINE

This has been interpreted as 'The mighty king Cunorix, son of the Holly', and it has been concluded that Cunorix was not British but an Irish chieftain. The tombstone has been dated to the latter part of the fifth century, and by inference it is suggested that he was a mercenary commander employed by the local citizens for protection. Such mercenaries were known as *feoderati*, which simply means 'allied'. The employment of these mercenaries suggests that organised life of a sort at Wroxeter survived into the sixth century; an assumption which is reinforced from the substantial sub-Roman buildings found within the city walls.

Early Anglo-Saxons in the Marches

The story of the Anglo-Saxon domination of the Welsh border is problematic. The political story alone is a confused one and it is far from clear how far political developments were accompanied by changes on the ground. Most important of all we do not know what the real degree of Saxon folk penetration was in the Marches; what linguistic and place-name evidence that does exist would suggest that as late as the ninth century the true Saxon element in the population was very small. Conventionally the initial conquest and occupation of the area later known as Mercia is attributed to the kings of Wessex in the late sixth century. The early Mercians were an obscure people, politically dependent on the northern kingdom of Deira. A crucial battle was fought at Chester in 614, when the Saxon Aethelferth defeated the combined forces of Gwynedd and Powys. Some centuries later Bede records the victory of the pagans over the Christians thus:

> The warlike king of the English, Aethelfrid . . . having raised a mighty army, made a very great slaughter of that perfidious nation [the British] at the City of Legions [Chester] . . . Being about to give battle, he observed their priests . . . Most of them were of the monastery of Bangor [on Dee] . . . Many . . . resorted among others to pray at the aforesaid battle . . . to defend them against the swords of the barbarians. King Aethelfrid being informed . . . said, 'If then they cry to their God against us, in truth, though they do not bear arms, yet they fight against us, because they oppose us by their prayers.' He therefore commanded them to be attacked first, and then destroyed with the rest of the impious army, not without considerable loss of his own forces.

It is generally accepted that this battle opened the route to north Wales, which was taken by Aethelferth's successor, Edwin. It has been suggested that it was at this stage, with an English army on the doorstep, that Wroxeter was finally abandoned as the political capital of the Cornovii (or indeed Powys) and a better protected site chosen.

In AD 628 the Mercians, led by a pagan king, Penda, broke into the region of the lower Severn and later together with the Welsh, defeated Oswald at the battle of Maserfelt (AD 641), better known as Oswestry (from St Oswald's tree). Oswald, a Christian, was later canonised and the Norman town founded afterwards was named after him. The resulting kingdom of the Magonsaetan embraced both Shropshire south of the Severn and the plain of Herefordshire. Boundaries of this territory are still preserved in the diocese of Hereford. Bishops of Worcester were frequently styled Bishops of the Hwicce (a tribal name) and by analogy it has been suggested that the Bishops of Hereford could originally have been regarded as the Bishops of the Magonsaete. The northern part of Shropshire formed part of the kingdom of the Wreocensaetan.

The transfer of economic and political power from Wroxeter to Shrewsbury which was the eventual consequence of these events may not have been a straightforward operation. Cynddylan, an early seventh-century British hero, was said to have lived in a great hall at Pengwern (Hall of the Welsh), a white town by the Alder woods. A number of ninth-century poems, notably the *Canu Llywarch Hen*, mourn the death of Cynddylan and his family. According to the poem, Pengwern is in ruins, the well known lands by the Tren (Tern) are empty and all Powys grieves; only Cynddylan's sister, Heledd, survives to weep:

My brothers were slain at one stroke,
Cynan, Cynddylan, Cynwraith,
Defending Tren, ravaged town . . .
White town between Tren and Trafal,
More common was blood on the field's face
Than ploughing of fallow . . .
The hall of Cynddylan, dark is the roof,
Since the Saxon cut down
Powys's Cynddylan and Aelfan . . .
It's not Ffreuer's death I mourn for tonight
But myself, sick and feeble,
My brothers and my land I lament. . .
Heledd the hawk I am called.
O God! to whom are given
My brothers' steeds and their lands?

The poem also contains other topographical references to places such as the river Severn, the Wrekin, Ercall, and Baschurch; it would also seem from the poem that Powys then covered the later county of Shropshire, a claim to be reiterated by the medieval Welsh historian Giraldus Cambrensis.

Various attempts have been made to identify the site of Pengwern, which appears to have been the intermediate centre between Wroxeter and Shrewsbury. Suggestions have included Wroxeter and Shrewsbury themselves, as well as Bury Walls to the south of Shrewsbury, but perhaps the most likely candidate is the Berth, a fortified glacial hillock surrounded by a rampart and inturned entrance linked by causeways across an area of marsh close to Baschurch where Cynddylan was buried. The site of the Berth is an evocative one today, silent and eerie, well suited as the home of one of the last British heroes. If such a hiatus in the history of settlement did occur, it would explain why Shrewsbury did not acquire a cathedral and the county of Shropshire became divided between the diocese of Hereford and Lichfield. For if Shrewsbury had been in existence as an important political centre in the seventh century at the time the diocesan map was being drawn up, it seems most unlikely that it would not have been able to have exerted control over the Wreocensaetan territory. It is also worth noting that other hillforts in the region such as the Breidden and Old Oswestry also appear to have been reoccupied at this time.

Penda himself was killed in 654 at a battle near Leeds. He was succeeded by his son Peada, who was baptised and founded a monastery at Lichfield. Another of Penda's sons was Merewalh, who is recorded as 'king of the Magonsaete'. Among his possessions was the land purchased from him for the founding of a convent at Much Wenlock in 618 of which his daughter Mildburg eventually became Abbess. A medieval version of the life of St Mildburg relates how her father was baptised in 650.

These decades in the middle and later part of the seventh century were crucial for the formation of the Marches. They saw the establishment of Anglo-Saxon political control over most of the region, control that was often unstable and which generally looked eastwards rather than westwards for support. 660 was the year of the so-called 'Tribal Hidage' which pushed the boundaries of Mercia to the Severn. These decades also saw the conversion of the new Saxon rulers to Christianity, and after the Synod of Whitby in 663 the Celtic Church bowed to the power of Rome and St Peter.

Despite the establishment of Anglo-Saxon political control by the seventh century, the process of Anglicisation in the Border was almost certainly slow and there must remain a large question mark over the nature and extent of the settlement by the English in the Marches. The absence of pagan Saxon cemeteries suggests that any actual English settlement which did occur was Christian in character, which places it firmly in the seventh century or later. Despite the fact that the majority of villages carry English place names there is no archaeological evidence to support the idea of a substantial English folk movement into the region during either the seventh or eighth centuries. English control was established through the towns and the church over a predominantly native British population and only gradually did Anglo-Saxon place names and language replace their British predecessors. The story of the survival of British/Celtic culture and language in the Borderland is not a simple one, and it has recently been pointed out by Dr Wendy Davies that there was considerable variation in the scale of the Celtic survival. Additionally, in parts of the Borderland Welsh customs and language were reintroduced from time to time.

It is therefore perhaps surprising that relatively few British place names survive. Amongst these however are Ercall, Hodnet (*hoddnant* – peaceful valley), Lizard (*llysgarth* – hall by the hill), and Prees (*prys* – brushwood); but Celtic names for hills and rivers such as Bredon, Neen, Dulas, Lugg, and Meole are far more common. The river Severn is a Celtic name and is alternatively known by the Welsh name *Hafren*, where the S has been replaced by an H. There are other indications of British survival – the place-name element *walh*, for example, was a term used by the Saxons for the Celts and in western Shropshire, for instance, there are nine Waltons and four Walcots. During the later Saxon period, though, the element *wal* was applied to settlements of serfs, who were not necessarily British. Important evidence for Celtic survival has also been provided by a study of the dialect peculiar to the Border shires. This shows that up to the eighteenth century a linguistic frontier between English and Welsh ran well to the east of the political frontier, from a point between Oswestry and Ellesmere through Upton Magna, two miles to the east of Shrewsbury, and then along the Severn to Bewdley. West of this line it appears that the inhabitants were the descendants of Welsh speakers and that the English of the region was traditionally a Welsh English.

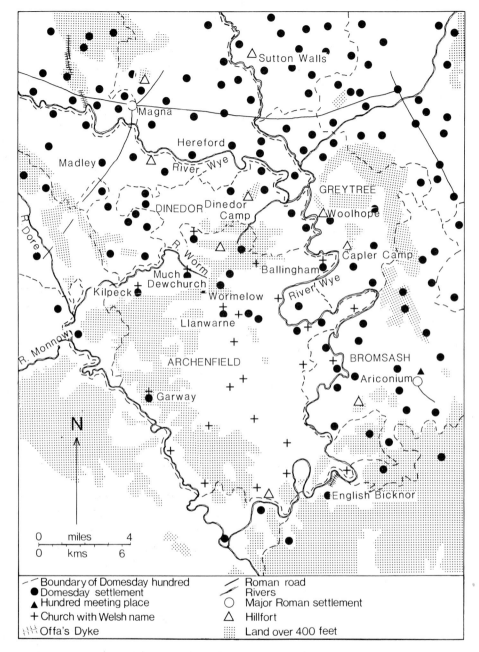

Fig. 6 *Archenfield and central Herefordshire, showing the survival*
of Welsh church dedications

There were other strong legacies on the English side of the border. Some
of these might have been reintroduced during one of the eastward Welsh
movements, or they could originally have been British. For instance,

throughout the Middle Ages in the western parts of Herefordshire and Shropshire, the system of Gwaeli Bond, a form of Welsh communal ownership, survived; also many western Shropshire manors had a number of Welsh inhabitants, known as the Walchera, throughout the Middle Ages. Welsh dues continued to be paid in parts of the Borderland – *trethnedion*, a tribute of oxen, was observed in the Clun region, and a special Welsh court was held at Clun throughout the Middle Ages. Welsh dues also survived at Oswestry until the seventeenth century.

In south-west Herefordshire the area of Archenfield, known as 'Herefordshire in Wales', remained part of the Welsh diocese of St David's until the nineteenth century. The river Wye formed the eastern boundary of Archenfield and the difference in the nature of the place names found in the Domesday survey on either side of the river underlines the totally different cultural history of the region. On the eastern bank are names such as Brockhampton, Fawley, Brompton Abbots and English Bicknor, while on the western bank we find Kilforge, Tryseck, Llanfrothen, Craddock, Daffaluke and Ganarew. Even today, over half the field and farm names in Archenfield are Welsh. Quite apart from the obvious Welsh characteristics of Archenfield there are a number of legends especially associated with the district. One of these was recounted by the early Welsh historian Nennius:

> In the district of Ergyng there is a tomb near the well which is called the Eye of Amr; and the name of the man who is buried in the tump was Amr. He was the son of Arthur the knight and he [the knight] slew him [the son] and buried him there. And men come to measure the tump. It sometimes measures in length seven feet, sometimes fifteen feet, sometimes twelve feet, and sometimes nine feet. Whatever measure you may make it at one time, you will not again find the same measurement. And I myself have proved this.

The brook Amyr is believed by some to be known as Gamber, and the *eye*, or source of the brook, is the round pool a few yards north of the buildings of the farmhouse known as Gamber Head. From this pool the Gamber has its origin, and is the boundary for half a mile between the parishes of Much Birch and Much Dewchurch. The tumulus in which Amyr the son of Arthur was buried was traditionally believed to be a place called Wormelow Tump, of which nothing now remains beyond the name.

The place-name geography along the border is far from straightforward. Over the centuries English names percolated westwards across the Welsh border and periodically Welsh names moved eastwards. For instance, many Welsh names were introduced into Herefordshire after the break-up of the Marcher lordships in the sixteenth century, which was followed by a large influx of Welshmen into England. The complexity of the situation is underlined by some examples from the Monnow valley. The settlement known as Michaelchurch (itself a Normanised Welsh name) in the thirteenth century by the sixteenth century had become Llanfihangel-eskley, but was then retranslated into English by eighteenth-century antiquarians and is now known as Michaelchurch again. Lower down the valley Silas Taylor reported in the seventeenth century that the Welsh Clodock 'hath lately taken the name Longtown'. Yet even at this time some English names were being crowded out by the Welsh: Foscombe and Burycombe, which were found in Longtown in 1540, are no longer there; and today considerably more than half the farm names in the area are Welsh. A few miles lower down the river, it was only at the end of the seventeenth century that the Welsh Pontrilas completely replaced the English Heliston. The process of gradual reconquest of territory by the Welsh language can be traced in the former county of Flintshire, where such typically English Domesday names as Preston, Westbury, Merton and Bishopstree have become the modern Prestatyn, Gwespyr, Mertyn and Bistre.

Places to Visit

Baschurch and the Berth

Baschurch is a village some eight miles to the north of Shrewsbury. Its Dark Age associations are with the hero of the legendary Welsh poems Cynddylan, and Baschurch is where he is reputedly buried. The church of All Saints, which is built of local red sandstone, is medieval and later and contains no obvious pre-Norman Conquest features. A mile and a half to the north of Baschurch, not far from Western Lullingfields, lies the Berth, a lowland hillfort which has been proposed as the site of Pengwern, a stronghold which appears to have been the centre of British power between the collapse of *Viroconium* and the rise of Shrewsbury. The site consists of two glacial hillocks, one about three times larger than the other, linked by causeways to each other and to the mainland. Although the earthwork fortifications are relatively simple the prominence of the two mounds rising from surrounding marshland makes them appear particularly imposing, giving them all the appearance of Dark Age sites such as Glastonbury and South Cadbury. As early as 1825 the historians Owen and Blakeway proposed that the Berth was the site to which Cynddylan, the prince of Powys, fled after his capital of Pengwern was destroyed by the Saxons. Others have subsequently suggested that the Berth was Pengwern itself. Cynddylan is known only from a series of poems known as *The Eulogy on Cynddylan* in which Cynddylan's sister Heledd, in a series of dramatic monologues, laments his death and the destruction of his homeland. It is generally believed that the poems were written in the early ninth century but were recalling events two centuries earlier. The reference to 'Eglwyseu Bassa' in one of the poems cannot very well be to anywhere else but Baschurch, but the actual site of Pengwern is much more difficult to pinpoint from them.

25 The largely Norman church of St Michael at Moccas. This is the probable site of an early Celtic monastery founded by St Dubricius in the sixth century. The church is built of tufa, a sponge-like rock which is formed by water running over calcareous rock deposits, of which there is a good source close to Moccas Court

Moccas, Herefordshire

Today Moccas consists of a fine country house, a park and a largely Norman church which sits by itself close to the river Wye. Although the church is of intrinsic interest as a Norman foundation built in an unusual material – travertine – it is the identification of Moccas with the early Middle Ages that makes it important.

The name Moccas is derived from the Welsh *moch* (plural of *mochyn*, meaning pig) and *ros* (moor). It was an area originally surrounded by water and is therefore characteristic of many early Christian sites. St Dubricius, or Dyfrig, the son of King Pepin of Archenfield and a predecessor of St David, founded a religious school at Hentland near Ross, and from there, accompanied by his disciples, he moved to Moccas. One legend among many says that St Dubricius left Hentland at the bidding of an angel who told him to found a monastery at a place where he would find a white sow with her piglets.

He found the place further up the river Wye 'well wooded and abounding in fish which he called Moccras [or the moor of the pigs]'. Although he founded other monasteries he lived chiefly at Moccas and is said to have died on Bardsey Island about 550. Among the stories told about him was one that he owned land in Caerleon and also that he crowned King Arthur there. These links with the Roman town point to his close connection with Romano-British Christianity. It is said that pestilence laid waste to Moccas about AD 600 and that the last known abbot of Moccas was Bishop Comereg in about 590. After him Moccas Abbey slipped into obscurity and was recorded in later charters simply as a church.

By the time of the Domesday Book Moccas was owned jointly by St Guthlac's Priory, Hereford, and Nigel the Physician. By the reign of Edward I the manor of Moccas had long been in the hands of the de Frene family when a royal licence was granted to Hugh de Frene to fortify his manor house. It is possible that this licence referred to a castle on the edge of a deer park which has all but disappeared.

The present church of St Michael and All Angels, which is largely Norman, was built of tufa or travertine, probably obtained close by at Depple Wood. Moccas is perhaps best known today for its fine deer park (now privately owned) so lovingly described in his diaries by Kilvert, who was for a while rector of the adjacent parish of Bredwardine in the nineteenth century.

Saturday, 22 April 1876

After they had left William and I walked up to the top of Moccas Park, whence we had a glorious view of the Golden Valley shining in the evening sunlight with the white houses of Dorstone scattered about the green hillsides 'like a handful of pearls in a cup of emerald' and the noble spire of Peterchurch rising from out the heart of the beautiful rich valley which was closed below by the Sugar Loaf and the Skyrrid blue above Abergavenny. We came tumbling and plunging down the steep hillside of Moccas Park, slipping, tearing and sliding through oak and birch and fallow wood of which there seemed to be underfoot an accumulation of several feet, the gathering ruin and decay probably of centuries. As we came down the lower slopes of the wooded hillside into the glades of the park the herds of deer were moving under the brown oaks and the brilliant green hawthorns, and we came upon the tallest largest stateliest ash I ever saw and what seemed at first in the dusk to be a great ruined grey tower, but which proved to be the vast ruin of the king oak of Moccas Park, hollow and broken but still alive and vigorous in parts and actually pushing out new shoots and branches. That tree may be 2000 years old. It measures roughly 33 feet round by arm stretching.

I fear those grey old men of Moccas, those grey, gnarled, low-browed, knock-kneed, bowed, bent, huge, strange, long-armed, deformed hunchbacked mis-shapen oak men that stand waiting and watching century after century, biding God's time with both feet in the grave and yet tiring down and seeing out generation after generation, with such tales to tell, as when they whisper them to each other in the midsummer nights, make the silver birches weep and the poplars and aspens shiver, and the long ears of the hares and rabbits stand on end. No human hand set those oaks. They are 'the trees which the Lord hath planted'. They look as if they had been at the beginning and making of the world, and they will probably see its end.

Oswestry

The field where the Roman Catholic church now stands is believed to be the site of the battle of Maserfelt in AD 641, when the pagan king Penda of Mercia defeated and killed Oswald, the Christian King of Northumbria, and the site was named after the defeated king.

Oswestry, although a Norman foundation planted with English settlers, eventually became thoroughly Welsh; and a proportion of the townspeople were and still are Welsh speakers or bilingual and many place names and street names within the town are Welsh or have Welsh equivalents. There were also important links between Welsh bonds and Oswestry, indicating the presence of a flourishing Welsh culture. In the fifteeenth century Gutor Glyn was made a freeman of the borough for his *cwydd* (poem) in praise of Oswestry, and other Welsh bards came to sing the town's praises. Religious life in the town, too, had a strong Welsh element and Welsh services were held in St Oswald's parish church up until 1814.

The town was a frequent bone of contention between the Normans and the Welsh tribes. King John burnt it down in 1215 and eighteen years later Llewellyn of Wales did the same. Owen Glendower sacked the town and almost demolished the church in 1400; and there were three accidental but disastrous fires between 1542 and 1567.

The result of all this destruction and pillage is that Oswestry is now largely a product of the nineteenth century. But odd traces remain: in the Norman foundations of the tower of St Oswald's church; in the original buildings of the Grammar School dating from 1407 and now divided into three cottages; and in the early seventeenth-century Llwyd Mansion in the centre of the town, a well-preserved black and white building bearing, strangely, on its wall the double-headed eagle of the Holy Roman Empire, arms granted to a member of the Llwyd family, owners of the mansion, for distinguished service during the Crusades.

Oswestry Castle, built originally by the Normans, was destroyed on Cromwell's orders after the Civil War and today only fragments of the walls remain. But the site has been made into a public park which offers fine views from the top. King Oswald's Well, which is still in existence, is fed by a spring which, according to legend, sprang from the spot where an eagle dropped one of Oswald's limbs after the battle of Maserfelt. Oswestry's other claim to fame is that it was once one of the country's major railway centres. The first line arrived here in 1848 and by 1866 the town had become the headquarters of the Cumbrian Railways, with extensive locomotive and carriage works.

CHAPTER FIVE

Offa and After – The Late Saxons in the Marches

THE ESTABLISHMENT of political dominance by the Mercians in the seventh century appears to have been followed by the westward movement of the Anglo-Saxon language and placenames. As we have seen, just how much English folk movement there was in the Borderlands at this time is a matter of speculation. Undoubtedly Mercian and Briton mingled over the years, a process indicated by the distorted place names that are in use today. Possibly a long, subtle and unrecorded take over of Celtic lands is remembered in the seventh-century poem of Llywarch Hen where he recalls:

> Mae Wyn, when I was of thy age
> No one trod on my mantle,
> No one without bloodshed ploughed my land.

Late in the same poem there are some lines which could refer to a small band of Mercians who took over land in the Golden Valley: 'A gift has been stolen from me, from the valley of Mafwrn.'

We have already seen that the distribution of English and Welsh place names on the modern map was not the result of one simple process of English settlement, but it is possible that groups of place names with '-ton' endings, such as those found well to the west of Offa's dyke in the Radnor basin, may reflect an early phase of Anglo-Saxon colonisation. Similarly, a group of English settlements in the Severn corridor, between the Welsh border and Montgomery, appear to have been cut off from their Anglo-Saxon base with the establishment of Offa's Dyke later in the century. After 700 Mercia's expansion into the Welsh Borderland proceeded more rapidly, and during the eighth century Mercia became the most powerful of all the Anglo-Saxon kingdoms in England. Aethelbad of Mercia was recognised as overlord of England south of the Humber and later in the century Offa was recognised by the Emperor Charlemagne as one of the princes of Europe. And so, for a brief period Mercia was in the ascendancy.

The Mercian Dyke Systems

Whatever the scale of British survival, by the middle years of the eighth century Anglo-Saxon political control had been established throughout the Marches and was expressed in one of the Border's most famous and intriguing archaeological monuments, Offa's Dyke. This is the most extensive linear earthwork in Britain and is named after Offa, King of Mercia (757–96). In the ninth century Bishop Asser described Offa as the king who 'ordered the construction of a large rampart the whole way from sea to sea between Britain and Mercia'. This frontier with the Welsh, using a combination of rivers and artificial banks and ditches, ran for over a hundred miles from the mouth of the Wye to the estuary of the Dee. There are a number of other shorter stretches of dyke which run more or less in parallel with Offa's Dyke and are believed to be roughly contemporary with it. Indeed if we take all the Marcher linear earthworks of this period they measure just under 150 miles in length. The dyke runs in and out of England still following part of Shropshire's border with Wales to the west of Chirk.

26 *A stretch of Offa's Dyke in the Clun Forest. The ditch here is on the Welsh side of the boundary*

The dyke follows the western margin of the Welsh massif tracing roughly the geographical line along which one might have expected the Mercian advance to have halted. In the south the dyke crosses the Hereford basin and reaches the Severn estuary by following the course of the river Wye, which would imply that the district of Archenfield to the west of the Wye was recognised then as being under Welsh control. In broad terms the present boundary between England and Wales follows the dyke, but today national boundary and dyke are rarely precisely coincidental. The greatest discrepancy is in north Wales, where Offa's Dyke (or possibly another dyke, Wat's Dyke) runs to the west of the present political boundary, and in the south, where the dyke cuts through the western part of Herefordshire and therefore lies to the east of today's boundary line. In its central section the dyke and the present border do not diverge to any great extent, but only along very limited stretches do they coincide. Recent research indicates that the dyke might have reflected a negotiated boundary between the Mercians and the Welsh, built perhaps to control trade between the Border peoples.

Over the centuries Offa's Dyke has been used as if it were a natural topographical feature in the same way as an escarpment or a stream influences later parish and field boundaries, although, significantly, relatively few parish boundaries (approximately 13%) follow the line of the dyke. It could be argued that if these boundaries were created after the dyke had been built the proportion should have been considerably higher. We are left with the intriguing possibility that many parish boundaries in this part of the world were founded earlier than the eighth century, originating perhaps as the margins of large tribal or family territorial units. Earthworks of this magnitude have traditionally attracted legend and superstition, often associated with supernatural forces, and a popular Marcher story is that Offa's Dyke was ploughed by the Devil in a single night.

Offa's Dyke may, however, have been the culmination of several attempts to define the border by means of linear earthworks. Some four miles to the east of Offa's Dyke in northern Shropshire and Cheshire runs Wat's Dyke, which appears to have been an earlier attempt to define the border, possibly the work of an earlier Mercian ruler, Aethelbald (716–57)). Further south, the Rowe Ditch crosses the flood plain of the river Arrow near Pembridge, some three miles to the east of Offa's Dyke. Sir Cyril Fox, the great historian of the dyke, interpreted this work as a barrier across the cleared valley land closing the gap between a forested area to the south and the hills to the north. To the west of Offa's Dyke there are a number of very short linear earthworks known as the Short Dykes. David Hill, who has studied the dyke system intensively over the past fifteen years, is of the opinion that all these works are more or less contemporary with Offa. Furthermore, he believes that Fox's interpretation of the northern section of Offa's Dyke is wrong and that Offa's Dyke stopped well short of the Irish Sea, being overlapped and replaced by Wat's Dyke for the final stretch, which reached the coast at

Fig. 7 The Mercian dyke systems in the Welsh Marches

Basingwerk, not Prestatyn as Fox believed. Although there is considerable logistical strength in Hill's argument the absence of dating evidence makes this or indeed any interpretation very difficult to demonstrate.

Hill and others have argued that two surviving documents, the Tribal Hidage and the Burghal Hidage, show that the country was already assessed in taxable units (*hides*) which were theoretically linked to the productive capacity of the land, and that each *hide* was responsible for supplying a certain quota of workers to build and repair and perhaps garrison the dyke if required. Although Sir Cyril Fox considered it to be 'the product of one mind and one generation of men', Offa's Dyke was almost certainly constructed by different groups of workers, possibly for different reasons, and possibly at different times.

The building of such linear earthworks by groups of men linked or tied to different geographical locations may have its precedents in prehistory. The Dark Age dykes perhaps echo the building of the Iron Age linear boundaries in southern England and also the great hillforts, which could well have been found erected and repaired by the inhabitants of a region in return for their use in times of trouble as safe refuges. It is therefore not too fanciful to suggest that the re-establishment of fortified towns known as *burhs* in the ninth century, in response to Viking incursions, was organised in a similar manner.

Anglo-Saxon Towns

During the later Iron Age many of the great hillforts of the Marches appear to have been developing urban functions, both politically and economically. The Romans effectively stopped the development of these proto-towns and replaced them with their own towns, and although occupation of a sort continued in some cases throughout the Roman period and afterwards, except in isolated cases and for brief periods, the hillforts ceased to operate as regional or even local centres. The fundamental disruptions which followed the collapse of the Romano-British way of life and the political upheavals associated with the Anglicisation of the border did not create favourable conditions for the rebirth of towns. None the less the establishment of an ecclesiastical framework involving the creation of diocesan and monastic centres, perhaps linked to evolving political centres, did bring places such as Hereford, Leominster and Much Wenlock into prominence and in the case of Hereford certainly aided its development as an important regional centre.

The relatively peaceful conditions of the mid eighth century appear to have acted as a stimulus to urbanisation on a modest scale and it is from this period that the first substantial references to Hereford appear, although it is another two hundred years before the other principal Marcher shire capital, Shrewsbury, begins to evolve as an important centre. Paradoxically it seems to have been the threat from another wave of invaders from the north, the Vikings, that gave a spur to embryonic town life in the Marches.

There were two main phases of Scandinavian settlement in England, the first between 866 and 880 when, despite successful local resistance by Wessex under Alfred, the Danes defeated and settled in the eastern part of Mercia, all East Anglia and all but the northernmost part of Northumbria. The second was in the early years of the tenth century when Scandinavians, chiefly Norwegians, along with some Irish, began the occupation of the country on the west side of the Pennines from the Wirral peninsular to the Solway. Alfred was able to hold his own and place a limit on the Danish-held area by a treaty with Guthrum in 886, which gave formal recognition to the northern domination of the Scandinavians in the area covered by the Danelaw. However, early in the tenth century the joint campaign of Edward the Elder and his sister Aethelfleda, the Lady of the Mercians, began to reduce the area under the Danelaw by means of military victories and progressive occupation. In due course the whole of the country as far north as the Mersey and the Humber, including the Welsh Marches, came under the Wessex kings. Ironically the English success against the Scandinavians coincided with the demise of the Mercian Dynasty, and the last king of Mercia was Ceowulf II, who died in about 886.

The Scandinavian advances appear to have resulted in the creation of fortified centres known as *burhs*. It is therefore not surprising that during the late Saxon period the terms 'town' and 'fortress' were synonymous. The need for an integrated system of defence against the Scandinavians was met by a rapid growth of defended centres in Wessex, accompanied by largely successful attempts to foster urban life. At the beginning of the ninth century a number of former sites which still had their Roman walls were refortified and a century later, during the reconquest of the Danelaw, the Roman defences of Chester were also restored. The process of urban fortification, however, spread well beyond former Roman towns, bringing into existence a brand new generation of towns, many of which were to become the shire capitals throughout the Middle Ages and later. The choice of places for fortification seems to have been determined largely by the communication system that had evolved during the post-Roman period; particular attention was paid to river crossings, where bridgehead fortifications were built on the opposite bank from the main settlement in order to maintain control of vital fording points.

In recent years the archaeological and topographical evidence for these centres has been widely studied. The most important surviving written evidence is contained in the Burghal Hidage, which in its present form belongs to the reign of Edward the Elder, but probably recapitulates practices which date from the time of his father, Alfred, sometime before 892. Defence had traditionally been the responsibility of local magnates (*ealdormen*) who led locally raised armies known as the *fyrd*. By the early tenth century the defence of Wessex was organised on new principles, laid down by the Burghal Hidage, which involved the building and manning of a widespread system of new local fortresses designed to restrict the movement of Danish armies. The Burghal Hidage lists some thirty-two places as fortified centres, but is concerned only with southern England. The distribution of these *burhs* was such that no place in Wessex was more than twenty-five miles from a fortified centre of refuge and resistance. The Mercian Register, which forms part of the Anglo-Saxon Chronicle, records how the building of these fortresses was carried out alongside the campaign of reconquest of the Danelaw begun in 910 by Edward the Elder and his sister Aethelfleda: Edward built ten and Aethelfleda built eleven. A number of these were located in the Welsh Marches, although not all the sites have yet been definitely identified.

27 Aerial view of Shrewsbury showing the siting of the early town within the loop of the river Severn. The Anglo-Saxon town probably lay in the area just above the railway station, which unusually has been partly built over the river

Along the Severn the main bridging points of Gloucester, Worcester, Bridgnorth and Shrewsbury were guarded by *burhs*. In 895 a Danish army broke
out from its blockaded camp near London, perhaps seeking to link up with
the Welsh, and built a *geweorc*, or work (a palisaded camp), at a place which
the Anglo-Saxon Chronicle calls *Cwatbryg* (Quatbridge), and reputedly spent
the winter there. (Later accounts call this place Bridge, which is the early
name for Bridgnorth.) In the Middle Ages there is a reference to the
'Heathen's ditch' some way to the south of Bridgnorth at the foot of the
spur on which Quatford church now stands – the term heathen was one
commonly applied to the Danes, who at this stage were still pagan. The
Danes were again at Cwatbridge in 910 after raiding areas to the west of
the river Severn and accordingly it is recorded that in 912 Aethelfleda built
a *burh* at Bridge. The precise location of Aethelfleda's *burh* at Bridgnorth
is something of a mystery. There are at least three possible locations. Shropshire's great nineteenth-century antiquarian the Reverend E. W. Eyton
argued that it was sited on Panpudding Hill, a fortified hillock which lies
to the south-west of the present town. Florence of Worcester, writing in
the twelfth century, was very precise about the size of the *burh*: it was, she
said, on the western bank of the Severn at a place called Bridge. Later
Florence stated that the Norman Robert de Bellême refortified Bridgnorth
in the early twelfth century. Topographically too the present castle site seems
to be the most attractive candidate, as a number of other Saxon promontory
burhs occupy very similar types of site. However, Bridgnorth was not
recorded in the Domesday Book although there was a *burgus* at Quatford
which was said to yield nothing. Quatford therefore has to be viewed as
the third candidate, but excavations here have failed to provide any cor-
roborative evidence and therefore the question of the location of the late
Saxon fortification must remain open. What is certain is that after the Norman Conquest a highly successful borough developed at Bridgnorth close
to the Norman castle.

The precise location of the Saxon fortification at Shrewsbury is also
unknown although it almost certainly occupied the highest part of the town.
It was in existence as early as 901 when it was recorded in a charter of
Aethelred and Aethelfleda. Coins were issued from Shrewsbury mint by
Aethelstan (929–39) and his successors right up until the Norman Conquest, so the town must have been fortified, as from the tenth century
onwards mints were only allowed to operate in defended places, known as
either *ports* or *burhs*. In terms of the number of moneyers found in Saxon
mint towns, Shrewsbury ranks fourteenth in England, compared to Hereford, which was twenty-fourth. Shrewsbury was also one of the most important and provides a textbook example of a river-defended site. The Severn
meanders around a sandstone outcrop creating an almost complete natural
moated circle, with a narrow gap on the eastern side. The logical location
for the defended settlement would have been on the highest part of the town

overlooking the eastern gap and it is from this area, particularly in the vicinity of St Mary's church, that mid and late Saxon material has been uncovered. It has been suggested that the Saxon *burh* was roughly co-extensive with the ancient parish of St Alkmund and it is possible that the High Street, Pride Hill and St Mary's Street defined the limits of the *burh*. Whatever the precise location of the Saxon town, however, by the time the Domesday survey was compiled Shrewsbury was sufficiently important to possess five churches, and its large population in the late Saxon period is reflected in the fact that when Roger de Montgomery added the outer bailey of his castle between 1074 and 1086 some fifty-one houses had to be destroyed. In 914 Aethelfleda built another *burh* at Eddisbury, presumably reoccupying the hillfort there, and in 915 another at *Cyricbyrig*, thought by some to be Chirbury, just a few miles to the east of Montgomery, where, despite its promising site with an undated earthwork enclosure close to Offa's Dyke and Montgomery, no evidence of Saxon occupation has yet been found.

28 An aerial view of Chirbury, close to Offa's Dyke. Although Chirbury is believed to be the site of the Anglo-Saxon burh *of Cyricbyrig, no archaeological evidence has yet been found to substantiate this theory. St Michael's church, in the centre, is all that remains of a house of Augustinian canons founded here in c. 1200*

Places to Visit

Hereford

The *burh* which has left the most impressive imprint on a modern townscape in the Marches is at Hereford, the centre of a bishopric since the late seventh century. A cross erected about 740 was said to commemorate Milfrith, king of the Magonsaetan, together with three earlier bishops of the diocese. There are also vague traditions of an earlier Celtic church here. The church of St Guthlac, on a site later enclosed by the more recent castle earthworks, was probably founded in the first half of the eighth century. Conflicts with the Welsh in the region were recorded after the kingdom of the Magonsaete was incorporated into Mercia, including a battle at Hereford early in the reign of King Offa in 760. A programme of excavations over the past twenty years has revealed a sequence of city defences, the very earliest of which may belong to the mid eighth century. This early town, almost square lying either side of an east-west high street and enclosing an area of about 40 acres, was approximately the same size as the Roman Kenchester which Hereford replaced.

The early rampart was subsequently enlarged and provided with a substantial timber revetment, possibly in the early tenth century at the time that other *burh* defences were being constructed. We know that Hereford had the status of a *burh* in 914 when it is recorded that the Danes were raiding Archenfield. In 1055 the city was besieged by the northern Welsh under Gruffydd ap Llewellyn and it was probably following this attack that the ramparts were provided with a stone face. Gradually the town's defences were extended to accommodate the growing population until they reached their maximum extent of some 120 acres during the later part of the twelfth century. Considerable traces of this line of defences can still be identified on the ground today.

The Saxon town was founded round St Aethelbert's cathedral and the crossing of the Wye. The grid of streets in the vicinity of the cathedral dates from this period and the modern inner ringroad precisely follows the line of the Saxon and mediéval defences. To the south of the river there was a bridgehead fortification to protect the crossing. The shape of the *burh* which has been revealed by excavation in recent years has been distorted by the insertion of a great Norman castle on the eastern side and by the growth of the cathedral precinct in the centre. The latter gradually pushed the bridging point further westwards until today the major Wye crossing is actually outside the area of the ancient city. The gradual expansion of the cathedral precinct and its associated buildings not only nudged the Wye crossing westwards, but effectively filled up the interior of the early Saxon town. Accordingly, when a new area to the north of the early town was enclosed within the defended area in the early Middle Ages, a broad new market area had to be laid out running east to west which was at total variance with the traditional north–south axis of the town. Subsequently this large market street has itself been all but infilled by encroachments. This process explains the apparently confused layout of the street pattern in Hereford, and similarly that of Shrewsbury which also expanded considerably during the period. The main reason for this is that the late Saxon towns made little effort to provide space within the defended area for trade and commerce, which tended to be carried out around churches or in narrow streets. It was not until after the Norman Conquest that broad open streets and market areas were deliberately laid out as an integral part of town plans.

During the first half of the eleventh century, Edward the Confessor appointed his nephew Ralph, the son of the Count of Vexin, Earl of Hereford in succession to Swein Godwinson. Ralph almost certainly had a castle built at Hereford – one of the first in the country – and significantly established a Norman garrison here well before the Norman Conquest. After Ralph's defeat in 1055 by a combined army of Welsh and disaffected English the city was sacked and burned and he was replaced by Harold Godwinson (later King Harold), who refortified the settlement and made it his base for raids against the Welsh.

The Domesday Book account makes it clear that Hereford already had many of the special characteristics of Saxon shire towns. The lordship was divided between the king, bishop and earl: the customs of the 103 king's *burgages* (merchants' houses and plots) and the twenty-seven owing allegiance to the earl are listed in unusual detail and resemble those of the other prominent military Welsh border outpost, Shrewsbury. There were six royal moneyers and six smiths who made the king's iron (presumably from the Forest of Dean) into horseshoes. There were women brewers within and without the city, and there was regular trading of salt with Droitwich where the church of St Guthlac appears to have possessed nine *burgages*. The trading character of the city is confirmed by the description of the bishop's share, recorded significantly under the heading 'Hereford port or market', a name already used on a number of earlier occasions in the Anglo-Saxon Chronicle. All in all, the picture is that of a thriving Saxon shire town.

Offa's Dyke

Offa's Dyke provides a tangible relic of the growing conflict between the newly established English and the Welsh. It is now much overgrown and crosses some of the loneliest countryside in England and is an evocative monument whose full story has yet to be told. The dyke runs mostly across the grain of the countryside, that is north to south, rarely following a straight line and tending to follow a switch-back course, constantly changing direction. The engineers who constructed the dyke made use of west facing slopes wherever possible, even if this meant taking the boundary eastwards. In the north the dyke is almost always accompanied by a western ditch, frequently with a counterscarp, but in the south there is less ditch and over short stretches an eastern ditch can be found. At its most pronounced the top of the bank is almost 20 feet above the bottom of the ditch, and originally was in the region of 24 feet above it, with the ditch averaging 6 feet in depth. In places it has been heavily ploughed and sometimes completely removed. The most complete section of the whole dyke is in south-west Shropshire in the Clun Forest, where it runs through some of the Border's wildest countryside.

Largely through the efforts of the late Mr Frank Noble, since the early 1970s the Offa's Dyke Path has been created, which offers the walker an unrivalled opportunity to admire both the earthwork and the magnificent countryside through which it passes. The Offa's Dyke Path runs from Prestatyn to Chepstow, about 140 miles, providing some of the most varied and exciting walking of any of Britain's long-distance footpaths. Particularly recommended are the lengths over the Black Mountains, across the Radnor and Clun Forests, and through the countryside between Llanymynech and the Clwydian range. A set of strip maps, route notes and other valuable information can be obtained from the Offa's Dyke Association, West Street, Knighton, Powys, where there is a visitor's information centre.

Bridgnorth

Bridgnorth lies on a ridge of Old Red Sandstone overlooking the river Severn. It consists of two parts, High Town on the west bank of the river, and Low Town on the east; these are linked by a cliff railway, the steepest and shortest inclined railway in the country, and by a bridge from which the town derives its name (Old English, *brycg*). The present bridge was built in 1822, but earlier bridges may well have used the islands, or bylets, which lie in the river Severn here. Only one of these survives, to the south of the bridge, but a late sixteenth-century map marks two, the 'great billet' and the 'weures billet'.

As already mentioned, the origins of the town are confusing. As early as 896 there was a bridge over the Severn at *Cwatbryg* (Quatbridge) and a *burh* was created on the river bank in 912 by Aethelfleda, the site of which is not known. Possibly, it is the earthwork known as Panpudding Hill, but Dr John Mason convincingly argues that the *burh* stood on the site of the present castle.

It is certain, however, that the present town of Bridgnorth was not founded until the beginning of the twelfth century. It is not known how long the bridge at Quatford continued to operate, but the use of the place name Bridgnorth to describe a second town upstream suggests that it was not completely forgotten in the thirteenth century. This second town followed the transfer of the military site from Quatford in 1101, when the twelfth-century Shropshire-born writer Ordericus Vitalis records that the rebel earl Robert de Bellême abandoned Quatford and transferred his castle, church (St Mary's) and borough to Bridgnorth. The new town lay originally within the large Anglo-Saxon parish of Morville, and St Mary's parochial dependence on the church at Morville reflects Bridgnorth's artificial origin.

Bridgnorth Castle, the remains of which now form the centrepiece of the town park, was originally built by Robert de Bellême and was later fortified by Henry II, who granted the town its first charter in 1157. Although Bridgnorth, along with Shrewsbury, was in the front line of defence against the Welsh in the eleventh and twelfth centuries, the defences were left to decay with the coming of more settled times in the late thirteenth century. By the early sixteenth century the castle was said to be 'totally to ruine' and it was recorded that townspeople were building themselves houses in the bailey.

29 *The promontory site at Bridgnorth overlooking the river Severn may be the site of a Saxon* burh. *The ruins of the medieval castle and Telford's eighteenth-century church of St Mary lie on the left-hand side and the strangely located medieval church of St Leonard on the right*

The new borough was probably laid out in the traditional manner during the later twelfth century, with a broad high street and a series of streets running off at right-angles. During this period a second church (St Leonard's) was built. Following the Welsh disturbances in the thirteenth century the new town was surrounded by a turf rampart and ditch between 1216 and 1223. Some forty years later the stockade was partially replaced by a stone wall, but by the time of Leland, Henry VIII's antiquary, the walls were all in ruin, although remains are still to be seen at the west end of Lisley Street and the Half Moon Battery off Pound Street. Of the five original town gates, only the North Gate, much remodelled in 1910, still stands. Whitburn Gate survived until 1761 and the Hungry Gate until 1821.

The area enclosed by the town walls was inadequate to accomomodate the late medieval expansion and new suburbs grew up outside the North Gate, in New Town and Littleburg, now known as Pound Street. A suburb also grew up at Low Town across the river. Although Leland dismissed it as 'a pretty long street of mean buildings', on early maps it appears to be as large as High Town, Bridgnorth.

Medieval Bridgnorth was an important route centre; the road from Chester to Bristol crossed the Severn here and the river itself was of major importance in the development of the town. Along with Bristol, Gloucester, Tewkesbury and Shrewsbury, Bridgnorth is one of five towns on the river Severn to be marked on Gough's 1360 map of Britain.

During the Middle Ages the textile industry was important and so too were tanning and brewing. In 1540 Leland, however, recorded that the town 'standeth by cloth, and that now decayed, the town sorely decayed'; by this time the textile industry was virtually extinct. Later it turned with only modest success to cap- and hat-making. Today there is little evidence of early cloth working, except the names Tainter Wall and Tainter Hill at the west end of Lisley Street; here freshly woven cloth was 'tented' or stretched out to dry. The carpet industry did not arrive until the end of the eighteenth century, when Joseph MacMichael established the first carpet factory in Lisley Street.

Because of destruction during the Civil War (much of High Town was burnt down), little remains of the buildings of medieval or Tudor Bridgnorth. At the bottom of the Cartway, which was the only way up from the river to High Town until the building of the New Road, stands Bishop Percy's House (1580), one of the few surviving half-timbered buildings in the town. An appeal to Parliament was made for aid, the fire having consumed 'almost the whole subsistence of the Corporation, consisting of very faire and ancient buildings, to the value of ninety thousand pounds' and the new town hall was completed in 1652 on a new site in the middle of the High Street, where it still stands today with the traffic flowing through it.

The real reconstruction, however, did not come until the eighteenth century when Bridgnorth emerged as a gracious and pleasant town with some fine Georgian terraces. In 1763, Bridgnorth was described as a 'place of great trade, both by land and water'. In Low Town new residences were built in Mill Street and St John's Street; the Post Office (*c.* 1700) is a very good example of this phase. In High Town, Anthony Weaver made a large-scale attempt to improve the inhabited area within the ancient limits of the castle. The ultimate sequel to these improvements came with the rebuilding of the fourteenth-century church of St Mary's (originally the chapel of Bridgnorth Castle), earlier described by Leland as a 'rude thing'. A new church in white freestone in the classical style was built by Telford at the end of East Castle Street in the late eighteenth century on a different alignment. This church was designed to blend with the spacious streets and buildings of this part of the town, which still possesses considerable elegance. During the nineteenth century a number of large fashionable residences were built around the edge of Castle Park.

As Bridgnorth lay only a few miles downstream from Coalbrookdale and the coalfield there, there were links with the iron industry in the town. From 1760 the Coalbrookdale Company leased the Town Mills as a forge and Thomas Cranage, the ironworker, was employed there as 'master Hammer-man' in 1766. On the east bank of the river behind Mill Street are remains of John Hazeldine's once-famous foundry. Crude iron was stored at Bridgnorth before being shipped downstream to Stourbridge; this trade was mainly controlled by the Knight family who had furnaces at Charlcote about eight miles from Bridgnorth and at distant Bringewood near Ludlow. Until the coming of the railway in the 1850s Bridgnorth remained a major river port. During the eighteenth and nineteenth centuries coal from the pits at Broseley and agricultural produce from the surrounding countryside were the main cargoes. The river warden's house built in the late eighteenth century can still be seen with an area of old wharves in front of it. Other surviving signs of the once-flourishing river trade include the flights of landing steps at the Old Quay, which originally included Skinner's Load, Friar's Load and Foster's Load. On a map of 1739 there are three dockyards on the Severn and in about 1800 it was recorded that the river at Bridgnorth presented a 'constant moving picture of boats and barges'.

The coming of the railway did not bring any immediate advantages to the town. Indeed the first consequence was to kill the river trade; the last barge to use Bridgnorth came down the Severn in 1895. Ironically this barge, which was carrying firebricks, sank after hitting one of the bridge piers.

CHAPTER SIX

Castle and Borough in the Marches

The Normans in the Marches

It is difficult to overestimate the impact of the Normans on the Welsh Border landscape, both in the short and the long term. The Normans came as conquering feudal lords to a region which in 1066 had very few towns and only a scattered rural population, and stamped their mark very firmly in the form of castles, towns, villages and churches. In the late Saxon period the Borderland had been restless, local border skirmishes were common and on a larger scale the region was coveted by both the Anglo-Saxons and the Welsh. Despite the continued existence of Offa's Dyke as a tangible western boundary and despite the recent formation of the Mercian shires during the eleventh century, there was no finite border between the Saxons and the Welsh. The historian Round sums up the position at the time of the compilation of the Domesday Book twenty years after the Norman Conquest:

> There is no fixed western boundary, only a border which was ever shifting with the ebb and flow of conquest . . . What Harold recovered with his light infantry, what William Fitz Osbern [Earl of Hereford] and his male horsemen can hold at lances point that at the moment of the great survey was all part of Hereford-shire . . . No more and no less.

Until the early 1060s the Welsh held the initiative, with the English continually on the defensive. This situation had arisen because of the emergence of two energetic Welsh leaders, Gruffydd ap Rhydderch of Deheubarth, who found the rich pickings of Gloucestershire and Herefordshire an irresistible temptation until his death in 1055, and after him, Gruffydd ap Llewellyn of Gwynedd. Wales was briefly, if uneasily, unified under the latter, who raided into England as far as Chester and Leominster, until his death at the hands of Harold and Tostig in 1063. Partly in response to this situation Edward the Confessor, who had been brought up in Normandy, introduced

Fig. 8 Distribution of castles in the Welsh Marches dating primarily from the eighth century

a number of Norman lords into positions of power in the Borderland in the 1050s. One of these Norman lords, called Osbern, established the lordship of Ewyas Harold in the Black Mountains, where he almost certainly built one of the first castles in England, while another Norman lord appears to have built a castle at Richards Castle, a little to the south of Ludlow, and Edward the Confessor's own nephew Ralph built himself a castle at Hereford. The Anglo-Saxon Chronicle recorded in September 1051 that, 'The foreigners had built a castle in Herefordshire in Earl Sweyne's territory and inflicted all injuries and insults they could upon the King's men in that region.' These early Norman lords were clearly unpopular and they were eventually ousted; this early Norman incursion into Herefordshire was, however, a mere trifle compared to their total domination of the Borderland after 1066.

It is not difficult to understand why the Normans acquired a strong taste for this region – Normandy itself had started life as a Marcher duchy. There were geographical as well as political similarities: gently undulating country with plenty of natural stone and timber for buildings, and politically a frontier zone with potentially rich pickings, in this case beyond the Welsh border. Additionally Wales was a hilly, misty, Celtic country, reminiscent of Normandy's coveted neighbour, Brittany, a kingdom tailor-made for the Normans, and it is no accident that they were so attracted to it, and that in their ambitions and their feuding they left behind such a deep impression on the landscape.

However, the apparent similarities between Wales and Brittany were to be dangerously deceptive. Brittany was a kingdom which had more in common with Cornwall than Wales. The Breton landscape of weathered granite rarely reaches above 1000 feet, so that in comparison with Welsh mountain geography it is gentle. Brittany had been a far more prosperous and integrated region in Roman Gaul than Wales had ever been in Roman Britain, and despite the legendary Celtic links between the two peoples, the Bretons shared more of a cultural and a political heritage with the rest of France than did the Welsh with Anglo-Saxon England.

The Norman Conquest of 1066 represented more of a watershed in the Welsh Borderland than perhaps anywhere else in Britain. Whereas the complete conquest of England was achieved within twenty years, the conquest of Wales took over a hundred years after the battle of Hastings and even that was far from complete. The risings which occurred between 1068 and 1070 must have first alerted William to the political and military problems of the Welsh. The geography of Wales made it a difficult country to control, but the divided and relatively weak nature of the independent princedoms in 1070 meant that at first the Normans had little difficulty in defeating or intimidating the Welsh. The main problem, however, was in maintaining political control after the initial Norman military victories, and there was a series of significant Marcher revolts in 1075, 1088 and 1100. Following a rebellion by Welsh princes in alliance with a Herefordshire thegn known as Eadric the Wild, William the Conqueror devised a scheme by which the Marches were administered as semi-autonomous earldoms based on the Saxon towns of Chester, Shrewsbury and Hereford. Within this framework the land was divided between the Marcher lords – in all some 153 separate lordships were created, functioning almost as little kingdoms, which, technically at least, did not revert to their mother counties until the Act of Union (1536). Recent research indicates that the units chosen for their lordships were pre-Norman, and coincided with the *commotes*, the social and territorial cells of the Welsh kingdoms. Within each lordship one or more castles were built, and these castles formed the nuclei on which the border boroughs were subsequently created.

The parts of Wales conquered by the Normans came to be known collectively as 'The Welsh Marches' (*Marchia Wallia*) to distinguish them from the unconquered parts, which were known collectively either as 'Wales' (*Wallia*) or 'Wales proper' (*pura Wallia*). The distinction between Wales and the Marches was not simply geographical, it was also legal and constitutional; 'Wales proper' lived under what was then conventionally called 'the law of Howel', i.e. the indigenous Welsh law, while 'the March of Wales' lived under what were called 'the customs of the March', under which the Norman Marcher barons were allowed a considerable degree of autonomy, and the rest of England was strictly under royal control.

There was therefore a real distinction between Normanised England and the Normanised March of Wales. The lords of the Welsh March were allowed to exercise extensive judicial powers in return for conquering the March. These lords had jurisdiction over all civil and criminal cases, high and low, with the exception of crimes of high treason. They established their own courts to try these offences and subsequently they executed sentences and collected fines. They possessed all of the royal perquisites – salvage, treasure-trove, plunder and royal fish. They could establish forests and forest law, declare and wage war, establish boroughs, and grant extensive charters of liberties. They also had unique rights of unlicensed castle-building and of waging what was conventionally called 'private war'. The Marcher lord was thus established in the position of a petty king, exercising both royal and lordship rights. In this respect, a lord of the March of Wales differed from a lord of an estate in England, for the latter enjoyed none of the royal privileges but held his lordship as a direct grant from the king.

The Marcher lord took responsibility for the defence of his own lordship, and though he regarded the king as his sovereign, the king had little right to interfere in the lordship except on the lord's death, when he had right of entry to conduct an inquiry as to the legal heir and to arrange for the succession. He could not, however, normally interfere with the succession, which usually passed from eldest son to eldest son, by the custom known as primogeniture; in the absence of male heirs, the lordship was divided equally among the daughters. If, however, the lord abandoned his territory, or if he were found guilty of treason or felony, the king could then confiscate the estates.

The three great territories based on Chester, Shrewsbury and Hereford were to be defended by castles both internally and, where possible, westwards into Wales. Hugh d'Avranches (made Earl of Chester in 1070) was based in the north with a forward defence under his cousin Robert against the Welsh at Rhuddlan. In the centre Roger de Montgomery, Earl of Shrewsbury, built an outpost on the Welsh side of Offa's Dyke in the region of Montgomery. In the south the Normans, headed by the Conqueror's friend William Fitz Osbern, Earl of Hereford, defended the Wye basin with castles at Wigmore, Clifford and Ewyas Harold, and following an invasion of Gwent, established the lordship of Striguil around Chepstow. By the time the Earl of Hereford returned to Normandy in 1070 he had pacified his section of the Border and had completed the organisation of the Marches from Ludlow to Chepstow. William Fitz Osbern was killed in Flanders the following year leaving as his legacy a chain of Norman strong points on the Welsh border as well as a number of infant boroughs which he had created in order to centralise Norman political control. The franchises and laws of his boroughs, such as Hereford, were based on the laws of Breteuil in Normandy and these served as a model for a considerable number of newly created towns in the rest of England and Wales. William Fitz Osbern was a powerful and ruthless man, typical of the eleventh-century Norman Marcher barons. Ordericus Vitalis dismissed them thus:

> Puffed up with pride they gave no heed to the reasonable complaints of his [the king's] English subjects and distained to wave them in the balance of equity. They shielded their men at arms who most outrageously robbed the people and ravished the women and those only incurred their wrath who were driven by these grievous fronts to be allowed in their remonstrances.

Time places a shield between us and the worst excesses of the Norman lords, but even at this distance they are not men to romanticise.

By 1086 the Normans held Caerleon and the line of the river Usk and in 1093, following the defeat of Rhys ap Tedwr, they extended their control over south Wales, with the establishment of the lordships of Brecon and Glamorgan. The sequence of military events was reminiscent of the Roman conquest of Wales. Roger de Montgomery, the Earl of Shrewsbury, attacked Wales along the Severn valley to gain control of a number of Welsh lordships, thus imposing Norman control on the waist of Wales, while from Oswestry the Normans pressed north-westwards into Welsh lands beyond Offa's Dyke and in the far north moved quickly along the coastal plains establishing castles at Deganwy, Conway and Caernarvon.

Castles of the Conquest

The castle was the first and perhaps the most important physical manifestation of the Conquest. Throughout the Borderland castles were built both of stone and of earth and timber to proclaim the new Norman dominance. Castles were clearly one of the reasons for rapid Norman success: they were built in virtually every town, village and hamlet and acted as strategic centres from which Norman political control was exercised and military dominance clearly demonstrated. Ordericus Vitalis believed that it was the castle which enabled the Normans to establish themselves in England: 'The fortifications called castles by the Normans were scarcely known in the English provinces, and so the English – in spite of their courage and love of fighting – could put up only weak resistance to their enemies.' Contemporary chroniclers sometimes implied that the castle was a secret weapon which gave the Normans an unfair advantage, and in 1137, during the civil war between Stephen and Matilda, the compiler of the Anglo-Saxon Chronicle was sufficiently moved to complain: 'They sorely burdened the unhappy people of the country with forced labour on the castles. And when the castles were made they filled them with devils and wicked men.'

The castle was not merely a defensive stronghold but was also a firm base for active operations. The Norman cavalry were able to use castles to respond swiftly and decisively to any uprising and to dominate the surrounding countryside, as well as for making sorties against besieging forces. The distribution of these castles to some extent reflects where the various uprisings against Norman control originated, for instance in the south-west and the Welsh Marches. But underlying this distribution there is clearly a pattern of political centralisation, not merely in response to specific uprisings but also as a means of intimidating any potential unrest in the form of an unambiguous statement of Norman superiority.

For these purposes the motte and bailey design was ideal. The motte (a Norman-French term for mound) was normally conical in shape, and could range in height from 9 to 90 feet. The mound was surrounded by a ditch from which the material making up the motte was extracted. There would have been a wooden bridge leading from the castle bailey to the motte, which was capped by a tower initially constructed of timber. The bailey was also surrounded by a ditch or ditches and a rampart, on top of which a palisade was built. Inside there were various buildings, such as a hall, chapel, stable, smithy and buildings for storage.

Motte and bailey castles appear to have developed from a seigneurial enclosure with a tower gate house that was found in north-western Europe during the Carolingian (pre-Norman) period, and, as we have already seen, castle-like structures had already been erected in the Marches by the Normans prior to 1066. In England the intermediate stage in private fortification appears to have been a tower and a circular area enclosed by a bank, but no mound – such castles have often left earthworks known as ringworks. The success of the practice of piling earth around the base of the tower to prevent it being burnt down easily may well be the reason why the motte became the principal feature of early Norman castles in England. The Bayeux Tapestry dramatically illustrates the point that firing fortifications was an important part of siege warfare and that wooden towers were very vulnerable to burning. The tradition of constructing ringworks continued into the twelfth century in the Marches but it has been suggested that in many cases the decision to build a ringwork rather than a motte seems to have reflected nothing more than the personal preference of the local lord or his castle builders.

30   The castle at Dinant in Brittany in the process of being attacked by fire as depicted on the Bayeux Tapestry. This is perhaps the earliest depiction of a motte and bailey castle of the type found in profusion in the Welsh Marches

The beauty of these early earth and timber castles was that they were relatively easily and rapidly constructed using materials that were readily to hand. There were no problems in finding quarries or masons, or arranging for the transportation of stone. All that would have been required were a number of carpenters and a force of men to dig the defences. In William's England this was not difficult, as the Normans could command an endless supply of labour. Thus, in troubled areas, the Crown or its representatives could rapidly establish a formidable presence capable of withstanding an all-out attack. The chroniclers recorded that castles were thrown up in a few days (it has been suggested just fifteen days for Hastings), but although considerable scepticism has been expressed about the accuracy of these accounts, there seems little doubt that the basic structure could be created within a few weeks.

31 Montgomery town and castle, showing the regular layout of the town which was created in the shadow of the new castle where building started in 1223. For many centuries Montgomery was a shire capital until local government was reorganised in 1974

Apart from the advantage of speed in the construction of the castle, the capacity for rapid rebuilding following destruction was also an important factor. At Hen Domen (Montgomery) a motte and bailey castle was constructed between 1070 and 1074 as a base for an attack on Cardigan by Hugh, son of Roger de Montgomery. The Domesday Book notes that the castle was built in an area of 'waste' used by three Saxon thegns as a hunting ground. During the next century and a half it was besieged on several occasions and changed hands frequently before a new stone castle was built at a new site in Montgomery town after 1223. The archaeologist Philip Barker has brilliantly demonstrated that wooden buildings within the bailey which have left only ephemeral traces were repeatedly destroyed or dismantled and rebuilt. The final-phase bridge is of the 'gangplank' variety so carefully depicted on the Bayeux Tapestry.

In the whole of England and Wales by far the densest concentration of earth and timber castles was in the Marches where the earthwork remains of several hundred such castles reflect the troubled conditions which persisted there. Many of the strategically important timber castles were later rebuilt in stone, to add to the range of stone castles already in existence. Mottes were not always easily converted to accommodate stone towers, and there are many records, such as those for Shrewsbury Castle, which tell of the collapse or slippage of masonry following such an attempted conversion. A compromise solution was to ring the top of the motte with a roughly circular or polygonal curtain wall following the crest of the mound, forming what is generally known as a 'shell keep'. There is an example of this at Snodhill, in Peterchurch parish in western Herefordshire.

32 The substantial stone remains of Hopton Castle in southern Shropshire sit on a low mound, which may be the vestiges of an earlier motte and bailey castle. The castle appears to date from the twelfth century. Hopton saw bloody action during the Civil War when it was the scene of violent reprisals by the Royalists against a band of Parliamentarians, whom they massacred

The castles were part of the apparatus of war and suppression, but despite their apparent permanence in the landscape, many Border castles had relatively short active lives. As Norman dominance of England grew, so the need for private defence on such a scale declined and those timber castles that were not rebuilt in stone fell into decay. Resident lords sometimes built themselves more comfortable manor houses close to the former castles, while others used the opportunity to move out of the village altogether and build their homes on completely new sites, often maintaining a semblance of defence in the form of a water-filled moat. Nevertheless the earthworks of the motte and bailey castle remain the most tangible and indelible element of the Norman contribution to the landscape. The sheer size of most mottes has ensured that although they lost their original function many centuries ago, they are not readily converted to alternative uses or eradicated from the landscape. With a few notable exceptions such as at Hereford, where the castle mound was destroyed in the nineteenth century, mottes of all shapes and sizes have survived into the late twentieth century, into an age when they are protected for their historical importance. Like prehistoric hillforts their very presence in the landscape has influenced what has come after them, and the subsequent morphology of town and village alike has been affected by these great monuments to Norman confidence and energy.

The Emerging Marcher Towns

It was the castle in conjunction with the town that was to confirm the Norman domination of England and the Marches. The impact of the construction of castles in existing towns is graphically recorded in the Domesday Book. Many early castles erected inside towns destroyed large areas. Prior to the Conquest the normal unit of settlement in Wales was the isolated family homestead or small hamlets which sometimes huddled around the courts of local chieftains. Groups tended to be self-sufficient, and there was little inter-community trade to stimulate the growth of market centres. The conditions necessary for urbanization were therefore not present. The coming of the Normans changed this situation drastically. It was soon found that the combination of a castle and a borough formed an economic unit of great vitality. The castle attracted merchants with its promise of protection and guarantee of a local monopoly of trade.

In Wales trade in each lordship was confined to the newly established boroughs, it being the monopoly of the burgesses (town merchants) who paid the lords a fixed sum annually in return for the right to collect the town dues and elect their own officers. These privileges were set out in the town charter under which the town was governed. The country folk of the locality were permitted, on payment of a toll, to trade their produce in the street at the weekly market, and at the town fair, held for several days once or twice a year, itinerant traders offered their wares for sale. The castle garrison would have provided the merchants and artisans of the borough with a basic market in the first instance and eventually the borough would have provided for the material needs of the castle, as well as bringing the lord a substantial revenue. The castle plus borough possessed a strength and unity which the combination of castle and manor had never exhibited.

The Normans quickly realised that such communities were the most effective method of settling and controlling newly conquered or disputed areas. To some extent the scale of town creation, unparalleled since the Roman period in Britain, reflected what was going on at the same time in the rest of England and indeed many parts of western Europe. In the Marchlands, however, the movement towards the creation of new towns and market centres was even more feverish than elsewhere. The territorial jigsaw of the Welsh border country, in the form of a mixture of baronies, lordships and earldoms, provided fertile ground for the establishment of new towns. Each unit of new political order needed central places where trade and government could be carried on and the logical focal point where these functions could be safely encouraged lay in the shadows of the walls of scores of new castles founded between 1066 and 1200. The new towns were largely inhabited by people from the surrounding districts, but there is some evidence to suggest that in the first instance Normans or Frenchmen were brought in; the Domesday Book indicates that the greatest concentration of Frenchmen in 1086 was in the Border countries of Cheshire, Shropshire and Herefordshire. There were, for instance, forty-three French burgesses in Shrewsbury in 1086.

It should be stressed that most of these new 'towns' were very small, often with only a hundred burgesses or so, and sometimes considerably less. They ranged in size from less than an acre within the walled area, as at Longtown, Herefordshire, to over 80 acres in the case of Ludlow. Their legal status also varied considerably: some were granted borough charters while others never achieved borough status – they did, however, all have common urban aspirations.

The late Frank Noble, who made a special study of the Border boroughs, identified four phases of borough creation in Herefordshire; these reflect the uneasy consolidation of the Welsh border and the various advances into Wales by the Norman lords. In the first phase, which dates from within a few years of the Conquest, new castles were built at Wigmore and Clifford and the pre-Conquest castles at Hereford and Ewyas Harold were rebuilt. These four were probably intended as bases from which to attack Wales and had boroughs attached to them at an early date. It has been suggested that perhaps Chepstow, Ludlow, Clun, Bishop's Castle, Caus, Oswestry and Monmouth date from this period as well.

33 *The castle and shrunken borough at Longtown, just to the east of the Black Mountains. The medieval castle in the foreground occupies a massive earthwork fortification. Beyond the castle the straggling vestiges of the medieval town can be seen. Abandoned burgage plots of former town dwellers appear as parallel linear earthworks on the left-hand side of the principal road*

34 *The typical Marcher motte at Longtown which occupies the north-west corner of a substantial square earthwork of unknown date. The circular keep dates from the late twelfth and early thirteenth centuries*

During the second phase of borough creation, which dates from the late eleventh to the early twelfth century, castles and boroughs were established by some of the lesser Marcher lords. The de Lacys created a borough and castle at Weobley which can still be identified from its large open market square, although it does not appear to have been fully defended, and also a new borough beside their castle at Grosmont. At White Castle there are hints of an unrecorded borough beside the castle and further south at Trelleck the village has the grid-iron plan of an undeveloped borough. Although there is no documentation of a borough at Dorstone, from the village topography and the castle it seems probable that there was an early borough plantation there as well. It is possible that the earthwork enclosure which incorporates the remarkable Romanesque church at Kilpeck, Herefordshire, also dates from this phase.

The third phase dates from the later twelfth century with the establishment of boroughs at places such as Huntingdon (between 1174 and 1190) and Hay, at Brecon and in the Black Mountains at the ridgetop and the now largely deserted site of Longtown (1185–95). The fourth phase dates from the thirteenth century when we have the consolidation of market boroughs in western Herefordshire at places such as Eardisley in 1233 and Pembridge in 1240. Another of these, Ploughfield, described as a borough in 1273, is today only a hamlet in Preston on Wye parish. In Shropshire there was a similar process with attempted town plantations at Baschurch in the late thirteenth century and close by at Ruyton-Eleven-Towns which was granted borough status in 1308 (Ruyton did not lose its municipal status until 1886). Burgage plots can still be identified in the property boundaries which lie along the broad high street running westwards from the church and along the northern extension of the town. There appear to have been many other attempts to graft new towns or more frequently market extensions on to existing settlements. Robert Burnell, for instance, attempted to extend Acton Burnell in the late thirteenth century: by 1315 there were thirty-six burgesses living here, but because of its comparative isolation this town, too, had been absorbed back into the rural landscape by the later Middle Ages.

Although the vast majority of the borough towns were Anglo-Norman creations, by the later thirteenth century there were attempts by the Welsh to establish towns comparable to their English neighbours. Llewellyn ap Gruffydd was proclaimed Prince of Wales in 1258, and in 1267, by the Treaty of Montgomery, Henry III recognised Llewellyn's title and conceded to him the territory of Cedewain. This included much of the area that was later to become the county of Montgomeryshire in the sixteenth century. Llewellyn decided to built a castle and attach a borough to it at Dolforwyn, a wild site on the upper Severn overlooking Montgomery. The proposal met with considerable English opposition and following Edward I's invasion of Wales in 1277 Dolforwyn was besieged and taken, and granted to Roger de Mortimer. With the acquisition of this new territory the Mortimer empire occupied a considerable slab of the central Welsh border well into Wales; and continuing the Mortimer tradition of borough creation, Newtown (Llanfair Cedewain) was developed.

The creation of the towns of the Welsh Marches is closely related to the westward expansion of the territories of the Marcher lords. Of the many towns in the region created in the late eleventh and early twelfth centuries Brecon illustrates, perhaps more clearly than most, the relationship between the westward advance of the Norman frontier and the planting of towns. By 1110 the army of Bernard de Newmarche had overrun the whole of the Dark Age Welsh princedom of Brycheiniog. In his wake three new towns, Brecon, Builth and Hay, were created. Brecon was planted at the junction of the river Usk with its tributary, the Honddu, draining in from the north.

The first element of the Norman settlement appeared on a steep western bluff overlooking the two rivers in the form of a motte and bailey castle constructed in 1092. Outside the north walls of the castle the foundations of the church of St John were laid, a church which later became a priory and is today a cathedral. Facing the site of the castle on the east bank of the Honddu the new town of Brecon appears to have been implanted at the same time as the building of the castle. Traditionally it is believed to have been created by Bernard de Newmarche, who was also the benefactor of the monks at Battle Abbey in Sussex, to whom he gave St John's church as well as lands in the town. Bernard himself came from Neufmarche in Normandy, a name whose literal meaning is Newmarket, thus emphasising the prevalence of new town creation in north-western Europe at this time.

We can still see today the elements of the Norman town engraved on the townscape. The centrepiece is the market place, in the form of a triangle which, as so often with successful new towns, has been encroached upon by later buildings. The oval-shaped defences of the walled borough, once crowned by ten equally spaced towers, can also be traced. It is believed that stone for the Norman defences was obtained from the Roman fort at Brecon Gaer, which lies three miles west of the town. Today minor changes of level and a curving street pattern that follows the inner line of the walk betrays the presence of the former ditch. In the thin parallel backyards of the back-streets of Brecon the shapes of the original burgage plots can still be identified. Both Builth and Hay also retain clear indications of their Norman origins in their street plans, and it is reasonable to assume in all three cases that they were laid out within a few years of the building of their castles.

With this consolidation of power by the Marcher lords in the late thirteenth century the urban geography of the Welsh border was largely complete. There were few attempts at borough creation during the remainder of the Middle Ages and further efforts towards urbanisation were not made until the Industrial Revolution. Not only had the political situation been largely determined, so too had the economic forces which had enabled towns to be created throughout the Borderland begun to deteriorate, and even by the time of the creation of Newtown some of the earlier town plantations had begun to decline. The truth is that town creation in the Welsh border had gone too far. It had been partly a response to the strategic situation and had partly mirrored the general process of town plantation throughout England in the early Middle Ages. From 1300 onwards, however, the economic tide had turned and whereas previously the climate was right for new and expanding towns, afterwards the position was very different and both towns and villages were being abandoned rather than created. Town desertion in the Welsh border appears to have occurred at a considerably higher level than elsewhere in the country.

The reasons for the success or otherwise of a border town appears to have been linked to its ability to change its function from military to economic, and a small minority of new towns enjoyed considerable success during the Middle Ages. This category is epitomised by Ludlow, founded by Roger de Lacy in the late eleventh century, which became the seat of the Council of the Marches during the later Middle Ages. Ludlow was able to combine its military function happily with thriving commercial activity, and by the middle of the fourteenth century it was rated as one of the most prosperous towns in England. (Monmouth and Chepstow fall into the same category of prosperous regional commercial capitals.) Less successful were a line of towns further to the west, Welshpool, Montgomery, Bishop's Castle, Clun, Knighton, Kington and Hay, which enjoyed moderate prosperity as minor market towns. Montgomery was, however, a county town until local government reorganisation in 1974. Oswestry and Clun were both Fitz Allen creations and, despite their size, acted as important centres where Welsh and English cultures could meet and mingle. Most of these towns, however, barely outgrew their medieval form, and this can still clearly be seen in their street layouts and the lines of their defensive fortifications. Some, such as Clun, have perhaps decayed since the Middle Ages and the topography of small market towns such as Pembridge and Weobley appears to have changed hardly at all over the centuries.

Failed Boroughs

Today the landscape of the Marches is littered with places that were once granted market charters and the rights of boroughs, places that have since failed completely. A rectangular-shaped field where sheep and cattle graze, as at Huntingdon, may be the sole visual evidence of a former market-place. Narrow high-hedged fields as at Richards Castle mark the plots that attracted the burgesses to a newly founded borough eight centuries ago. Deep lanes and foot paths indicate the lines of former streets; and the once formidable castle of a forgotten founding Marcher lord is no more than an overgrown mound, dangerously steep to ascend and defended now by brambles, nettles and scree.

Some of the most evocative landscapes in the Borderland have been produced by these once proud and dominant towns. At Caus in the parish of Westbury, in the foothills of the Long Mountain a few miles from Shrewsbury, there are the earthworks of a massive fortified town and castle created by the Corbet family. The place name of the new town echoes the name of the Norman homeland from which the founder, Roger Corbet, came – the *Pays de Caux*, which lies to the north of the Seine estuary. Sited on a high ridge Caus commanded the valley road from Shrewsbury to Montgomery. The ruins of an enormous earthwork and stone castle with outer fortifications now have to be disentangled from the undergrowth; nothing except earthworks and the odd chunk of masonry remains of the borough. The town was created by Roger Corbet in 1198 and it is recorded that by 1349 there were fifty-eight burgesses living here. In the mid fifteenth century much of the town was burnt down during the rebellion of Sir Griffith Vaughan and by the time a survey was made of the site in 1521 the castle was recorded as being in 'grete ruyne and decay'; thus the borough of Caus faded away in the later Middle Ages and now only its earthworks, its place name and a single farm remain. In the words of Professor Maurice Beresford, Caus was like 'a prehistoric monster crushed beneath the weight of its own armour', unable to adjust to the new economic conditions of the later Middle Ages. The great tree-covered motte and bailey and the line of the town ramparts can be clearly identified, but here and there are more subtle remnants of this once locally important town. Tucked behind one of the farm's outbuildings are two great stone buttresses that originally must have reinforced the massive town wall. In the inner bailey of the castle a stone-lined well can still be found and at the northern entrance tree roots and the passage of animals through the centuries has revealed part of the town wall over 8 feet wide. Prehistoric pottery which has been found underneath the wall here suggests that the town may originally have been the site of an Iron Age hillfort.

A failed town with a rather similar history lies further into Wales beyond New Radnor, Cefnllys, which is another reoccupied hillfort. The site of Cefnllys stands on a rocky spur 300 feet above the wooded gorge of the river Ithon. The Mortimer family built a castle here between 1240 and 1246, at the same time as other outposts at New Montgomery and Paincastle. It is recorded that in 1332 Cefnllys had twenty burgesses and a survey of 1360 records it as a borough. But this highly exposed settlement had little chance of subsequent success and was already in decline by the time that Edward I led his attack on Wales. By the late fourteenth century there were only ten burgesses at Cefnllys. Like other border boroughs of its type the earthworks of the actual town are difficult to disentangle. Only a short stretch of street with possible burgage plots can be identified within the ramparts of the Iron Age fort, and like so many of these lost towns it has been fairly extensively plundered for its stone. Like Wigmore and Richards Castle it is dominated by massive motte and castle defences. At the close of the sixteenth century the antiquary Campden described Cefnllys as a 'lonely ruin', but surprisingly it survived as a rotten borough into the early nineteenth century. In 1832 the parliamentary boundary commissioners' report showed that there were still sixteen burgesses there who had the right to return a member of parliament, but they were living in just three farms and one cottage.

Moving south-eastwards we come to Huntingdon where the borough was created in the late twelfth century as part of a policy of political reprisal. In 1173 after a rebellion against the king the honour of Kington, a planted borough close by, was suppressed and absorbed into the new Marcher kingdom of Huntingdon. This was granted to William de Braose and as a result Kington castle was abandoned sometime before 1230 and the government of the lordship was moved to Huntingdon. The outlines of the new borough were sketched out between the castle mound and the church. Ironically Huntingdon failed to make any real progress and the successful town in the area was Kington-in-the-Fields, which had been laid out in a valley bottom some distance away from the old borough of Kington. Huntingdon is today perhaps one of the most spectacular of the failed border boroughs occupying as it still does a little territorial enclave which projects into Wales; the boundary of the borough is still marked in an identation in the national boundary. The earthworks are in the form of an extended outer bailey marking the town precinct, and the lumps and bumps that remain of the medieval settlement indicate former town houses. Its situation, however, is so rural that it is difficult to imagine that the settlement ever harboured urban ambitions.

35 The huge earthworks and masonry ruins of the castle at Huntingdon. The castle actually occupies a little territorial enclave which projects into Wales. During the thirteenth century it formed the apex of a medieval borough which was never really successful and always subsidiary to nearby Kington. In 1403, the Countess of Stafford was ordered to fortify the castle and rebuild a tollgate which had been destroyed by the Welsh; by 1521 the castle was reported to be derelict, except for one tower in which prisoners were kept

Another site where today it is difficult to imagine there ever having been a town is Richards Castle, near Ludlow. This site was important because before the Conquest a Norman, Richard le Scrob, was given land at Orleton and built a castle there. By the beginning of the next century a small town known as Richards Castle had developed. For although no trace of a borough charter survives, there is little doubt than an urban community flourished here for some three centuries after the Norman Conquest; a document of 1304 records 103 burgesses. However, like Huntingdon, Caus and Cefnllys, Richards Castle went into a decline in the later Middle Ages. Today the only remnants of the ancient town are in the form of the church of St Bartholomew, noted because of its detached tower, and the outlines of the borough which still survive as earthworks, providing us with one of the most exciting examples of a failed borough anywhere in the Borderland. Like many of the failed border boroughs there is a triangular green at Richards Castle which marks the former market area. The reasons for its failure are the familiar ones: the town's inability to change from a military to a trading community; sitting on a high bluff looking eastwards it was rather uncomfortably situated; and as Ludlow's fortunes waxed in the later Middle Ages so the commercial fortunes of Richards Castle declined. A new village with the same name was created at some later date down in the valley on the road from Ludlow to Leintwardine. A little to the south, Wigmore occupies a very similar situation and although a village survives here, together with its market place, only the enormous earthworks of the castle and those of the former borough give some indication that this was the capital of the great medieval Mortimer kingdom.

The castle-dominated settlement was not limited to just urban or proto-urban centres, but was to be seen in small villages as well; for instance, the renowned Romanesque church at Kilpeck lies within the shadow of a considerable Marcher castle and at the apex of a rectangular-shaped fortified enclosure, now identifiable only in earthwork form. Similarly at More, near Bishop's Castle, a defended deserted village lies immediately to the west of a ringwork castle and the evidence suggests that the settlement here was a post-Conquest creation contemporary with the castle and church. More, which was carved out of the great Saxon manor of Lydham, was granted a charter by Grand Searjentry in the reign of Henry I; this service is described by the nineteenth-century antiquary the Revd R. W. Eyton: 'The Lord of More, as a Constable of the King's host, to assume the command of two hundred foot-soldiers whenever the King of England crossed the Welsh Border in hostile array. The said Constable was to march in the vanguard of the army, and with his own hands to carry the King's standard.' The topography of the surviving settlement, with the earthworks of the castle at the west and the church at the east, demonstrates clearly its planned origins. The church has a squat Norman tower, typical of the Clun region and found in other settlements which are suspected as having similar origins.

Places to Visit

Shrewsbury Castle

Major castles were built in places such as Shrewsbury, where Roger de Montgomery constructed a large motte and bailey in the narrow neck of the loop of the river Severn between 1067 and 1069. The sixteenth-century Shropshire poet Churchyard said that Shrewsbury Castle was built 'in such a brave plott that it could have espyed a byrd flying in every strete'. In 1069 'the Welsh, with the men of Cheshire, laid siege to the king's castle at Shrewsbury aided by the townsmen under Eadric the Wild'. It survived the ordeal successfully until the town was relieved, at which point the insurgents burnt down the town and retired. The castle was rebuilt in stone under Henry II, but by the thirteenth century, in common with many other Border Castles, an enquiry of 1255 found that the motte had been undermined by river erosion, a condition attributed to the recent construction of a mill by the Abbot of Shrewsbury. During his campaign of north Wales (1277–83), Edward I made Shrewsbury the seat of his government and rebuilt the castle. In 1790 Thomas Telford converted the castle, then in ruins, into a residence for Sir William Pulteney: among his additions was Laura's Tower, a red sandstone octagonal structure that overlooks the castle and town. The castle now houses Shrewsbury District Borough's council chamber. (See Chapter Ten for details of Shrewsbury town.)

Clun

Clun lies at the heart of one of the emptiest parts of the Welsh Marches, known since the Middle Ages as the Clun Forest, but which is hardly wooded at all. The famous traditional lines 'Clunton, Clunbury, Clungunford and Clun are the quietest places under the sun' are frequently attributed to A. E. Housman, but they are actually a traditional jingle which he used for a preface to one of the poems in *A Shropshire Lad*. The castle at Clun, which today is a picturesque if somewhat precarious ruin overlooking the little town of Clun and the Clun valley, began life as a motte and bailey. It was rebuilt in stone in 1195–6 by the Fitz Allens (later Earls of Arundel) after the battle of Radnor, when we hear that Prince Rees had besieged Clun Castle and reduced it to ashes. At the same time there appears to have been an attempt to stimulate a town community here and the grid layout of the town clearly demonstrates its deliberately planned origins. This Norman settlement lies to the north of the river on a site that was laid out on waste ground – the ancient centre of Clun was around the church of St George on the opposite side of the river.

The attempt at urbanisation here was only partially successful, for although Clun was an important meeting place for Welsh and English, its vulnerability and remoteness meant that it never really flourished, a condition reflected in a borough rental of about 1300 which records that some sixty tenements were lying empty and worth nothing.

36 Clun Castle and town – a place where the English and Welsh met over the centuries to trade and, occasionally, to fight. The town appears to have been planned within the shadow of the Fitz Allen Castle. St George's church in the foreground marks the site of the original ancient settlement centre

The church has a squat Norman tower and is typical of the region. The bridge which crosses the river Clun and joins the ancient centre with the Norman plantation is a medieval saddleback with five arches. Otherwise the town is not particularly well endowed with historic buildings, although the splendid Holy Trinity Hospital, a group of seventeenth-century almshouses with a chapel, is well worth visiting.

Bishop's Castle

Not far from Clun is Bishop's Castle, another castle town which similarly enjoyed only modest success. The castle was erected by the Bishop of Hereford in 1127 in the western part of the 18,000-acre parish of Lydbury North, now a small village three miles to the south-east of Bishop's Castle. The castle lay at the top of a hill with a long road running down to the church of St John Baptist, originally a chapel belonging to Lydbury North. The town was developed between the church and castle. The solid squat form of the Norman church tower, a characteristic of several churches in this area, suggests that it played a role in the defence of the community. Ironically, the castle which gave its name to the town has all but disappeared and doesn't feature in the modern townscape of this delightful little settlement. Apart from this, Bishop's Castle has hardly changed in shape or size since it was created, and until 1967 could boast of being the smallest borough in England. However it still maintains its other claim to fame, The Three Tuns, a seventeenth-century inn which brews its own beer to this day.

37 Bishop's Castle was a medieval borough planted by the bishops of Hereford between the diminished remains of the castle (top) and the church of St John the Baptist (bottom). The town is still largely contained within its medieval layout, with the parallel lines of the burgage plots still acting as property boundaries

Ludlow

In contrast, a few miles to the south-east of Bishop's Castle lies Ludlow, a Norman castle town whose plantation was an unqualified success. Ludlow Castle, which was begun by Roger de Lacy in 1085, was constructed in local sandstone. The castle was soon to acquire a remarkably beautiful round Romanesque chapel in the middle ward – part of the improvements made in the 1130s by Sir Joyce de Dinan, an enemy and rival claimant to the Lacy castle. The two turbulent decades of his occupancy and the heroic recovery by the Lacys of their home are described in graphic detail in the thirteenth-century romance *Geste of Fulk Fitzwarine*. Subsequently five generations of Mortimers lived there, and it was probably they who were responsible for the impressive fourteenth-century buildings of the north front.

38 Inner bailey of Ludlow Castle with the circular Norman chapel on the right and the medieval and later apartments on the left; some of these were built specifically at the time Ludlow Castle became the quarters of the Council of the Marches

The castle was later to become the seat of the Lord President of the Council of the Welsh Marches, of whom the most illustrious was Queen Elizabeth's favourite, Sir Henry Sidney, father of Philip. The building of the gate house on the north side in 1581 was part of the extensive architectural improvements carried out under his tenancy – originally the entrance to the castle had been through the Norman keep. Milton presented his pastoral entertainment *Comus* here as a spectacular last act to close the castle's long active history. Although the castle was not seriously damaged in the Civil War, almost immediately afterwards the defences were dismantled. Vandalism in the reign of George I, when the lead was removed from the roofs, contributed to its decay which continued throughout the eighteenth century.

Ludlow town, which is packed tightly around the castle, has long been recognised as a classic example of Norman town plantation. In 1967 Professor Maurice Beresford wrote a book entitled *New Towns of the Middle Ages* in which he drew attention to the large number of English, Welsh and French towns which had been deliberately laid out during the early Middle Ages, and whose plans still reflected their origins. Over half a century earlier W. H. St John Hope had drawn attention to the planned nature of Ludlow's layout. Even earlier, however, Mr Hudson Turner, in his book *Some Account of Domestic Architecture in England from Edward I to Richard II* (1853), wrote a description which could have been based entirely on observations of Ludlow:

> There is, however, still another class of towns which were entirely founded in the Middle Ages, built from their foundations on a new site for some specific object, which have not been specifically noticed. These towns are more regular and symmetrical than most modern towns, and are built on an excellent scientific plan, combining very close packing with great convenience for individuals, while the principal streets are wide, open and straight, crossing each other at right angles only. There are always two parallel streets at a short distance one from the other and connected by short streets at frequent intervals; between these principal streets and also in parallel lines are narrow streets or lanes corresponding to the modern mews and employed for the same purpose: by this means each plot of ground for building on is of a uniform size and shape, a parallelogram with one end facing a principal street and another a lane. In some towns each building plot, or when built upon, each house, was also divided by a narrow passage or court leading from the principal street to the lane, serving as a water course and surface drain. Sometimes when a large house was required two plots were thrown together and the passage omitted; and in some towns these narrow passages were not used at all.

Ludlow was probably originally created by the de Lacys in the eleventh century immediately after the castle had been established. The new town sat in the parish of Stanton Lacy, and ancient parish boundaries to the north of Ludlow clearly demonstrate how the land was divided between St Peter's church, Stanton Lacy, and St Lawrence's, Ludlow and later St Leonard's, Ludlow. Up until the late nineteenth century part of the keep of Ludlow Castle still sat in Stanton Lacy parish.

The wide High Street which extends eastwards from the castle gates was laid down in the twelfth century and originally formed the old market place. The terraced shops at the eastern end of the High Street were contemporary structures and effectively represent 'fossilised' market stalls, with a narrow alley, Market Street, running behind them. Old Street, which does not conform to Ludlow's regular grid plan, may pre-date the town, and could have been the original north–south routeway that crossed the river Teme some two hundred yards to the east of Ludford Bridge, the present crossing point. Ludford Bridge, which sits close to the medieval St John's Hospital, dates from the fifteenth century.

39 A vertical air photograph of the 'classic' medieval planned town at Ludlow. The castle (top right) and town walls are clearly visible, as is the regularly laid out street pattern

Mill Street and Broad Street have a slightly bow-shaped street form often linked with medieval town plantation, designed possibly to enable a maximum amount of market area within the new town. West of Mill Street the plan has been considerably altered, but a narrow lane, originally known as Christ Croft, ran parallel with it towards the river. This was probably an original road as on its western side sits the twelfth-century chapel of St Thomas of Canterbury. There is a strip of ground between this lane and Mill Street extending north and south which itself is now divided into gardens and was apparently one of the original town streets. The abandonment of streets like this was almost certainly associated with the addition of the new outer castle bailey at the end of the twelfth century, which cut off the western end of the High Street, making redundant those roads immediately to the south of the castle.

St Lawrence, the largest parish church in Shropshire, was given a block of land to itself to the north-east of the High Street. The present church was built later in the Middle Ages by the wealthy wool merchants of the town and the Palmers Guild. The imposing church and tower cannot be fully appreciated from within the town and later medieval infilling in the High Street has completely obscured the fine southern porch. When approached from the north, it is the church along with the castle that dominates Ludlow. St Lawrence's has many fine features including a set of late medieval misericords depicting scenes from everyday life.

There is no doubt that the plantation at Ludlow was successful, for by 1377 there were over 1000 taxable householders here. Not only had there been a considerable movement of population to the new town, but Ludlow also took over the important north–south route previously controlled by Stanton Lacy. Ludlow maintained its prosperity throughout the Middle Ages, but many of its fine medieval timber houses were later encased in brick. As the majority of standing buildings are ostensibly Georgian the overall impression that Ludlow gives today is that of a fashionable eighteenth-century town, and indeed there were plans to turn it into a Salopian version of Bath. Ludlow is in many respects the most pleasant and best preserved of Border towns. None of the other new Border castle towns was as successful as Ludlow, and although places such as Hay on Wye, Knighton and Montgomery enjoyed a modicum of prosperity, today they carry an air of detached obscurity.

Hubert de Burgh's Three Towns

Among the undulating hill country between the main valleys of the Wye and Usk in the former county of Monmouthshire we find the traces of a number of failed urban experiments. The construction of White Castle began in 1184–5 in the parish of Llantilio Crossenny. White Castle is traditionally associated with Gwyn ap Gwaethfoed, who is said to have been a native princeling of the region. The name White Castle was in use as early as the thirteenth century, and must be taken to refer to the white plaster coating of the masonry, of which fragmentary remnants can still be seen. The castle stands about one mile from the village of Llantilio Crossenny on the summit of a high west-facing hill; it forms the strategic centre of the region enclosed by the northward bend of the river Monnow.

In 1201 King John granted White Castle, Grosmont and Skenfrith to Hubert de Burgh, an officer in the royal service who later distinguished himself in the French war by a prolonged defence of Chinon. In 1205 the castles were transferred to William de Braose, a local magnate who already held the neighbouring lordships of Brecknock and Abergavenny. William fell from royal favour and lost his lands in 1207, but his son regained White Castle and other neighbouring strongholds during the confusion and civil war at the end of King John's reign. In 1219 the king's court once more confirmed that the three castles belonged to Hubert de Burgh, then at the height of his power as Justiciar and Earl of Kent.

In 1232 Hubert de Burgh himself fell from royal favour and was forced to surrender the three castles, and custody was granted to Peter des Rivaux, a nephew of the Bishop of Winchester, who then acquired a key position in the royal administration. Peter des Rivaux fell from power in 1234, the three castles reverted to the Crown and were placed in charge of a royal officer, Waleran the German. Matthew Paris, the medieval historian, recording the fall of the once powerful Hubert de Burgh and his surrender of the three Monmouthshire castles and of Hatfield Peveril in Essex, states that these were the most prized of his possessions, on which he had spent an immense sum of money.

Waleran was still in charge of the three castles in 1244, when a new hall, buttery and pantry were erected at White Castle. In 1254 the three castles were granted to the King's elder son, later crowned King Edward I. In 1267 they were transferred to his younger brother Edmund Crouchback, Earl of Lancaster. It was in this period that a serious threat to the western Marches developed. Llewellyn ap Gruffydd, the Welsh ruler who had succeeded to the united principality built up by his grandfather Llewellyn Fawr, took the offensive during the English civil war between King Henry III and Earl Simon de Montfort. The Welsh tenants of the Border lordships rose in 1262 and a report to the King in the following spring records the disaster and the consequent loss of many of the English-held castles, stating that the frontier then held by Llewellyn lay only a league and a half beyond Abergavenny. It became clear that should that castle fall, White Castle would constitute the next line of defence. The Lord Edward is known to have been raising money in that year for certain urgent business of the King in the Marches. Even when the English civil war was over and peace returned the threat remained, for the Treaty of Montgomery (1267) recognised the Welsh conquests and Abergavenny was still a frontier fortress. Only in 1277 was the English position re-established. The campaign of that year forced Llewellyn to surrender his conquests and the subsequent advance and the final subjection of the Welsh a few years later robbed White Castle of the strategic role it had filled for a few years in the third quarter of the century.

After the Edwardian conquest of Wales, White Castle remained an administrative and financial centre. It was the place at which levies for the Scottish wars were mustered and where the rents and dues from the extensive manor could be collected. The White Castle continued in the possession of the Earldom and later Duchy of Lancaster until this honour was merged in the Crown on the accession of Henry IV. The castle is shown as already roofless and derelict in a survey of the sixteenth century. Medieval records make reference to town merchants at White Castle, but for centuries there has been no trace of a town here apart from earthworks in the field around the castle that conceal the house-plots of its former burgesses. Today White Castle is a delightfully lonely place – the rather menacing calm which prevails provides an appropriate memorial to its epic history.

At Skenfrith which lies on the west bank of the river Monnow on a site which still commands one of the then main routes from England to Wales, a small town appears to have been created about 1200. The borough of Skenfrith scarcely added to the primary elements of church and castle in the centuries after its foundation. Skenfrith probably failed to take off as a market town because of the overshadowing rivalry of its neighbours on the Monnow, Monmouth and Grosmont.

Scarcely three miles above Skenfrith, the ruined keep of Grosmont stands perched above a precipitous river cliff. Castle building had started at Grosmont in Henry II's reign, about the same time as the foundation of the other strongpoints of the defensive triangle. As the head of a Marcher lordship, Grosmont had acquired the right to hold markets and fairs; its status as a borough lapsed only in 1860. It is possible to recognise in Grosmont all the basic elements of the medieval townscape. Between the castle and the church lies an empty market place with a nineteenth-century market hall. The parish church bears witness to the declining population and prosperity of Grosmont over the centuries; most of the building dates from between 1200 and 1400. Its elaborate cruciform plan and fine octagonal tower suggests a busy and prosperous urban settlement, but for centuries St Nicholas has been too big for the dwindling population of Grosmont, which since the fifteenth century has found sufficient accommodation for its ecclesiastical needs in the chancel and has used the abandoned nave as a graveyard. Around the market place the cottages stand on narrow rectangular strips of ground, the burgage plots which were sketched out early in the thirteenth century when Hubert de Burgh established his new town. Some of them have lost their buildings and are now used as allotments.

Montgomery

Shortly after the Norman Conquest Roger de Montgomery, who had been left in Normandy as co-regent, received large tracts of territory in Sussex and in Shropshire and was created the Earl of Shrewsbury, where the castle already established by the Conqueror in 1069 became his principal seat. Roger came from Sainte Foy de Montgomery in the department of Calvados in Normandy. Sometime between 1070 and 1074 Roger built a castle in what was then the Shropshire hundred of Witentreu (a name which may survive in Whittery Farm and Whittery Bridge in Chirbury parish) which he named after his ancestral home in Normandy. This, however, was not on the site of the present castle, but was the earthen motte and bailey of Hen Domen one mile north of the town; and any reference to Montgomery prior to 1223 therefore refers to this site known as the Domen (the Old Mound) and not to the present castle.

40 View of the recently restored castle remains at Montgomery, which belonged to the second generation of medieval Marcher fortifications. They occupy a spectacular hilltop site overlooking the planned borough of Montgomery

Earl Roger died in 1094 and was succeeded in his estates in this country by his son Hugh. During Hugh's tenure the castle was sacked in 1095 by the Prince of Powys. Hugh was killed in Anglesey in a fight with the Norwegians in 1098 and was succeeded by his elder brother, Robert. Robert was prominent among those who sided with Duke Robert of Normandy against his brother Henry I, and as a result was deprived of his estates in 1102. After a further turbulent career, he died as Henry's prisoner in Corfe Castle in about 1131. The castle at Montgomery was then granted to Baldwin de Boulers, whose son, Stephen, and grandsons, Robert and Baldwin, succeeded him. The lordship was eventually sold to Thomas de Erdington, of Erdington (Warwickshire), in 1214–15 and although this sale was confirmed by King John he handed the lordship to Gwenwynwyn, Prince of Powys, in 1216; but he was almost immediately driven out by Llewellyn ap Iorwerth (Llewellyn the Great), Prince of Gwynedd. John died on 19 October in the same year and the effective history of the first castle came to an end.

In the autumn of 1223 the royal army under Henry III, which had relieved the de Braose castle of Builth from siege by Llewellyn ap Iorwerth, advanced through Hereford, Leominster and Shrewsbury to Montgomery, where it arrived on 30 September, the eve of the young King's sixteenth birthday. Montgomery was, however, such a keypoint of the Marches that, though King John had believed it worth while to secure the alliance of Gwenwynwyn by a grant of Montgomery, ultimate control of the town by the English Crown was inevitable. The contemporary chronicler Matthew Paris says that it was then that the young King was shown, probably by Hubert de Burgh, 'A suitable spot for the erection of an impregnable castle' on the high rock a mile south of Hen Domen. Orders had already been given to the chief forester of Shropshire to admit the King's carpenters into Shirlett Forest for the purpose of making brattices, or wooden palisades, to fortify Montgomery 'when the need shall arise . . .' Orders were also issued for the dispatch of twenty miners from the Forest of Dean to work on the new castle. By November work was sufficiently advanced for the King to be referring to his 'new castle of Montgomery' and to make arrangements for mass to be said in its chapel. A castle erected so swiftly can only have been of timber and the purpose of the autumn building campaign of 1223 must have been to erect a temporary castle which could subsequently be replaced by a stone one. In 1224–6 £2000 was spent on the castle, including the wages of the garrison and the cost of clearing the surrounding area of trees and undergrowth.

On 27 April 1228 the King granted the castle to Hubert de Burgh for life, with 200 marks (about £130) a year for its upkeep. The still uncompleted castle was attacked by Llewellyn ap Iorwerth in August, but the Welsh prince failed to take the castle either then or in a subsequent assault in the summer of 1231, though on the latter occasion he did succeed in burning the new town which had grown up below the castle rock. The castle was again attacked without success by Dafydd ap Llewellyn in 1245.

In 1229 Hubert received a further grant of £166 13s. 4d. towards 'enclosing' the castle. The work probably included 'the new bailey running from the road to Bedewin [i.e. Cedewain] to the castle'. This new bailey was most likely the complex outworks which lie between the present farm building on the site and the middle ward. In the autumn of 1223 'The Tower' was roofed in lead, probably marking the completion of the castle, but in the previous year, when Hubert lost the King's favour, he also lost Montgomery together with his other Marcher castles. In 1249 a survey listed the castle 'within le donjon' and a number of brattices, together with chapel, granary, stables, penthouses 'which cover the timber without the five brattices', a tower outside the gate, the house of the arblaster, or crossbow master, and a guest house.

Llewellyn ap Iorwerth had died in 1240 and much of his work for the unity of Wales was undone by the treaty of Woodstock in 1247, but his grandson Llewellyn ap Gruffydd reversed the course of events. The Treaty of Montgomery, confirmed by the King at Montgomery on 19 September 1297, marks the high water mark of his fortunes. By it he secured the King's acceptance of his considerable territorial gains and of his title Prince of Wales, giving official recognition to his status as feudal lord over most of the smaller independent Welsh rulers.

In 1272 Prince Rupert ascended the throne as King Edward I. The first few months of the new reign brought new trouble in the Marches. Llewellyn ap Gruffydd started to build a stone castle at Abermule, four miles south-west of Montgomery. On 15 June 1273 he was ordered to stop this work; however, he felt himself strong enough to ignore this order and it was not until 1277 that the English attacked and captured this new castle, called Dolforwyn, which sat on a commanding hilltop high above the left bank of the Severn at Abermule. All this led to a strengthening of the defences of the town and castle at Montgomery, the outstanding development being the replacement of the wooden palisade around the town by a stone wall in 1279–80.

With the Edwardian conquest of Wales, Montgomery lost its importance as a frontier fortress, and the scene of castle building was tranferred to north Wales. In 1299 Montgomery was granted to Margaret, the second wife of Edward I, but was transferred to the Prince of Wales in 1301.

The antiquary John Leland, whose tours in Wales extended from 1536 to 1539, visited Montgomery on more than one occasion. He observes of the town, which he said had been 'defloriched by Owen Glindour', that 'great ruines of the waulle yet apere *ad vestigia* of gates thus cawlyd, Kedewen Gate, Chyrbyry Gate, Arthur's Gate, Kery Gate. In the waulls yet remayne broken towerets, of the wiche the white towre is now most notable.' But he speaks of the castle itself as 'now a late re-edified'. This 're-edification' was due to the energy of Rowland Lee, Bishop of Coventry and Lichfield and President of the Council of the Marches in Wales from 1534 to 1543. The castle site was later occupied by a brick-built mansion house which was the home of the Herbert family. This fine building was destroyed after the Civil War in 1649. Montgomery Castle was an overgrown ruin until 1960, when the Welsh Office undertook a vigorous programme of clearance and restoration. The site is now open to the public.

CHAPTER SEVEN

The Early Church in the Marches

The Late Saxon Church

At the time of the Norman Conquest the Church in the Marches was in a relatively weak position. Anglo-Saxon monasticism was limited, there were few houses in the Marches, and the process of parish churches creation, which in other parts of the country was virtually complete, appears to have still been in its infancy in the Borderlands. As we have seen, the question of the survival of Romano-British Christianity in the Marches is a difficult one to analyse. It is clear, however, that Anglo-Saxon Christianity began to penetrate the region during the seventh century and a number of important ecclesiastical centres were founded, possibly sited on or close to already existing religious establishments. Apart from the cathedral at Hereford there were two monastic institutions in the area, one in Shropshire and one in Herefordshire, at Much Wenlock and at Leominster. The histories of these two ecclesiastical centres run in parallel. Both appear in the records for the first time in the middle years of the seventh century, possibly reflecting an Anglo-Saxon takeover of a pre-existing Celtic religious centre; both were endowed with considerable estates, which probably represented sub-Roman or even Romano-British territorial units. During the later Saxon period both seem to have been involved in ambitious programmes of land colonisation and the early stages of the creation of subsidiary parish churches. Both, too, were afflicted first by Danish and then by periodic Welsh attacks.

Early in the eleventh century there was an attempt to revitalise Leominster by Earl Leofric and his wife Godiva, but by the middle of the century it had been 'dissolved for its sins', after the Anglo-Saxon Chronicle for 1046 recorded that 'in this year Earl Sweyne marched into Wales . . . when he was on his homeward way he had the Abbess of Leominster fetched to him and kept her as long as he pleased, and then let her go home'. None the less the secular importance of Leominster is recorded in the Domesday Book where it appears as one of the largest manors in England, consisting of some eighty *hides* divided into six scattered manorial units. A new Benedictine priory was established here after Henry I granted the manor of Leominster to Reading Abbey in 1153. The nave of the great priory church, which still serves as Leominster's parish church, was consecrated in 1130.

At Wenlock the state and status of the monastery during the early part of the eleventh century is far from clear although it was still endowed with extensive estates in south Shropshire and Herefordshire. The most recent assessment of Wenlock suggests that in 1066 it seems to have been operating as a typical Borderland minster, with an extensive parish in the hands of a number of peripatetic canons who followed their own particular rules.

41 A watercolour drawing of the church of St Milburgh at Stoke St Milborough by the Reverend E. Williams, 1791. The church here created a considerable number of daughter chapelries in the late Anglo-Saxon period, including that at Heath

Roger de Montgomery established a Cluniac house (a daughter house of the great French abbey at Cluny) house at Wenlock between 1079 and 1082 when he granted most of the lands of the Saxon minster to the newly established monks. One of Wenlock's daughter churches at Stoke St Milborough had already been active creating dependent chapelries on the lower slopes of the Brown Clee.

The Church at the Time of the Domesday Book

Other minster churches which catered for the pastoral needs of large territories in the Borderland in the late Saxon period included Bromfield,
Morville and Stanton Lacy, in Shropshire, and Bromyard, Hereford,
Withington and Moreton, in Herefordshire. Churches at Chirbury, Maesbury
and Oswestry also appear to have performed similar roles. Chirbury manor
had two churches, one of which was St Michael's in Chirbury itself, the
other a daughter chapelry at Church Stoke, which now lies on the Welsh
side of the Border. Stoke is a place name normally applied to daughter
churches or chapels who were dependent in some way upon a mother
church. It is clear that in the case of Chirbury and Church Stoke we are
dealing with an early example of a dependent chapelry. Chirbury parish
was originally very large, constituting almost the whole Domesday hundred
of Witentreu. Such extensive parishes were commonplace in the western
part of the Marches prior to the Conquest. Writing of Clun before 1086 the
Reverend E. W. Eyton noted, 'Here was one of those great Saxon foundations
whose parishes we hardly venture to define for fear of falling short of reality.'
Such parishes covered large tracts of forest and open heathland on the edge
of the Welsh massif. Subsequent to the Conquest Chirbury founded other
chapels at Montgomery, Snead, Forden and Hyssington. As we shall see,
this was a process followed elsewhere in the Borderland.

In addition to places where churches were specifically recorded in the
Domesday Book such as Shrewsbury, which is attributed with five churches,
priests without churches were also recorded in a considerable number of
Border manors. It is assumed that such a reference implies the existence
of a pre-Conquest church or chapel; even so, in the case of Shropshire, out
of a total of 630 entries in the Domesday survey only fifty churches are
recorded, while in Herefordshire, out of 313 places recorded, only forty-one
had priests or churches allocated to them in 1086. Even given the relatively
immature parochial structure in the Borderlands it would seem unlikely that
as few as 10% of settlements had some permanent form of place of worship.
It is clear that much is hidden in the blanket assessments of the Domesday
Book, where large tracts of land containing many settlements are often
bundled together for the sake of administrative convenience. It becomes even
clearer that this is a considerable under-estimate when we look at those
churches which contain substantial late Saxon architecture, and appear
only by inference in the folios of the survey. Indeed outside the *burhs* the
most important visible Saxon legacies in the Marches are those churches
which were wholly or partly built before the Norman Conquest. A remarkable group of churches containing Saxon material survive in south Shropshire – these include St Peter's, Diddlebury, St Giles's, Barrow, and St
Andrew's, Wroxeter. The most notable of these, however, is St Peter's at
Stanton Lacy in the Corvedale. In the case of St Eata's, Atcham, the church

not only contains Anglo-Saxon architecture but it is known that the historian Ordericus Vitalis was baptised there in 1075, although there is no church recorded at Atcham in 1086.

The New Norman Church

The massive transfer of land following the Norman Conquest was accompanied by the refounding of monasteries such as Wenlock and the creation of a new Benedictine abbey at Shrewsbury by Roger de Montgomery. Other Border barons followed suit and founded new monastic establishments at places such as Wigmore and later Abbey Dore while minsters such as Chirbury were refounded as monasteries or priories. The second stage in monastic foundation in the Marches was the most important. All the new houses were established within a few miles of existing communication routes, normally in wooded regions that were just being opened up for cultivation, and these helped to meet some of the needs arising from the transformation of the Saxon Church. The old minsters served scattered chapels in huge parishes, and they also provided hospitality along the main routes and in centres of local government. Both the abbey at Buildwas and Shrewsbury's dependent cell at Morville were expressly founded with an obligation to provide hospitality. There seems to have been a similar obligation at Bromfield where a dependent cell of Gloucester Abbey replaced the older collegiate establishment in the early year's of Henry II's reign.

The Normans came to England not only as conquerors but also as latter-day missionaries. The Conquest itself had been seen as a holy war, blessed by the Pope. In return William agreed to reform the English Church and after his victory at Hastings he sent the Pope the defeated English King Harold's banner. When they arrived the Normans did not like what they saw of the established Anglo-Saxon Church and set about its immediate reformation. Quite apart from its administrative structure they disliked the archaic Roman liturgy, the Anglo-Saxon architecture and its incomprehensible learning. Initially the Normans had little respect for the English saints, and Archbishop Lanfranc wrote:

> These Englishmen among whom we are living have set up for themselves certain saints whom they revere. But sometimes when I turn over in my mind their own accounts of whom they were, I cannot help having doubts about the validity of their sanctity.

At Evesham Abbey Abbot Walter (1077–1104) burned the saints' bones to test their authenticity and only those that survived were deemed to be genuine. The hostility towards the English saints did not, however, survive the first generation of Norman clerics: the writings of contemporary chroniclers did much to re-establish the reputation of the most famous saints and the Church began to appreciate the financial importance of their relics in attracting pilgrims.

William needed bishops whom he could trust absolutely and who could serve as vice-regents in his newly won kingdom. He therefore delayed only a few years before investigating a radical restaffing of the English Church, and, prompted by clerical involvement in the northern risings, William set about the systematic replacement of the upper sections of the Anglo-Saxon Church hierarchy. So complete was the eventual foreign 'takeover' that William of Malmesbury, writing in about 1125, claimed that

> England has become a residence for foreigners and the property of aliens. At the present time there is no English earl, nor bishop nor abbot; strangers all, they pray upon the riches and vitals of England.

In the case of Hereford there was, however, no dramatic change, for in 1060 Edward the Confessor had already installed there a French bishop, Walter of Lorraine, chaplain to Edward's wife, Queen Edith. In 1079 he was succeeded by a fellow countryman Robert Lorraine (Losinga) who was responsible for starting the rebuilding of the cathedral in the new Norman style. The policy of appointing Norman bishops and abbots in England and drafting monks from Normandy naturally led to a strong Norman influence on English architecture elsewhere. Despite the fact that several major English churches had been rebuilt in the tenth or early eleventh centuries, the Normans considered Anglo-Saxon architecture inferior and missed no opportunity to erect new buildings. As soon as a Norman prelate had taken charge of an English see or monastery a new church was begun. Such was the scale of rebuilding that it prompted a contemporary, Raoul Glaber, to write: 'One would have thought that the world was shaking itself to cast off its old age and was clothing itself in a white robe of churches.' The Conquest, therefore, presented an opportunity to start afresh, and with the arrival of the new school of Norman Romanesque, these elements combined to produce one of the great periods of architectural history.

Worcester was one of the very few cathedrals to retain an English prelate and some of its English customs, nevertheless the cathedral was rebuilt. Wulfstan had survived the political upheavals and ecclesiastical reforms associated with the Norman Conquest, and had been bishop for over twenty years before he turned his attention to any major building work. The *Worcester Annals* (compiled in the early fourteenth century) state: '1084. The beginning of the work of Worcester Minster by St Wulfstan.'

The circumstances surrounding the new work are detailed in a charter issued by the bishop in 1089. It reads:

> I Wulfstan, by the grace of God, pontiff of the church of Worcester, desiring to enlarge the monastery of the holy Mother of God, Mary, built in the episcopal see by my predecessor of pious memory, that is by blessed Oswald – to enlarge it with greater honour and dignity, not only in the building and adoring of the

church, but indeed also of the monks serving God there, I have sought to enrich it by an augmentation of property.

The charter indicates that Wulfstan on his appointment to the see in 1062 had founded a small community for whom the old cathedral buildings were probably quite adequate; subsequently he had set about its reform within the context of Lanfranc's wider reform movement after 1070. By this time the size of the community had increased to nearly fifty monks, which must have rendered the old buildings practically unusable. It was St Oswald's church of St Mary that was to be replaced by the new building to which the dedication was transferred. By May of 1089, the new building was sufficiently far advanced for the monks to move into it. This must indicate that the area of the choir together with the presbytery were virtually completed within a space of only five years.

William of Malmesbury gives further historical information about the state of the works around 1089 and, perhaps more interestingly, provides an insight into Wulfstan's own views about what he was doing. This information he derived, as he says, from Nicholas, who was an eyewitness at the time, and who became prior of Worcester in about 1113. William says that

> when the work of the main church, which he had begun from the foundations, had advanced to that stage of growth that now the monks might move into it, the old church which blessed Oswald had built was ordered to be unroofed and destroyed.

William goes on to record that Wulfstan

> yet then completed the new church, and you could not easily find the ornament that did not decorate it, so marvellous was it in single details and singular in all parts.

The move into the new church in 1089 must have been accompanied by the removal of the relics from the old church of St Mary and their re-enshrining in the new. The most important of these relics were those of St Oswald, and William of Malmesbury says that Wulfstan contributed 72 marks of silver towards embellishing the shrine which contained them and also many other relics. Worcester, which was started in 1084, was the earliest major church undertaken after the Conquest in the Severn valley, and can hardly have had significant local Romanesque traditions upon which to draw. In a recently published survey Richard Gem has pointed out that the main direct source of inspiration for the new cathedral at Worcester lies in what had been happening in the previous decade at Canterbury, at Christchurch and St Augustine's. It is clear that Worcester itself also influenced buildings in the region, as it formed the foremost Romanesque building in its area and clearly influenced buildings such as Great Malvern Priory (founded c. 1085), the abbey church at Gloucester (begun

1089) and the abbey church at Tewkesbury (founded in the early twelfth century).

In the century and a half following the Norman Conquest the process of creating new parishes and daughter chapelries continued at a frantic pace. This process was in some cases initiated by monasteries, in others by large wealthy mother churches. Typical of this process was the minster church at Morville in Shropshire, which according to the Domesday Book was the only church in the whole of the Saxon hundred of Alnostreu. In the late Saxon period it had been served by eight canons, who were obviously operating over a vast area. In the century following the Conquest, however, a number of new chapels were planted in Morville's territory. Chapels were founded at Billingsley, Oldbury, Taseley, and Aston Eyre, all before 1140.

42 Christ's entry into Jerusalem as depicted on the unusual Norman tympanum at Aston Eyre

The latter chapel contains a remarkable tympanum showing Christ's entry into Jerusalem, considered by many to be one of the finest pieces of Norman sculpture in the whole of the Marchlands. Further chapels were founded in Morville parish at Aldenham, Underton, and Astley Abbots. Significantly the chapel at Astley Abbots was endowed with some 'assart' (recently cleared) land, indicating that chapel creation was in some cases associated with woodland clearance. The original chapel at Bridgnorth too was initially dependent upon Morville. Although all traces of the chapels at Underton and Aldenham have disappeared, along with the hamlets which they served, the remainder all emerged later as parochial centres.

In many other large parishes there was a similar burst of activity. St Mary's church at Shawbury founded chapels at Acton Reynald, Moreton Corbet, Grinshill, and Great Wytheford. A certificate of Bishop Roger de Clinton dated 1140 tells of the time when these manors were without chapels and that he himself had consecrated three of them. In the more hilly districts chapels were planted along river valleys and a line of such chapels, later to become parish churches, follows the county boundary between Herefordshire and Shropshire along the Teme valley at Bedstone, Bucknell, Stowe and Llanfair Waterdine.

A considerable number of these chapels simply disappeared in the late Middle Ages with the desertion and shrinkage of the settlements they served. Duke, in his *Antiquities of Shropshire* (1854), records some 105 lost chapels in the county. One of these, at the deserted hamlet of Bold in the parish of Aston Botrell, was later incorporated into the outbuildings of the surviving farm and was drawn by the Reverend Williams in one of his invaluable watercolours of Border churches at the end of the eighteenth century.

Monasteries in the Marches

The Middle Ages saw a dramatic rise in the importance of religious houses in the twelfth century and an equally dramatic fall in the sixteenth century. The impact of both events on the landscape had considerable significance. The relative poverty of parts of the Marcher landscape since the early Middle Ages has meant that the new Norman churches were never rebuilt, with the result that throughout the Border, buildings in the distinctive Romanesque style of the Normans can be readily found. The earliest of monastic foundations were Benedictine and include St Werburgh's at Chester and Shrewsbury Abbey, built by Roger de Montgomery. The robust abbey church which lies a little way to the east of the English bridge in Shrewsbury incorporates a substantial amount of simple but competent Norman work, but the outlying buildings have been ravaged since the dissolution of the monasteries. The final blow came when Thomas Telford drove his A5 road through the claustral buildings. A few scrappy remnants including the refectory pulpit sit forlornly in a builder's yard, now totally divorced from the church.

Following in the wake of the early Norman foundations (which were normally attached to urban centres), in the middle years of the twelfth century came the Cistercians. This monastic order with its vows of poverty and simplicity normally located its houses in isolated settings well away from large existing settlements. The first of the great Cistercian houses in the Marchlands appeared with the establishment of Tintern Abbey in the deep gorge of the lower Wye in 1131. Tintern is a much visited site in a splendid setting, but to the north, high up in the deeply engraved valleys of the Black Mountains, lies the ruins of a monastery which exemplifies the Cistercian search for solitude far better, Llanthony Priory, built between 1175 and 1230.

Not very far away, at the mouth of the Golden Valley, lie the remains of Abbey Dore, which was established in the mid twelfth century. The records of this Cistercian monastery begin quite simply with the phrase, 'In 1147 was begun the Abbey of Dore.' A party of white monks from Morimond in France were sent to the Golden Valley and within thirty years the first monastic buildings had been completed. The great sight at Abbey Dore is the church, which consists of the massive chancel and crossing of the abbey church and gives some impression of the scale of the medieval foundation here. The size and the splendour of the surviving Cistercian medieval buildings at Abbey Dore reflect the accumulated wealth of the monastery, which was one of the most active in reclamation and possessed the most extensive estates in the whole of the Welsh Marches. Abbey Dore properties included seventeen granges, of which nine were in the Golden Valley. It is clear that this fertile corridor, isolated from the Wye valley by an irregular wooded sandstone ridge and screened to the west by the menacing plateau of the Black Mountains, owes the outline of its present rural settlement pattern to the pioneering activities of the Cistercians in the twelfth and thirteenth centuries. Granges founded in the Golden Valley include Morehampton Park Farm, a moated site close by the river Dore, New Grange, Blakemore Grange, Whitehall Grange, Hollins Grange and Backton Grange. The abbey also had estates in further flung places such as northern Monmouthshire. It was the wool trade which gave the abbey its wealth and a late thirteenth century account reveals that the Abbey Dore flock consisted of almost three thousand sheep. In an important account of the medieval wool trade, *La Patrica Della Mercatura*, it is recorded that Abbey Dore wool commanded the highest price among all the English fleeces.

The establishment of the monastic farms appears to have involved considerable woodland clearance. It is recorded that the monks of Abbey Dore were allowed to 'till, assart, enclose and deal with their pleasure'. The term 'assart', or 'essart', comes from the Old French *essarter*, which literally means to grub up, but was extensively applied in the early Middle Ages to land which had been cleared of wood and scrub in order that it could be cultivated. It is commonly found as a field or place name in the Marches, often in marginal areas. In the early thirteenth century King John granted Abbey Dore an area of former royal forest, Trivel Wood, with permission to assart. John also allowed the monks to enlarge and raise a mill pond in Trivel Wood and it has been suggested that this was the forerunner of the ornamental lake which now fills the floor of the shallow valley on the edge of Whitfield Park.

The reclamation activities of the Cistercians were not, however, universally applauded and Giraldus Cambrensis commented adversely about the economic activities of the monasteries following his tour of Wales in the closing years of the twelfth century. He accused the monks of 'changing an oak wood into a wheat field', and added that Abbey Dore's reclamation of the clearance of a tract of woodland because it was 'wild and rough and offered secure refuge to the Welshman and robbers' was nothing more than a lame excuse. The records of the monastic institutions show quite clearly that there were still sizeable areas of rough land available for reclamation in the Marches. We cannot be certain if this land had been previously cultivated and had reverted to waste, or if it represented the residue of poorer land which had never been seriously farmed. There certainly appears to have been a larger reservoir of land available for clearance in the Marches than in Midland England just to the east. Quite apart from the 'assart' place names, many field names in marginal areas carry elements such as 'marsh', 'moor' and 'heath', indicative of their condition in the early Middle Ages.

43 The substantial nave and chancel ruins of the church of the Cistercian monastery at Buildwas, which sits on the banks of the river Severn close to the Ironbridge Gorge

Close to the Ironbridge Gorge in Shropshire the monks of Buildwas Abbey (founded *c.* 1148) were also occupied with land reclamation in surviving pockets of waste. Later in the Middle Ages Buildwas, along with a number of other Shropshire abbeys, was involved in exploiting the mineral resources of the Shropshire coalfield and creating the foundation on which the Industrial Revolution was later to develop. The basis of Buildwas's wealth, however, lay in the land. In a taxation document of 1291 it is clear that the major wealth of the monastery came from its agricultural activities. It was assessed at the formidable figure of £113 19s. 5d., of which over 60% came from stock farming and over 20% from arable farming. Wool was not specifically included in the valuation, but the monks were certainly exporting wool at this time and it must have contributed substantially to their revenue. Buildwas possessed the right to wash sheep in the river Severn at Cressage and to load barges there, which suggests that wool was being shipped downriver, perhaps as far as Bristol. Earlier in 1264 we hear that Buildwas was one of the abbeys which was selling wool to Flemish merchants and it is the only one of the Shropshire monasteries to figure in Pegolotti's list of monasteries supplying wool to Italian merchants. If these figures are reliable the gross profits of the wool must have been between £150 and £200 a year, which is more than the estimated annual value of all the other income put together. The site of Buildwas Abbey is of interest because the local topography determined that the claustral buildings were built on the northern side of the church with drainage towards the river. There is also an interesting set of fishponds to be found to the north of the ruins of the main abbey buildings. Buildwas lies close to the river Severn but today its hidden buildings and earthworks have to be sought out as they are surrounded by a thick belt of trees.

The Hereford School of Romanesque Architecture

The Cistercian order, which was dedicated to simplicity, as one would expect built in plain and austere Romanesque styles, but many churches in the Borderland often contain much more flamboyant Romanesque architecture. During the middle decades of the twelfth century Norman architecture began to develop many more decorative elements and a number of regional schools developed in England with their own distinctive styles and designs. Especially noteworthy are the twelfth-century carvings of the Herefordshire School which was responsible for the decoration of a number of churches in Herefordshire, Gloucestershire and Shropshire. The most splendid example of their work was at Shobdon in northern Herefordshire, but the church was destroyed in the nineteenth century and only a few decaying fragments of this marvellous early medieval work have survived and are displayed in Shobdon Park. The Herefordshire School is now best represented in the little church of Kilpeck, where the sculpture shows that the School drew its inspiration from Anglo-Saxon, Continental and Viking art. Attention has also been drawn to the similarity between the work of the Herefordshire School and carvings found in the great pilgrimage churches of eastern France, such as Autun and Vézelay. Even more interesting, however, are the links between these Marcher churches and churches along the pilgrimage route which runs along western France and northern Spain to Santiago de Compostela in Galicia.

44 Samson fighting the lion as depicted on the tympanum at Stretton Sugwas. This sculpture is one of the finest executed by the Hereford School. It shows similarities in design with contemporary carving in churches in western France, which lay along the pilgrimage route to Santiago de Compostela

Evidence of the pilgrimage link is to be found in the tympana at Brinsop and Stretton Sugwas, which lie about two miles apart from each other. That at Brinsop depicts St George who is represented as a contemporary knight with hawks, on horseback, thrusting his spear into the dragon, whose snake-like body is being trampled on by the horse. The tympanum at Stretton Sugwas shows Samson battling with a lion, whose jaws he is forcing open. In western France there are a number of sculptures showing riders defeating enemies, which appear either in the form of dragons, serpents or in some cases infidels. The origins of this sculpture appear to be based on a Roman equestrian statue of Marcus Aurelius, but in the minds of the medieval sculptors it appears to have become confused with both Constantine the Great and Charlemagne, who features in early stories of the Christian fight against the Moors in Spain. Work of the Herefordshire School is to be seen at Leominster priory and Rowlestone, but a considerable number of other places in northern Herefordshire and southern Shropshire have tympana or fonts which were either influenced or executed by the School. The church at Kilpeck is a little gem and still lies almost completely intact. Other churches at places such as Holdgate and Tugford show partial elements of their work.

In the works of this group of sculptors it is possible to detect for the first time since the Norman Conquest the strong influence of continental centres on English sculpture. In comparison with the Southern English School of architecture, which developed between 1120 and 1140, the Herefordshire School demonstrates an important change in patronage. The greatest works of the Southern School were founded in the monastic houses and they show a close similarity of style with contemporary illuminations made in the mother monastic centres, but the works of the Herefordshire School were executed for lay patrons.

Another nearly complete example of the small Norman church is at Heath, hidden on the plateau below Brown Clee hill in south Shropshire. This isolated church, despite some insensitive restoration at the beginning of this century, is almost completely mid-twelfth-century. With its Norman font and box pews and decaying wall paintings, surrounded by the lumps and bumps of a deserted village, Heath represents the very essence of the Welsh Border landscape. Other examples of Norman architecture are to be found scattered throughout the isolated rural parts of the Borderland, mainly in settlements which decayed during the later Middle Ages and where subsequently there was no money or impetus for rebuilding. One interesting peculiarity of the Norman Border region churches already noted are the squat square Norman bell towers, found particularly in northern Herefordshire and southern Shropshire. The most spectacular are the low squat buttress towers to be found at places such as Bishop's Castle, Clun and Lydham.

The survival of so much Norman architecture can be attributed to the quality of the original buildings and to the later comparative poverty of the area. The Normans brought previously unknown wealth and skill into the Borders which led to the construction of these churches but the wealth which in the later Middle Ages was gained from trading in wool and textiles on the whole found its way back into secular buildings, markets and guild halls, rather than new churches. Places such as Leominster, Weobley, Pembridge and Ludlow all possess fine churches, paid for in part at least by the profits from wool, but with the possible exception of Ludlow there are few wool churches on the scale of those found in the Cotswolds or East Anglia.

Places to Visit

Kilpeck

The finest surviving church of the Herefordshire School is at Kilpeck, which lies about nine miles to the south of Hereford in the former Welsh area of Archenfield. Indeed the place name Kilpeck is Celtic, the first element of which means 'retreat' or 'corner'. It has a long military and monastic history – a Benedictine priory, of which nothing remains, was founded here in 1135. The parish church has a wealth of sculpture lavished on its doorway, chancel arch, corbels and windows. The doorway has been extraordinarily well preserved because of a wooden porch which protected it until it was unwisely removed in the nineteenth century. The main arch of this doorway is carved with a series of flamboyant designs characteristic of later Norman architecture. These include beaked heads, monsters and an angel, which is placed at the apex. There is also a chain motif, each ring of which contains birds, monsters and fishes. The doorway jambs are covered with thick bodies of twisting snakes and one of the shafts with figures of warriors interwined with foliage, while the other is carved with foliage and a pair of doves at the base. The capitals are decorated with animals and a grotesque head, while on the tympanum there is a symmetrical vine scroll.

45a Detail of the doorway at Kilpeck, showing a warrior with foliage

45b Tympanum showing the tree of life with outer arches depicting grotesque heads and the signs of the zodiac

The exterior of the church includes a richly carved west window and a magnificent corbel table fashioned in the form of grotesque heads and animals and bearing also a Celtic fertility symbol. Projecting from the angles of the nave and from the centre of the west front there are a series of large heads of dragons which are reminiscent of Scandinavian art, and a number of other features in the church, including some of the corbels, also suggest a strong Viking influence.

Inside the church the chancel arch is richly carved with Anglo-Norman designs and the shafts are designed in a way which until the mid twelfth century was unknown in England. Each shaft is decorated with a figure of three apostles, one above the other. The inspiration for this appears to have been the famous early twelfth-century doorway the Puerta de las Platerias at the cathedral of Santiago de Compostela in north-western Spain. In addition to the important stylistic links between the Herefordshire School and the Santiago pilgrimage route there is a remarkable document preserved in the university library at Chicago which records the circumstances of the foundation of Shobdon, which contained carvings very similar, if not superior to those at Kilpeck. Shobdon was founded by Oliver de Merlimond, chief steward of Hugh de Mortimer, Lord of Wigmore. When the building was begun, Oliver went on a pilgrimage to Santiago de Compostela to pay homage to the relics of St James Along the route, particularly in the Poitou and Charente areas of western France and in old Castile in Spain, he came across the pilgrimage style and it would appear that he either made extensive drawings or more probably returned with one of the craftsmen involved in the ornamentation of these pilgrimage churches.

Just to the west of the church are the extensive remains of a motte and bailey castle, and to the east are the earthworks of a rectangular defended settlement. It would seem likely that these represent the remains of a former 'borough' laid out adjacent to the church and castle, but which, like so many of its neighbours, failed to adapt to the trading requirements of the later Middle Ages.

Diddlebury

The unusual name of this Shropshire village reflect its Saxon origin. It means 'the burgh [or settlement] of Duddela', an Old English personal name, presumably that of an early lord. St Peter's church at Diddlebury is one of a group in southern Shropshire which boast significant surviving Saxon remains. One of the reasons for this early group of substantially built churches is perhaps the wealth produced by the rich grazing land and the high quality wool of the Corvedale region in the later Saxon period. The Saxon origin of St Peter's is evident from several notable characteristic architectural features. The infilled north door is narrow and round-headed with plain hood mouldings. The church has long and short stonework on the quoins of the north end of the chancel at the base. The herringbone pattern of stonework of the north wall of the nave, which can be seen on the interior only, is one of the finest examples of this eleventh-century method of construction. What is particularly unusual is that the stones have been especially cut for this pattern. It also has a number of other Anglo-Saxon features including a small double-shafted window of dressed stone, a horseshoe-shaped doorway and some interlaced sculpture. The chancel is basically Norman, although there are a number of features which suggest that it had a Saxon predecessor.

46   The interior north wall at St Peter's church, Diddlebury. The faced Saxon herringbone masonry is some of the best work in this style in England; on the left is a blocked Saxon doorway with large shapeless block-like imposts

After the Norman Conquest Roger de Montgomery gave the church of Diddlebury and its land to Shrewsbury Abbey. The rest of Diddlebury was part of the Earl's manor of Corfham which before the Conquest belonged to Edward the Confessor. Corfham stood a mile to the east of Diddlebury and by the twelfth century boasted a substantial castle belonging to the Clifford family; apart from some earthworks nothing now remains above ground. An illuminating sixteenth-century account of Corfham Castle records:

> Cofham hath been a manor of great fame, and had in it a castle compassed about with a mott and a strong cour wall, strong towers, wereof one doth remain called Rosamund's Tower, but can't long stand for it is uncovered and the lead taken away. The forsaid courts was also compassed about able to withstand any suddain invasion, but nowe all decayed, ruinated and destroyed.

Henry II gave Corfham and Diddlebury to Walter Clifford, whose daughter Rosamund was Henry II's mistress. She produced two sons, one of whom became Archbishop of York, and a well near Corfham bears her name. Rosamund eventually retired to Godstow nunnery near Oxford. Today Diddlebury is a delightfully quiet spot in the peaceful Corvedale now far removed from its brief association with national political intrigue.

Much Wenlock

Recent excavations at Wenlock Priory suggest that the settlement here may have a Romano-British or possibly prehistoric origin. The first religious house at Wenlock was a nunnery, which was founded by Merewalh, King of Mercia, about 670 for his daughter, St Mildburg. Mildburg was reputedly a gentle lady to whom miracles were attributed in her lifetime, and she died an abbess in about 715. This nunnery was destroyed by the Danes when they raided Mercia in the late ninth century. The second foundation at Wenlock was a minster built by a friend of Edward the Confessor, Leofric, the powerful Earl of Mercia. Leofric founded several religious houses in the mid eleventh century including Coventry, Stow, Wenlock and Leominster. In 1086 in the Domesday Book it is recorded that Earl Roger 'has made the church of St Mildburg into an abbey. The same church holds Wenlock and held it in the time of Edward the Confessor.'

The refounded monastery was dependent upon La Charite in France and was clearly well endowed with lands in southern Shropshire. A small number of monks came from La Charite to take possession of the lands of the church of St Mildburg and the newly installed monks decided 'to open the silver shrine which was believed to hold the body of St Mildburg'. The story relates that the shrine was empty, but soon afterwards a servant of the monks called Raymond was working in the monastery of the Holy Trinity, which lies close to the church of St Mildburg, and there found on an altar an old box. Inside it was a document which stated that the saint's body was buried before the high altar of the church of the Holy Trinity. The monks then asked St Anselm, Archbishop of Canterbury, for advice, who divined that this had happened 'not by the will of man'. He told them to dig up the ground and search and as a result they found the bones. The monks deposited the bones in a new shrine and the story continues that miracles followed to confirm the truth of the discovery.

By 1169–70 the monks of Wenlock had become so numerous that they were able to send a prior and twelve monks to found the Cluniac monastery of Paisley in Scotland. They also sent a prior and a small number of monks to three small dependent priories, Dudley, St Helen's in the Isle of Wight, and Church Preen, a few miles from Wenlock and one of only four churches once served by Cluniac monks in this country which are still used as parish churches.

47 Aerial view of the surviving parts of the Cluniac priory at Much Wenlock. Although an attempt was made to save the church at the time of the dissolution, by recommending that it should form part of a new joint bishopric with Chester, it was eventually demolished. The prior's lodging (centre right), which dates from c. 1500, was turned into a magnificent private residence

Dramatic events at Wenlock are recalled in a letter addressed to the prior of La Charite from the prior and monks of Wenlock written about 1163. This recalls a local uprising by the priory's agricultural tenants.

The villeins who held lands by rendering of feudal service had rashly lifted up their heel against us and wished to depose the prior and put another in his place . . . They carried their complaint to the king's court, and although they met with little favour, a writ was sent to the sherriff to inquire into their grievances . . . The prior offered an inquiry by the tenants in chief and his own free tenants. At last the villeins were convinced of their error and they took a solemn oath over the body of St Milburga that they would be faithful in all things to the priory. But the next day they went back on their oath and their last error was worse than the first when they threw down their ploughshares . . . It was Tuesday in Whitsun week . . . and as was our custom we went out from our church in procession carrying the shrine of St Milburga and with a great company of men and women following us. After a sermon had been preached to them we put forth a sentence of excommunication against those who wrong the church.

When our villeins heard that sentence they hastened back to Wenlock before us and beset the three doors of the church, and when we came back they barred our way crying out, 'Seize the unjust man and kill him.' By the mercy of God and with the help of the knights who accompanied us we escaped them, but they threw stones and cudgels after us and some of our monks and servants received severe blows. After this outrage they consented that six monks and four knights should hear their grievances, and both they and the prior would accept the decision of these judges. This was done. The villeins submitted and on the morrow they intended to come back and plough the land. But the messengers whom they sent to you to complain of our prior have come back from La Charite with letters from you. The villeins have gone back on their pact and lifted their horns. Saving your reverence you have acted incautiously, for judgement is not to be given in absence. If you have any mercy, if any virtue of charity, if any bowels of compassion restrain the rage of these wolves while there is time ... We would rather die than give in to them.

We do not know how this story of a very early version of the Peasant's Revolt ended, but peace seems to have returned to Wenlock fairly rapidly.

The oldest parts of the buildings which still survive, the chapter house and the lavatorium, are twelfth-century. The blind arcading in the chapter house and the carved scenes on the side of the lavatorium are some of the finest architectural features in the priory ruins. The church was rebuilt in the first half of the thirteenth century, and the priory received many gifts of money and materials for the work, including timber from Henry III, who was several times a guest of the priory. In 1295 war broke out between France and England, and alien priories like Wenlock came under suspicion because they owed allegiance to foreign houses. For the next hundred years Wenlock was subject to severe restrictions and heavy taxation, which only came to an end when the links with La Charite and Cluny were finally broken in 1395.

The monastery was dissolved on 26 January 1540. There were proposals for using the church and revenues for a new diocese; one was that there should be a see of Chester with Wenlock, another Shrewsbury with Wenlock, but they came to nothing and most of the buildings were destroyed. The eastern block, however, which contained the prior's lodging (c. 1500), was converted into one of the finest houses to be created out of a monastic building anywhere in England.

Apart from the remains of the priory, Wenlock has plenty to see including Holy Trinity church which incorporates a Norman nave and chancel. Elsewhere there is a mixture of building styles and building materials closely packed along narrow streets. The sixteenth-century half-timbered guild hall is a building of considerable charm, with its open ground floor. It is still used as a court and also houses the parochial council chamber. In the courtroom, over the magistrate's chair, is an unusual inscription, in which the nouns of the top line have to be linked with the verbs immediately below them in order to make sense.

Much Wenlock is an unlikely place to search for the origins of the modern Olympic Games, yet here in 1850 Dr William Penny Brookes founded the Wenlock Olympian Society and staged annual Olympian Games from that date. Despite the presence here of some of the country's leading athletes in the 1870s and 1880s the contribution of Dr Brookes to the Olympic movement was all but forgotten until recently. The achievement of Dr Brookes and the Wenlock Olympians is particularly remarkable when the background to his life and work is considered. The population of the small, declining market town of Much Wenlock was just under 2500 in 1841. Its character was primarily agricultural, and although the largest non-county borough in England, Kelly's Post Office Directory of 1864 characterised Wenlock as

> chiefly agricultural, but there is a considerable trade in malting and tanning, and in lime and limestone for which this neighbourhood is famous.

It was from this obscure and conservative background that Brookes struck a spark of the Olympic ideal, served on committees of national importance and became well known amongst continental pioneers of organised sports.

Leominster

Leominster lies in the valley of the river Lugg, just to the north of its confluence with the river Arrow, and for many centuries the town was one of the great wool markets in England. It sits a few miles to the east of the principal Roman road running from Wroxeter to Kenchester. Leominster's status during the Roman period is unknown; however, it seems to have emerged in the mid-Saxon period as one of the major political and ecclesiastical centres in the Welsh border when its history is linked with the Saxon tribe the Magonsaetan. It has been argued that the original pre-Roman central site in the region was at Sutton Walls, but in the immediate post-Roman period this site was abandoned and a new one established somewhere to the south of Leominster, possibly at Maund.

A religious community was founded on the site of Leominster by Merewalh, the Saxon prince of the Magonsaete, brother-in-law of Aethelred. In about 660 it appears to have served as the ecclesiastical centre of the Magonsaete until the foundation of Hereford cathedral. Despite the transfer of ecclesiastical power the vestiges of the original political importance of the Leominster region appear in the Domesday Book as enormous estates, and it is tempting to see that the Domesday Book's account of the great manor of Leominster reveals something of the territorial organisation of the Lugg valley before the Saxon settlement.

In 1123 Henry I gave Leominster to Reading Abbey and soon after this much of the fine Romanesque work built in local sandstone which still survives in the nave was begun. The Norman nave was consecretated in 1130, by Robert de Bethun, bishop-elect of Hereford. In its original state, the priory was a large cruciform building. The nave of the priory was always reserved for townspeople but this led to disputes with the monks, as was so often the case, and in 1239 the splendid central nave was built as the original parish church. A further large extension was made in 1320, when the south nave was built, and within the next century the great west window had been inserted and the western tower raised to its present height. This period was almost certainly the zenith of the priory, and its gardens, orchards and fishponds must have made an extremely attractive picture.

48 *All that remains of the Benedictine priory of St Peter and St Paul at Leominster is part of the church which now serves Leominster. Twelfth-century Norman work can be seen in the tower, but most of the remaining visible architecture is thirteenth-century. The church is unusual in that it has three almost identically sized naves*

All this was swept away in 1539 when the Monastery of Reading, with its cell at Leominster, was dissolved and dismantled. The last Abbot of Reading, Hugh Cook, was hanged before the gates of his own monastery but the fate of John Glover, last Prior of Leominster, is not known. Immediately after the dissolution the work of destruction began and the whole of the eastern end of the priory, together with the central tower, was demolished. The parishioners, however, were eager to maintain their rights and erected the present eastern wall to safeguard the fabric of the naves, so that now the church, curiously, consists of three naves, each about the same size.

The earliest surviving part of Leominster's street plan seems to date from this period when a community developed outside the western entrance to the church. Corn Square appears to have been used as a market square and New Street and Burgess Street to the west show signs of deliberate western extensions during the Middle Ages. Quite apart from its central geographical position (for it was able to attract trade from northern Herefordshire and central Wales), Leominster's wealth developed on the wool trade, or the Leominster Ore as it was called, and was renowned by the late Middle Ages. The town hall, now the offices of the district council, and the market hall were built by a local architect, John Abel, in the late sixteenth and early seventeenth centuries and are obvious signs of the prosperity of the wool trade in the centre. The great rebuilding of the seventeenth century in particular is shown through the wealth of timber-framed buildings to be found in the town, particularly in the area of Corn Square, Drapers Lane and School Lane.

Stanton Lacy

Stanton Lacy was a centre of considerable importance before the Norman Conquest; in fact it was the predecessor to Ludlow. St Peter's church was built to a cruciform design and although reconstruction, halted through lack of funds, took place in the thirteenth century, it still has some fine Saxon features, including pilaster strips and Saxon carvings. Indeed it is the finest of all the Saxon churches in the Marches. Built of local limestone, the west end looks particularly beautiful in the light of the evening sun.

Llanthony Priory

A group of Augustinian monks formed a community at Llanthony at the beginning of the twelfth century, but before long local warfare between the Welsh and the Normans drove them away in search of security. They established a new home, called Llanthony Secunda, near Gloucester, and although a fresh start was made in the Vale of Ewyas in about 1175 there was continued rivalry between the old and new establishments. The two eventually became independent in 1205 but it was the Gloucester community which flourished; in 1481 it received royal authority to take over the older priory, which was by now almost deserted.

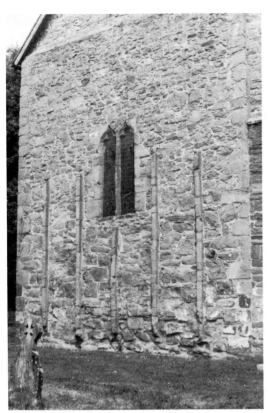

49 *The west end of the Saxon church of St Peter at Stanton Lacy. The vertical sections of parallel stonework are known as pilaster strips, and may be imitation of timber work in contemporary or earlier churches*

50 *The lonely ruins of the Cistercian abbey at Llanthony high up in the Vale of Ewyas*

When both communities were dissolved in 1538 Llanthony passed into private hands and fell into disrepair. A shooting lodge was built into the ruins at the beginning of the nineteenth century, and in 1807 the whole establishment was bought by the poet Walter Savage Landor, who had ambitious plans to develop the estate. Living temporarily in the shooting lodge, he started to build a house above the ruins, but intense local hostility and a stream of litigation forced him to leave, virtually bankrupt, in 1815. A special fund was set up to pay for the restoration of the ruins, but it was not until the 1930s that systematic work began.

In recent years the shooting lodge has become a small hotel, but it is worth visiting the remaining ruins, preferably out of season or late in the evening, when some of the atmosphere that attracted the original settlers can still be sensed. The ruins mainly comprise the two magnificent towers of the west end, a centre tower, and the north nave arcade. The gate house, now used as a barn, stands apart from the main site close to the road.

The long, low building that was probably once the infirmary is now the parish church of St David. The plain interior is relieved by a remarkable group of slate memorial tablets on each side of the chancel. Above the priory there is a short walk which passes some of the woodland planted by Landor and also the remains of his ill-fated house.

Four miles further up the valley at Capel-y-Ffin – 'The Chapel on the Boundary' – was the scene of a remarkable episode at the end of the nineteenth century. The Revd Joseph Leycester Lyne, born in 1837 and ordained a deacon in the Anglican Church in 1860, became a famous figure of the Anglo-Catholic revival, calling himself Father Ignatius and claiming to have been called to re-establish English monasticism. He tried to buy Llanthony Priory for this purpose, but having failed he decided to build a new monastery at Capel-y-Ffin, calling his community Llanthony Tertia.

By means of a series of preaching tours he raised enough money to start building in 1870. His charismatic personality was sufficient to attract recruits, and the establishment survived rather precariously until he died in 1908. His successors failed to achieve the drive and fund-raising success of the founder, and the community eventually linked itself with a monastery on the island of Caldy, whose members entered the Roman Catholic Church in 1913.

All that now remains of the monastery church is the roofless nave and chancel containing the grave slab of Father Ignatius, maintained by a Memorial Trust set up in 1968. The residential quarters, privately owned, are nearby. They were bought in 1924 by the sculptor and designer Eric Gill with the aim of setting up another community, this time of artists. This venture also failed, mainly because of the poor communications in the valley.

CHAPTER EIGHT

Woodland, Park and Forest

PRE-DOMESDAY KINGS created hunting reserves in the Marches, at, for example, the Brown Clee hill in Shropshire and an area around Hereford, which both appear to have been associated with the hunting activities of the Saxon monarchy. Under Edward the Confessor it is recorded that three thegns held land in Dene (Forest of Dean) free from rent in return for the services of guarding the woodland. Although immediately after the Norman Conquest King William began the process of forest creation the Domesday coverage of woodland and forest is unreliable and often ambiguous: there are some hints about the nature and extent of newly created forest areas, for instance under the entry for Shrewsbury, where it is recorded that the sheriff was to provide thirty-six beaters when the King hunted at Marsley and Stiperstones Forest. The term 'hay' occurs with some frequency in the Domesday Book for the counties of Shropshire, Herefordshire, Worcester and Chester, but it is found most frequently in Shropshire where there are over sixty hays recorded for thirty-six localities. Hay literally means hedge, but the Domesday hays seem to have been enclosures used for the control of deer, a term found only in the Marches. Two manors, Lower Churton and Stretton, had five hays each, two others – Wentnor and Worthen – had four and there were five at Clunton. These hays were constructed for the purpose of either capturing game, usually roebuck, or in some cases for rearing game. At Corfton Manor the Domesday survey expressly stated that the hay was 'for the taking of roe deer', and at Lingen in Herefordshire, a heavily wooded area, there were three hays for the same purpose. At a later date the term hay was used in the Welsh border context to mean larger enclosures, particularly in connection with debased forests – for example, the hay of Lythwood, immediately to the south of Shrewsbury, and the hay of Wellington, which was the residue of the forest of Mount Gilbert (the Wrekin), frequently appear in the documents.

It would appear that there were still substantial areas of woodland left in the Marches during the Middle Ages, and Marcher timber, particularly from Shropshire, is often mentioned in connection with building operations in other parts of the country. When Abbot Faritius (1100–1135) rebuilt his abbey at Abingdon, we are told that 'for all the buildings which the abbot made he caused beams and rafters to come from the district of Wales, for he had six wains for this purpose, twelve oxen for each of them, six or seven weeks was the journey coming and going, for it was necessary to go as far as Shrewsbury'. The timber from Shropshire used in the south of England was sometimes referred to as 'Walschborde'.

Throughout the Middle Ages there was a consistent demand for timber for a wide range of uses. The building and repair of castles, churches and houses required enormous quantities of wood, and there are numerous references to these activities; for instance in 1213 William Cantelupe was licensed by the Crown to take timber from Aconbury Wood for the purpose of fortifying and repairing Hereford Castle and in 1286 Edward I licensed Robert Burnell, Bishop of Bath and Wells, and Hugh Burnell, his brother, to fell and take away whatever great and small timber they required for their manors within the bounds of the forest of Shropshire. Industrial activities similarly required a constant source of timber and although oak trees were reputedly 'the weeds of Herefordshire', eventually conservation measures had to be taken even in that county. Thus in 1226 Henry III ordered a temporary cessation of the work of the iron forges in Penyard Wood in order to prevent its complete destruction. Court rolls contain persistent references to infringements of local conservation regulations. As late as the sixteenth century one defendant at Lingen was accused of having 'felled and carried away for his own use [in his pottery kilns] 500 great oaks and saplings', over a period of seven years.

Royal Forests in the Marches

Quite apart from the building of castles, churches and new towns the Norman Conquest had a dramatic effect upon the Marcher landscape in another way – the creation of Royal Forests. The Anglo-Saxon Chronicle for 1087 bemoans that:

> The King, William, set up great protection for deer and legislated to that intent that who so ever should slay hart or hind should be blinded . . . He loved the high deer as if he were their father.

After the Norman Conquest much of Shropshire, parts of Herefordshire and a large portion of Gloucestershire in the Forest of Dean were designated Royal Forest. Forest in this context was a legal term applied to areas in which only the Crown and its delegates had exclusive hunting rights. The establishment of such forests, which frequently incorporated villages and fields, did not involve the expropriation of private property, but did initiate the imposition of a special code of Forest Law on its inhabitants. At one stage in the twelfth century, up to a third of England was Royal Forest and subject to the Norman Forest Law. It is, however, doubtful whether the Forest Laws were ever as harsh as contemporaries described them, and certainly by the thirteenth century a considerable degree of lassitude had crept into their implementation, largely because of the immense difficulty of enforcing laws over such vast tracts of land. Many of the fines for encroachment were in reality no more than an annual rental, and fines imposed for tree felling represented a form of timber trading. Although the Forests of Wyre, Morfe, Brewood and parts of Long Forest were wooded, Royal Forests were not necessarily tree-covered. At the height of forest creation at the end of the twelfth century more than half the county of Shropshire was operating under Forest Law and was collectively known as the Forest of Shropshire. The area of Royal Forest in Hereford covered a considerably smaller area and consisted of two principal forests, a section of the Forest of Dean and an area of indefinite limits to the west and north of Hereford, possibly demarcated as a physical buffer between the Marches and Wales. This latter area was subsequently broken up into a number of chases known as Mocktree, Deerfold and Bringewood.

51 Brown Clee hill, with its upland plateau in the foreground. All this area formed part of the Clee Forest and later Clee Chase in the Middle Ages. The regular fields in the centre were created by parliamentary enclosure in the nineteenth century

The Crown's interest in the forests was in the first instance principally, but not exclusively, for the 'deer' (wild pigs were normally classed as deer, as were hares in some cases). The forests, however, provided other resources and sources of revenue such as timber, underwood and, in the case of the Forest of Dean, minerals. In 1237 the Constable of St Briavel's was ordered to 'cause to be erected mobile underwood forges' and 'to sustain those forges . . . with thorn, maple, hazel and other underwood; so that no oak, chestnut or beech be cut down; and to cause the area felled and allocated . . . to be well and sufficiently fenced lest any deer or other beast be able to get in to browse there'.

The status of many forest areas is far from clear during the Middle Ages, as they appear under different guises at different times. For example Brewood Forest was deforested in 1209, when it was recorded that the knights and men of Brewood in Shropshire gave the king 100 marks 'to secure the disafforesting of that part of Brewood Forests for themselves and their heirs'. Yet in 1256 six thousand oak trees in Tong Wood, which had recently been taken out of Brewood Forest, were felled. Another Royal Forest district which enjoyed a short life was the Stiperstones, a prominent landmark in western Shropshire which was granted by Henry II to Roger Corbet and was subsequently operated as a hunting chase by the Corbet family.

The Long Forest took its name from its length, extending along the continuous ridge of Wenlock Edge, but also covering a considerable area on either side of the Edge, embracing the whole of the Domesday hundred of Condover, and large portions of adjacent hundreds, and also incorporating three large hays. Another extensive medieval forest was that of the Wrekin, normally known as the Forest of Mount Gilbert. It embraced nearly the whole of the Domesday hundred of Wrockwardine and extended into the liberties of Shrewsbury. The forest was divided into two areas, known as the Bailiwick of Haughmond and the Bailiwick of Wombridge, both post-Conquest ecclesiastical establishments. By the mid fourteenth century the hay of Wellington was all that survived of the former forest, but in the 1260s it had a fully paid-up hermit – Nick de Denten. In 1267 the Crown granted him six quarters of corn 'to give the hermit greater leisure for his holy exercises', and in 1273 he was given a further grant; but subsequently he was involved in some misdemeanour and was obliged to quit his post.

The Forest of Shirlett, which abutted on to the Long Forest, was originally enormous. This forest, which remained partly under royal control until the sixteenth century, appears to have been the original 'shire forest', perhaps representing the residue of the early Shropshire forests. Shirlett in fact means a 'share of the shire' and it may have performed the same role as the Forest of Dartmoor did in Devon, providing common grazing and other rights for the whole county. In 1233 two of the King's carpenters were sent to Shirlett to make bottices to fortify Montgomery Castle, 'when the need arises'. A decade afterwards oak trees were sent throughout the county as 'the men of Llewellyn were in many places rising'. Wood from Shirlett was constantly being sent to Shrewsbury Castle and Jail for repairs and fuel. A survey of Shirlett in 1235 noted a great amount of recent timber felling and recorded, 'The custody is good as regards oak trees and underwood, except that great deliveries have been made by order of the king to the Abbeys of Shropshire, Buildwas and Wenlock . . . there is small abiding of beasts except in coming and going from other forests.'

By the late twelfth century references to a wide range of activities within the forests were common. A fine roll of Shropshire forests for 1179, for instance, demonstrates that there was considerable activity within the forest areas. The Abbey of Lilleshall paid a mark for a mill within the forest bounds and there are references to encroachments, house building, assarts, the enclosure of wastes, and the cultivation of newly cleared land. The crops raised on these new enclosures are listed as winter rye or oats. On the same roll there is a reference to the sale of the King's lead obtained from within the forest, which was sold for the considerable sum of £55 when all the other income of the forest only amounted to £45. Other interesting, if somewhat incidental, information about the operation of Forest Laws in Shropshire comes from the forest pleas of 1209, when it was reported that a hart had entered Bridgnorth and guards took it to the castle. When the news reached the forest officers they demanded that Sheriff Thomas de Urlington, then in charge of the castle, should report on the fate of the hart. He acknowledged the offence and promised that his men would appear before the justices; in the event the whole town of Bridgnorth was fined for this violation of Forest Law.

Another interesting case involved the question of sanctuary, and relates to the forests as the resort of criminals and heretics:

> Richard of Hotton, Wilkin of Eastlegh, Hulle of Hinton and Hulle Roebuck, the serjeants of the county, found venison in the house of Hugh le Scot. And Hugh fled to the church and when the foresters and verderers came thither, they demanded of Hugh whence that venison came. And he, and a certain other person, Roger of Wellington by name, acknowledged that they had killed a hind from which that venison came. And he refused to leave the church, but lingered there for a month, and afterwards escaped in the guise of a woman. And he is a fugitive, and Roger of Wellington likewise. It is ordered that they be exacted; and unless they come let them be outlawed.

Deerfold Forest seems to have been traditionally a place of refuge, and it is recorded that anchorites (hermits) settled here in the early Middle Ages. It has been suggested that some of these became the first nuns at the nunnery at Limebrook, which was founded by Robert de Lingen in the late twelfth century. During the early fifteenth century Deerfold became known as an area where persecuted Lollards (religious reformers) could take refuge, in particular Sir John Oldcastle, who led an abortive Lollard rebellion in 1413–14 and hid at Chapel Farm for three years before his capture and execution.

The Royal Forests were at their most extensive in the late twelfth century and by the mid thirteenth century, when records of individual forests become plentiful, they were already in decline. Although the process by which the forests were disbanded, known as disafforestation, was a protracted one extending over several centuries into the nineteenth century, many of the legal and administrative trappings survived throughout the Middle Ages. The true Royal Forests were nevertheless relatively short-lived features of the landscape. Only the Norman kings at the very height of their authority could impose and maintain such a system. Few physical traces of Royal Forest survive today, but as the forests gradually fell out of royal control, in many places the monopoly of hunting rights was taken over by individual lords who created chases or parks for their own sport. A line of such private deer parks created in the thirteenth century, for instance, which ran along the back of the Wenlock escarpment, had earlier been part of the Long Forest.

The record of forest offences shows that red deer predominated in the thirteenth century in Shropshire. In one year alone charges were heard concerning the illicit killing of 22 harts, 9 hinds, 3 roe deer, and 3 fallow deer. In April 1274 an order was given by Edward I to the Sheriff of Shropshire for all the venison taken from the forest for the King's use to be carried without delay to Westminster and deposited at the King's larder. A Crown licence was issued in 1279 to Adam Atwell 'to take foxes throughout the Forest of Shropshire, by traps or other means and to carry them away'. Two years later Roger de Mortimer obtained a licence to hunt the fox and hare with his own hounds in all the forests of Shropshire, outside the coverts, providing he took none of the King's great game or deer. In the same year there is a reference to Peter Corbet obtaining authorisation to take wolves by the aid of man, dog or traps, wherever they could be found in Shropshire, Staffordshire, Gloucestershire, Worcestershire or Herefordshire, and the bailiffs and minsters of the forest were to give him all the assistance he required. This is one of the last references to wolves in England.

The process of disafforestation was erratic, but in Shropshire by the middle of the fourteenth century only the Forests of Morfe, Shirlett and the hay of Lythwood survived as Royal Forests. A century later a survey taken by Geoffrey Lee of all the King's and Queen's woods, forests and chases in the county of Shropshire showed that the Forest of Morfe covered some 1200 acres. Morfe was one of the longest surviving forests in the Marches outside the Forest of Dean, and originally it occupied the area where the counties of Shropshire, Stafford and Worcestershire converge in the Severn valley. Ranolf, Earl of Chester, Sheriff of Salop 1216–23, sold 1700 oak trees during his period of office and is also recorded as supplying timber for the fortifying of Bridgnorth. By the early fifteenth century records show that the wood was being fairly systematically cropped for timber.

The process of clearance and colonisation within the forest is shown clearly, indeed pathetically, in a map of 1582. This was drawn as evidence in an enquiry about grazing rights, and shows the remnant of the forest consisting of saplings and stumps. During a further enquiry into the extent of the forest held in 1615, John Hatton of Claverley said that he knew the 'great waste common called Morfe Wood reputed to be a forest but he never did knowe any deare to be there in his memorie, neither is theire any woode or underwood, but few trees in many miles compass'. Some of the destruction had been on a large scale, for at an earlier enquiry in 1592 a witness recalled the cutting of 4000 oaks for Lord Dudley and 4000 for the Queen. He also commented that when the Council of the Welsh Marches met at Bridgnorth, two or three hundred cartloads of timber at a time were sent from Morfe to the town.

Morfe was important to its peripheral settlements, and to those that developed within the forest, for its grazing. At yet another enquiry, held in 1589, witness William Potter listed the numerous villages and hamlets that had rights of grazing, some lying within and some without the forest. According to another witness, John Billingsley, each of the inhabitants of the named places holding a yardland was entitled to graze 100 sheep, twelve cattle and two horses and to take three loads of fuel. From these records it is possible to trace the extension of arable farming into the forest. By the late thirteenth century the assart land in Claverley totalled as much as $63\frac{1}{2}$ acres. In the forest proceedings there are many references to newly assarted land which had been planted, usually with oats. In 1272 Hereward de la Syche held small assarts like this at Claverley, Bobbington and Nordley, and the Abbot of Haughmond had an acre at Beobridge. Buildwas Abbey was also involved in the clearance of woodland. Much of the dispersed character of the settlement within the once wooded parts of the Royal Forest must be attributed to the assarters, and their names are a vivid reflection of their work – William atte Mor, Robert atte Ok, Robert atte Lee, Richard atte Feldehouse.

The remnants of the waste left after medieval assarting and Tudor destruction were finally enclosed about 1812. The resulting pattern of regular fields, often enclosed by quickset hedges, can be seen clearly today, as for example along the A458 between Bridgnorth and Enville. This regular pattern contrasts with the parts of the forest which were settled earlier, with their winding, deep-cut lanes and irregular fields representing elements of a more ancient landscape.

The Forest of Dean

The Forest of Dean represents one of the most important survivals of the Royal Forests of England. During the reign of Henry II its boundaries extended from Gloucester, via Newent, to a point a little south of Ross to the north, and to the confluence of the Severn and the Wye at Chepstow to the south, forming a rough triangle bounded on the east and west by these two rivers. Encroachment and disafforestation steadily reduced the forest area, and successive records of the perambulation of the forest boundaries clearly demonstrate this process. By the time of Edward II the area had been reduced by more than half. The earliest record of interest in the protection of the Forest of Dean on the part of the Crown is contained in the Domesday Book, which states that Edward the Confessor had exempted the forest from taxation. The Domesday Book also contains an interesting reference to ships 'giving to the wood', when dealing with the lands beyond the river Wye. Under the earlier Norman kings the forest was administered by the Constables of St Briavels Castle, who were also Wardens of the Forest of Dean. Wood from the forest was used for the smelting of iron, for mining and for domestic purposes.

The Constable of the Forest presided over the Court of the Hundred of St Briavels, for the laws of the forest were superimposed on the civil administration. Furthermore, he presided over the Mine Law Court, though this was rarely held at the castle. The Verderers had their Court of Attachment before which offenders against the *vert* (any clearance of growing wood) of the forest were brought for preliminary examination. Malefactors were sent for trial before the Forest Justices at Gloucester, where the Foresters-in-fee and other witnesses gave their evidence. The tombs at Newland Church exhibit the costumes of some of these officials. The justice rolls of the thirteenth century tell us of the corruption of many forest officials, and of offences against the 'king's beasts' by, among others, the clergy, even the canons of Hereford, who stole venison and took it to their house at Lydney. A great deal of the venison and timber stolen from the forest went to Bristol.

During the Edwardian wars of the thirteenth century St Briavels was a great armaments centre. The industry was in the hands of the Malemort family for three generations; they seem to have specialised in bolts for crossbows, and had a considerable export trade to Scotland and the Continent. It was the abundance of iron and timber for smelting that made this industry possible and more than seventy forges are recorded to have been working at this time. Nails were also produced, and at a much later date, pins. The George inn at Mitcheldean was formerly used for making pins and shot, while Guns Mills, near Flaxley, derives its name from the cannons made there in the seventeenth century.

The iron industry made serious inroads on the timber of the forest, and from time to time the Crown bargained with forge owners, such as Flaxley Abbey and the Lady of Blakeney, for the exchange of their rights. It was in this way that Abbot's Wood, near Cinderford, came into being, granted as it was to the abbey in exchange for a right to cut timber in the forest. There were other woods which were granted by the king to individuals or religious houses, but which were carefully monitored in order to protect the King's game. At first the royal concern was mainly for the preservation of game cover, but in the course of time the timber acquired new importance for iron-smelting and shipbuilding and, as the coalmining industry developed, for pitworks.

Outcrops of coal were being worked from at least as early as the thirteenth century. In the seventeenth century Dud Dudley experimented here with coal, as distinct from charcoal, for smelting iron. Late in the following century the invention of the steam-engine and the development of a nationwide road system opened the way for a large-scale coal trade. The Free Miners of the Dean Forest are first mentioned in a record entitled 'The Laws and Customs of the Miners in the Forest of Dean', compiled about the year 1300. Until recently they still retained peculiar privileges in the opening and working of the small shallow collieries that are scattered throughout the coalbearing areas. Between 1668 and 1777 a unique Court of Mine Law met at intervals to deal with disputes amongst the miners. It was presided over by the Constable of St Briavels Castle, with the Gaveller and Clerk of Court attending and verdicts being given by a jury of twelve miners. An example of court procedure is given in the following extract from *The Book of Dennis*:

> Ye Miner shall present the debtor in the Mine Law w'ch is Court for the Mine and there debtor before the Constable and his Clarke the Gaveller and the Miners and none other Folke to pleade onely the Miners shall bee there and hold a sticke of holly and then the said Myner demanding the debt shall putt his hand upon the sticke and none other with him and shall sweare his Faith that the said debt is to him due.

The Gaveller, whose office still survives, superintended the opening of the mines, and kept an eye on the King's interests there.

During the seventeenth and eighteenth centuries the forest was farmed out from time to time to favourites of the reigning kings. The office of Constable persisted, but forest management under this regime was never systematic. Dean timber had acquired a reputation as being good for shipbuilding, and there was considerable interest in the forest at the time of the Spanish Armada. John Evelyn, the famous diarist, in his classic work on forestry, *Silva* (1662), mentions that he had heard

> that in the great expedition of 1588 it was expressly enjoined the Spanish Armada that if, when landed, they should not be able to subdue our nation and make good their conquest, they should yet be sure not to leave a tree standing in the Forest of Dean.

From the Elizabethan period onwards the history of the forest was largely one of exploitation and mismanagement by successive court favourites. There was a change of heart by the Crown in 1638, when a survey clearly demonstrated the parlous condition and stocking of the woods and some 17,000 acres were ordered to be enclosed. The scheme merged, however, into the famous (or infamous) sale of the forest to Sir John Winter by Charles I in 1640. Winter's patent was annulled by the Commonwealth, but during this period there was extensive felling and the timber sold for the benefit of the government. In 1656 a bill was passed for the preservation of the timber in the forest. Reafforestation was, however, fiercely resisted by the inhabitants, and little permanent good seems to have been done. Winter's 'rights' were restored to him by Charles II, greatly to the displeasure of the neighbourhood. At this time a new survey showed that the mature timber in the forest was reduced to 25,929 oaks and 4,204 beeches. In 1667 hardly any trees remained. In the meantime a committee of the House of Commons had been appointed to investigate local complaints, and they came up with the following proposal:

> Imprimis, That 11,000 acres of the wastle soil of the forest of Dean, whereof Lea Bayly and Canopp to be part of the said wastle, may be enclosed by his Majesty, and discharged for ever from all manners of pasture, estovers and pannage; and if ever his Majesty, or his successors shall think fit to lay open any part of the said 11,000 acres, when to take in so much elsewhere, so as the whole enclosure exceed not at any one time 11,000 acres.

By 1668 the Crown was empowered to enclose common waste of the forest for timber, provided that the total area enclosed at no time exceeded 11,000 acres, and this limit still holds. The enclosures authorised were to be freed from common rights so long as enclosure continued, and when the trees had grown up beyond damage the areas could again be thrown open for grazing and an equivalent area enclosed elsewhere. In 1675 the forest was divided into six walks or districts; six lodges were built and for each walk a keeper was appointed. It is stated in a return made in 1691 that, except in 'Lea Bayly', where the fences had been thrown down by dissatisfied commoners, the plantations were 'generally very well grown'. Again, in 1705 there is a report that the woods were full of young trees, two-thirds of which were beech which were overtopping the oaks. By 1788 the actual area still enclosed had dwindled to 765 acres. From the days of Charles II until 1808, the total area of the Forest of Dean suffered no appreciable reduction. In 1808 measures were again taken to ensure a supply of oak timber for the Navy, at which time it covered some 18,500 acres, together with between 600 and 700 acres of freehold land also held by the crown.

At this time the rest of the forest was very sparsely covered. It was estimated that 24,000 old oaks remained on the ground, of which large quantities were cut and used for naval construction. Few of these old oaks are now left, but there are still about a dozen standing in Churchill Enclosure, and a couple of others elsewhere. Tree felling for the Navy finally ceased in 1863, by which time iron was supplanting oak as the material used for constructing warships.

Medieval Parks

As the Royal Forests went into a gradual decline parks became increasingly more fashionable. To some extent the forests can be viewed as a dramatic, but relatively temporary, interval in the story of the management of wild animals. The park was a far more effective means of controlling animals, although the creation of medieval parkland could involve considerable capital outlay. Just as the greatest nobles aspired to the ownership of forests so, too, the acquisition of a park became an important status symbol which permeated to much lower levels of the social strata.

The medieval park differed from the forest in that it was normally demarcated by a boundary consisting of a ditch and wooden pale, or in certain areas, a stone wall as compared to the forests which had little or no boundary markers. Parks varied in size considerably from just a few acres to well over 1000 acres. Most of the medieval parks have subsequently been cleared and enclosed for agriculture, but their curving linear earthworks survive as modern boundaries, and place names such as Park Farm, Park End or Park Lodge often indicate the site of a former park which has long since disappeared. For example, Park Farm, close to Heath in south Shropshire, was created out of a medieval deer park, the boundaries of which are still identifiable on the ground. In 1334 there was a reference to the King's parks in Herefordshire at Stretton Sugwas, Ledbury, Donningwood, Colwall, Bromyard and Ross-on-Wye, but by the late fourteenth century the vast majority of parks were in the hands of private individuals. The parks were essentially intended for the retention of deer, at first roe and red deer, but later exclusively fallow deer.

There are numerous references in medieval documents to Marcher parks which have disappeared without trace. For example, in 1336, two parks at Wigmore are recorded as containing 'many great woods and great oaks', while a park with deer and a water mill is recorded at Asperton in the same year. Others survived into the post-medieval period and were turned into landscaped parks attached to country houses. Many of these parks feature prominently on Saxton's sixteenth-century maps including Hodnet Park, for example, which is first referred to at an inquest held in 1275, when it was found that it would not be to the public detriment if Sir de Hodnet enclosed two footpaths which ran through Hodnet Park, on the condition that he provided alternative footpaths around the park. Saxton also marks two parks close to Hodnet, at Stanton and Shawbury. At Shawbury, Giles de Erdington received a licence, in 1253, to make a deer-leap into his park. In 1297, Edward I licensed the Abbot of Haughmond to enclose 20 acres of his wood in the Bailiwick of Haughmond, and Edward II, in 1313, extended this licence to 60 additional acres in the same forest; these grants were probably the origins of the large park at Haughmond featured on Saxton's map. The extensive park at Acton Burnell also appears on Saxton's map.

On the borders of Shropshire and Cheshire, Saxton marks four nearly adjacent parks, Blakemere, Ightfield, Shavington, and Adderley. The last of these still exists; it was emparked by Walter de Dunstanville, Lord of Adderley,

52 The ruins of the late thirteenth-century fortified manor house at Acton Burnell. The castle formed the centrepiece of an extensive medieval deer park which measured four miles around its circumference

by permission of Ralph, Abbot of Shrewsbury, between 1175 and 1190. Blakemere, which originally belonged to the Le Stranges, is described thus by Leland, when making his progress through the county:

> From Whitchurch a mile and a half, I cam by the pale of the large parke of Blakmer longying to the Erle of Shrewsbiri, wherin is a very fair place of loge. The Park had both red deer and falow. In the park (as I herd say) be three fair poles, of wich I saw by the pale the largest, caullid Blakem, whereof the park is named.

At Ightfield, Leland records that:

> Syr Richard Manoring, chefe of that name, dwelleth a three miles be est from Price village at a village cauleld Hightfelde, having a Parke and great plenty of wood about hym.

To the south of the Severn, both Leland and Saxton notice a park at Willey, on the bounds of the Forest of Shirlett, and south of this Saxton marks a park at Upton Cressett (discussed in Chapter 10). In the centre of the shire, but south of Shrewsbury, Saxton shows parks at Langley and at Plaish and another at Rowton, eight miles west of the county town. In the south of the county other important parks are at Oakley, to the west of Ludlow, and Stoke St Milborough, a little to the north of Ludlow; also Dean Park, near Burford, on the Worcestershire boundary, and the large park of Cleobury in the south-eastern part of the Forest of Wyre. Before the First World War there were eleven deer parks in Shropshire, four of which had ancient origins and were on the sites of early forests.

Places to Visit

Millichope

An interesting reminder of the nature of forest landscapes in the early Middle Ages is provided at Upper Millichope on Wenlock Edge, where there is a fourteenth-century building which traditionally has been regarded as a hunting lodge. This was part of the Long Forest which covered Wenlock Edge and adjacent areas. There are other hunting lodges in the region but none which dates from the period of the Royal Forests.

Brown Clee Hill

Clee was one of the smaller Shropshire forests, no more than 24,000 acres in extent, and it remained directly under the control of the Crown for only a short time. The Clee ceased to be true Royal Forest in 1155, but it was later operated on the lines of a Royal Forest by the Cliffords from Corfham Castle in the Corvedale. Its history, however, illustrates some aspects of landscape history which are significantly different from the true woodland forests. The Clee Forest, constituting Brown Clee hill and its surrounding area, was almost certainly originally joined with the Long Forest to the north and Shirlett Forest to the east. The name Brown Clee does not appear until the fifteenth century, before which the hill and forest were known as 'Les Clives'. The name is probably derived from *claeg*, which was Old English for clay. Brown was later added to distinguish this hill from neighbouring Titterstone Clee and is an obvious allusion to the reddish-brown soils of the area.

It is possible to reconstruct the boundaries of the forest from ecclesiastical parish boundaries, which radiate from the three most prominent points on the Brown Clee, giving each foothill township a proportion of wood and wasteland on the hill. Where these boundaries run as straight lines they presumably reflect unexploited woodland or heath, which had not been subject to any territorial control before then or at any rate had not been demarcated till then. Earnstrey Park, now in Abdon parish, was part of the forest and the medieval hay there probably represents the residue of a Saxon park, the boundaries of which can clearly be identified on the ground today.

Apart from the manorial woodland attached to each village, most of the remaining timber was cleared during the early Middle Ages, principally by Wenlock Priory and Shrewsbury Abbey. In 1465, when a new fence was required for Earnstrey Park, the timber had to be bought outside the forest and by the time Leland visited the area in about 1540, he observed, 'There is no great plenty of wood in Clee Hills.'

A most interesting document of 1612 called 'A Description of Clee' demonstrates the persistence of the common rights of all the townships that had lain within the ancient forest. Common rights on Brown Clee included agistment and pannage (grazing rights for livestock), turbary (right to cut and collect turf) and estovers (right to take wood for repairs and fuel). These rights, however, were reserved for those townships that actually lay on Brown Clee, the inhabitants of the old forest area being allowed only common rights of considerably less importance. In return for these privileges, the 'out-commoners' were subject to a modified form of Forest Law – in particular they were to refrain from disturbing deer found among their crops.

The out-commoners had to follow very precise routes from their townships to the grazing areas on the Clee. These roads were known as 'driftways', 'straker ways' or 'outracks'. Many of them were deeply entrenched and can still be traced as sunken or 'hollow' ways. These routes were still in use in the seventeenth century when it was claimed that 'the driftways are long and tedious because the strakers were to drive the lands and commons belonging to other lordships before they could reach Clee soil'. The name 'outrack' is still given to a sunken road in Ditton Priors leading to Brown Clee, and other outracks survive on the Long Mynd and in other hilly parts of the Marches. The term 'straker' probably refers to the method of calling the inhabitants of the forest by a horn (Middle English *strake* means to blow a horn as a summons). Gough in his *History of Myddle* refers to 'streaking' in connection with similar movements of animals to commonland. An interesting footnote to this story was that at the time of parliamentary enclosure (1809), Thomas Mytton, Lord of Earnstrey, tried to claim extensive allotments on Brown Clee as 'lord of the Clee Chace'; in reality this was an attempt to claim rights from the Royal Forest which had been disbanded some six centuries earlier.

The Brown Clee is still an interesting place to visit and incorporates the remnants of three major Iron Age hillforts as well as extensive areas of open moorland. It is best approached from Heathamgate on the west of the hill which gives ready access to commonland and the hillfort at Nordybank.

Limebrook Nunnery

The site of Limebrook Nunnery is not a place to visit for its architectural glories, as today all it consists of is a few stumps of its former buildings. It does, however, occupy an immensely attractive site, located in a beautiful position on the narrow level floor of the valley of the Lingen Brook in the Deerfold Forest with steep hills rising from each side. In the area around wild strawberries reputedly grow and the surrounding woods are said to contain herbs grown originally for medicinal purposes. The nunnery, which was Augustinian and dedicated to St Thomas à Becket, who was murdered in 1170 and cannonised in 1173, was reputedly founded in 1189 but there is no positive evidence to confirm this date. The records of the nunnery suggest that although it frequently claimed poverty, the nuns were not particularly poor. Throughout its history the nunnery gradually acquired property, much of it on the best farming land in the area. In 1536 when, strictly speaking, under the terms of the dissolution of the monasteries it should have been dissolved as being valued under £200, the nuns purchased 'per-petual continuance' by payment of £53 6*s*. 8*d*., which hardly seems the act of a body of poor nuns. However, in 1539, Limebrook, along with all the remaining religious houses, was dissolved and the nuns pensioned off – their payment had prolonged their existence for only three years. A recent survey of Limebrook Nunnery property in places such as Aymestrey, Brim-field, Croft, Lingen, Pembridge, Stoke Bliss and Wigmore suggests that its houses, many of them of late medieval 'cruck' construction, were quite large.

CHAPTER NINE

The Later Middle Ages

DURING THE later Middle Ages Shropshire and Herefordshire enjoyed mixed fortunes. The various attempts by medieval kings to subdue Wales had resulted in the tide of national conflict moving further west leaving hundreds of small motte and bailey castles high and dry. With this came more settled conditions, but periodic Welsh raids occurred right up until the time of the Union with England in 1536 and, as elsewhere in medieval England, baronial conflict was endemic in the Marches. During the Baron's Revolt of 1321 it was recorded that Roger de Mortimer 'seized wools, meat, grain, livestock and other goods valued at more than £141 from the unwilling villagers in Herefordshire'. Other acts of barely disguised piracy were common, although as the number of fully functioning castles decreased, so the offences tended to be of a more petty nature.

Battles in the Borderland

Occasionally the Marches featured on the stage of national politics. At the battle of Shrewsbury in 1403, Henry IV defeated Sir Henry Percy (Hotspur). The battle, which is perhaps principally remembered today as forming the climax of Shakespeare's play *Henry IV (Part I)*, took place on 21 July 1403 between an army led by the Lancastrian King Henry IV and a rebel army led by members of the Yorkist Percy family. In July 1403 Sir Henry Percy and about 200 men, including some former Scottish prisoners, rode south from the Scottish border. Travelling by way of Northumberland and Lancashire they reached Chester on 9 July. Here Sir Henry stayed at the home of Petronilla Clark who, along with other inhabitants of Chester, eventually lost her property for siding with the rebel. Indeed most of the rebel army was raised in Cheshire and both city and county were later heavily fined for their support of the rebellion. The other rebel leaders came from north Wales, Lancashire, Shropshire, Herefordshire, Northumberland and Yorkshire.

Henry IV was, ironically, on his way to the Scottish border to aid the Percys against the Scots, and it wasn't until he reached Nottingham that he heard that the Percys had risen against him. Henry then moved rapidly west by way of Derby to Lichfield. After an abortive attempt at a negotiated peace at Saniway in Cheshire, both armies reached the vicinity of Shrewsbury on 19 July. Shrewsbury was the principal town on the route taken by the Percy army and was important both as a major crossing of the river Severn and as a potential source of supplies. The rebels' intention was to join up with another group of Welsh dissidents led by Owen Glendower.

The Percy army arrived first with the intention of fighting for Shrewsbury and stopping Henry's army crossing the river, and were preparing to attack the town when the banners of the King's army were seen approaching from the east. The early arrival of Henry caught the rebels by surprise and Percy retreated a little to the north and spent the night at Berwick. According to one story Percy was dismayed at leaving his sword at a place where it had been foretold he would die. The royal army apparently forded the Severn at Uffington on the night of 20 July and drew up in battle array near Haughmond Abbey. On the morning of 21 July the Percy forces marched east towards the enemy. The precise site of the battle has not been identified, despite many attempts which have been made to locate it, including one by Charles Darwin, a native of Shrewsbury, who reported finding 'a surprising number of iron arrowheads . . . in a grass field . . . on the northern side of the Severn'. On 21 July the two armies faced each other for several hours out of arrow shot while negotiations took place to see if a bloodless settlement could be reached. Envoys between the two sides included the Abbots of Shrewsbury and Haughmond for the royal side and the Earl of Worcester from the rebel army. Finally, however, two hours before sunset the peace talks broke down, partly because the King feared that the talks were being protracted because the rebels expected reinforcements the following day.

After the King gave the battle order the royal vanguard moved forward under the Earl of Stafford to meet the rebels led by the Earl of Douglas. The archers dismounted and opened fire 'so thick and fast that it seemed to the beholders like a thick cloud'. The Percy archers were more successful in this initial contest, for, as one chronicler wrote, the royal vanguard fell 'like apples falling in the autumn, when . . . stirred by the southwest wind'. After the arrows were exhausted hand to hand fighting began. Percy and the Earl of Douglas led a mounted charge apparently aimed directly at the King himself and succeeded in killing the Royal Standard Bearer, Sir Walter Blount; the Earl of Douglas was severely wounded. After the initial Percy successes the royal army counter-attacked. One account says that the tide of battle turned when Prince Henry (later Henry V) joined the battle with his troops. But the decisive moment appears to have been when the rebel army learnt that Henry Percy had been killed. The precise circumstances of Percy's death are not known and there are several versions, all of which tend to emphasise his bravery. A considerable number of his supporters died with him and some important rebel leaders, including the Earls of Worcester and Douglas, were captured. The battle had lasted for only just over two hours and when it ended many did not even know who had won. They were scattered over several miles of Shropshire countryside, 'they sank down in all directions, a chance medley of weary, wounded, bruised and bleeding men'. The contemporary chroniclers emphasise the exceptional number of casualties, and one wrote, 'Now those who were present said they never saw or read in the records of Christian times so furious a battle in so short a time or of larger casualties than happened there.' The total number of dead varies according to whom you read. A charter of 1445 mentions burials over an area of three miles, and different chronicles record the dead as numbering from 5000 to 9000 men. One unusual feature of the battle is the exceptionally high proportion of casualties suffered by the victors. Sixteen Royalist and eight rebel knights were killed. Sir Henry Percy was buried at Whitchurch in Shropshire soon after his death and it is reported that before he was buried King Henry wept at the sight of his body. Nevertheless, soon after, the King gave orders that the body should be put on show to prevent rumours that Percy was still alive. The body was exhumed and displayed in Shrewsbury and was later cut into quarters. The quarters were then displayed at Newcastle, London, Chester and Bristol and the head at York. In November 1403 the remains were returned to Percy's widow who is said to have had them buried in York Minster.

Monumental brasses were set up to the fallen knights in the church of Battlefield which was erected a few years after the battle. Attached to this was a chancery chapel where prayers were said for those who had died in the battle, but this was dissolved in the middle of the sixteenth century.

During the Wars of the Roses another decisive battle was fought at Mortimer's Cross in 1461 when Edward, Duke of York (later Edward IV) defeated a Lancastrian army led by Jasper Tudor and the Earl of Wiltshire. The Lancastrian army consisted largely of Welsh, French and Irish troops, the latter having been partly raised on Wiltshire's Irish estates. Wiltshire landed at Milford Haven at the end of 1460 and after joining forces with Jasper Tudor moved forwards in an attempt to defeat their enemies in the Welsh Marches and then link up with Queen Margaret. From Presteigne the Lancastrians moved towards Leominster with the intention of crossing the Severn at Worcester. However, at Mortimer's Cross on the river Lugg to the north of Hereford they found themselves facing a Yorkist army which had been mustered in Hereford under the command of Edward, Earl of March.

53 *The church of St Mary Magdalene, Battlefield, which was founded by Henry IV as a chantry to pray for the souls of those that died in the battle of Shrewsbury (1403). The church is now used just once a year: a service is held on 21 July every year to mark the anniversary of the battle*

On 2 February 1461 the Yorkists won, but little is known of this important battle apart from the report of a strange apparition seen in the sky when:

> There were seen three suns in the firemament shining full clear, where the people had great marvel, and there of were aghast. The noble Earl Edward them comforted and said, 'Be of good cheer, and dread not; this is a good sign . . .'

Edward, who was only eighteen years old at the time of the battle, later took the Sun in Splendour as a personal badge and was proclaimed and installed as King Edward IV on 4 March 1461. Following the battle of Mortimer's Cross, Jasper Tudor and the Earl of Wiltshire escaped, but Owen Tudor, who had accompanied the Lancastrian forces on the march through Wales, was captured and taken to Hereford where he was beheaded.

Edward's ancestral home was at Wigmore, just a few miles away from Mortimer's Cross. Had the Percy–Glendower alliance been ultimately successful, schemes afoot to dismember the kingdom into three parts – one each for Glendower, the Percys and the Mortimers – might have dramatically changed the course of British history. Wigmore Castle is today a massive ruin sleeping quietly in the Herefordshire countryside, and only its size hints at the momentous historical events with which it was associated.

The Welsh Marches also featured prominently in the ultimate phases of the Wars of the Roses, when the Tudors fared considerably better. On 1 August 1485 Henry Tudor sailed from Harfleur in Normandy with an expeditionary force for Wales. He landed just to the north of Milford Haven on 8 August and marched up the western coast of Wales collecting followers on the way. By 13 August Henry was at Welshpool close to where he met up with a contingent led by Sir Rhys ap Thomas; the combined armies spent the night on the Long Mountain in western Shropshire. The following day the army marched on Shrewsbury, taking Montford Bridge, about four miles west of the town, and Forton about two miles north of the Severn. Messengers were sent to Shrewsbury requesting admission, but the town's senior magistrate, Thomas Mytton, refused entry and closed the town gates. The next day, following further negotiations, Henry was allowed into the town and recruited further troops there. The bloodless taking of Shrewsbury provided a major morale boost for the Tudors and it was just one week later that Henry's army, having continued their eastwards thrust, successfully confronted Richard III at Bosworth Field and effectively ended the civil war.

The End of the Marcher Castles

The mosaic of Marcher lordships enjoying legal independence from the Crown had long made them offensive in the eyes of the English sovereigns. Ironically their demise came with the Crown acquisition of Marcher lands during the later fifteenth and early sixteenth centuries in the wake of the Wars of the Roses, which effectively made the King himself the biggest Marcher lord of all. The battle of Bosworth brought Henry VII not only the English Crown, but also the vast estates of the House of York around Ludlow and Wigmore and further westwards into Wales. In 1495 Chirk, Bromfield and Yale were forfeited and in 1521 the fall of the Duke of Buckingham gave the sitting monarch, Henry VIII, further extensive Marcher lordships. So, by 1530 most of the larger Marcher lordships were in royal hands, and the way was therefore clear for the Act of Union which was to extend English common law to Wales and divide the Welsh portions of the Marches into shires on the English model. In order to maintain order in what hitherto had been a notoriously disorderly part of the country, the Tudor government created the Council of the Marches with extensive judicial and administrative powers. The Council of the Marches of Wales remained in existence until the Civil War and was not finally abolished until 1689. Throughout its history it was based at Ludlow Castle, the ancient centre of Yorkist power in the Marches. Council members, however, made frequent journeys throughout Wales and the Marches in order to maintain order and exercise the Crown authority in a variety of matters. As they were accompanied by a considerable retinue, they required extensive lodgings. At Shrewsbury the Corporation maintained the Council House for their use; frequently, however, they were obliged to stay in royal castles, which partly explains the survival of some of these medieval fortifications into the post-medieval period. The principal royal castles of the Welsh Marches during the later Middle Ages were Ludlow, Wigmore, Chirk, Montgomery, Brecon and Monmouth.

54 The finely carved gate house of the old Council House in Shrewsbury built in 1502 and used by the Council of the Marches when it visited Shrewsbury in the late sixteenth and early seventeenth centuries

Bishop Roland Lee, president of the Council in 1534, deplored the state of the royal castles saying that they were 'fit for neither war or peace'. Ludlow was in such decay that the Council could not remain there until repairs had been carried out. Wigmore he found 'utterly decayed in lodgings, and awful want of reparation in time'. Despite some repairs two years later more work was required at Ludlow, while at Brecon 'there is a piece of the castle fallen and another piece at Chirk, and all must be done: God send money'. The dissolution of the monasteries brought some welcome windfalls in the form of building materials: stone from Wigmore Abbey, timber from monastic houses in Ludlow and lead from Basingwerk. However the burgesses of Shrewsbury who attached much importance to maintaining close and amicable relations with the Council tried in vain to save the claustral buildings of Shrewsbury Abbey. In 1540 they petitioned for the use of the abbey as 'a residence for the use of the princes grace or any other nobility of the realm that shall resort to this town'. Later, in 1590, they sent an emissary to London to ask for the 'ruinous castle to be repaired and builded, hereafter to be a place both to reserve the Council as also a convenient place for the prisoners of the Shire'.

During the seventeenth century, however, the only building regularly maintained by the Council was Ludlow Castle, the other ancient centres of royal authority in the Marches having been by then either passed to other owners or abandoned to decay. It would appear that when the Council was in session both Ludlow and the castle must have been extremely lively. The winter courts were famous social occasions enlivened by a round of banquets and masques of which the most famous was Milton's *Comus*, first performed at Michaelmas 1634, to celebrate the installation of the Earl of Bridgwater as Lord President. It was primarily for these functions that the old medieval castle was adapted during the sixteenth and seventeenth centuries. During the Commonwealth, the Council of the Marches was in abeyance and Ludlow Castle was left to its own devices. Some work was done after the Restoration, but in 1689 the Council was abolished and the castle ceased to have any further political usefulness. For a while it continued to be looked after by a resident keeper, who in the reign of Queen Anne was still being reimbursed by the Treasury for his occasional expenditure on repairs. After this, however, it was finally abandoned and after the lead was removed from its roof in the eighteenth century it rapidly fell into decay and became ruinous.

Economic Decline and Deserted Villages

The political events which brought the Welsh Marches on to the national scene did not exempt the region from the general agricultural decline which occurred in the fourteenth and fifteenth centuries. The Black Death, which was an important, if not the prime, reason for agricultural recession, affected the Border as badly as anywhere else in the country. The agricultural recession was accompanied by the shrinkage or total abandonment of large numbers of hamlets and villages.

The arable open field system, which operated in one form or another throughout most of England, had been adopted in highly marginal areas in the Borderland, probably in the eleventh and twelfth centuries, where its chances of success were low anyway. This system was adversely affected by a combination of factors in the fourteenth and fifteenth centuries, including climatic deterioration and failed harvests as well as the Black Death.

Fig. 9 Plan of deserted villages of south Shropshire most of which shrank gradually during the later Middle Ages

Thus over large areas, open field arable farming was abandoned and replaced by enclosed pastoral farming at a relatively early date. In contrast to these negative developments there was a substantial degree of prosperity brought to the region by the wool trade in the later Middle Ages. The Border, with its large open moorland spaces combined with nearby lush pastures and ample water power to treat the wool, was an ideal environment for a successful textile industry. Furthermore towns within the Borderland such as Oswestry, Hereford and Shrewsbury benefited substantially from their ability to monopolise the trade both in Marcher and Welsh wool for many centuries.

However, the underlying agricultural decline still inevitably led to both shrunken and deserted villages. There are something like 400 settlements in Shropshire and Herefordshire which can be classified as deserted, shrunken or shifted. Not all of this movement occurred in the late Middle

55 *The earthworks of a typical deserted medieval Marcher village at Sidnall in the parish of Ditton Priors (Salop). The former street pattern can be identified in the form of hollow ways; internal village boundaries can also be seen. Above the village there are slight traces of ridge and furrow representing part of a former open field agricultural system. The village appears to have shrunk during the later Middle Ages*

Ages, for many settlements were abandoned later as the result of the emparking associated with the creation of country houses between 1600 and 1800. Nevertheless, a large proportion of them do seem to have disappeared at this time. Because many of them were originally small and because the process of shrinkage was very slow, the identification of sites on the ground is more difficult in the Borderland than in the central Midlands, where large earthworks frequently mark the site of former villages. There are, however, a number of Marcher sites where there are earthworks to be seen on the ground and a number of these have recently been identified through aerial photography. A particularly good example is called the Bold, near Aston Botterell, a typical deserted Border hamlet now contained within a single modern field. The aerial photograph indicates that there could have been as many as twenty families living on the site in the Middle Ages, but like so many other Border townships, the Bold gradually declined to the size of a single farm. The remains of a chapel which once served the former settlement here is incorporated into the modern farm complex. Such abandoned chapels are a common feature of deserted hamlets in this area, and Duke in his *Antiquities of Shropshire* (1854) records some 105 lost chapels in Shropshire.

A valuable source of information about village mortality in the Border area is contained in the *Assessment of the Ninth* (1341), a taxation record which adjusted parish tax assessments which had originally been made in 1291. The assessors tell a story of almost universal hardship throughout the region. It is true that many of the original assessments seem to have been unrealistically high, but even allowing for this and exaggeration of poverty brought about by a natural reluctance to pay taxes, in almost every parish there was a substantial reduction. At Upton Cresset, for instance, known mainly for its fine Tudor gate house, the assessment dropped from 36s. 8d. to 17s., because it is said, 'The land lay untilled and the tenants of the same have withdrawn because of penury.' Reasons given for the reduction in other parishes include taxation, pestilence among cattle and sheep, bad harvests, and the destruction of crops by storms.

The main reason traditionally given for the disappearance of villages was the Black Death of 1348–9. It is recorded that over half the clergy in Shropshire/Herefordshire died then. In Hereford so many clergymen died that unusual arrangements had to be made for the canons to take services and the bishop complained bitterly of the 'recent unprecedented plague'. Precise references to the impact of the Black Death on rural settlements are rare, but it is clear that pestilence was a factor in undermining the village structure. Records for the year following the Black Death show that many manors were said to have been reduced in value because of plague and a few are known to have succumbed completely. For instance a small township in Stanton Lacy manor called Yeye is last recorded in 1350 as being ruinous. Similarly, Broomcraft, a township in Kenley parish, had been depopulated by 1363 when it was said to be uncultivated because of lack of tenants.

Ecclesiastical records are one way of finding out quite how much the Black Death affected the area. The parish of Knill in the deanery of Leominster was one of two benefices which were vacant twice during the pestilence. In the deanery of Frome both the parishes of Great and Little Collington were vacant twice and in 1352 they were consolidated. It was then stated, that 'because of the pestilence the diminished value of both livings was itself hardly sufficient to maintain one priest'. One observer declared that the deanery of Archenfield 'was the plague-patch of the diocese'. However, Ross-on-Wye, which was an important river port in the fourteenth century, seems to have suffered particularly badly and it is possible that the deanery of Ross was the real plague-patch of the diocese. Thirteen of the twenty-six incumbents in the district around Morville died of plague within four months of 1349. Two vicars of Ellesmere and one vicar of Welsh Hampton died in the same year of the pestilence. An inquisition at Lilleshall Abbey taken in 1353 found that the underwood of a park there was then worth nothing because all the customary buyers had perished in the 'Great Plague'. The inquisition also mentioned 'a certain foreign wood, the underwood of which used to be worth before the pestilence 3s. 4d., and now it is only worth 12d. beyond the sustentation of the house'. It also recorded that the land belonging to the abbey, which was worth £15 in 1330, was worth only £10 after the pestilence because there were no tenants and that 'One Abbot died 1350'.

A register of loss of rents in Shropshire after 'The Great Pestilence' provides further insight into the decline of the area. At Yockleton the rents of assize of free tenants fell from £8 to 30s.; at Colmere and Hampton, from £4 to 10s.; in the hundred of Bradford, from £16 to £8; at Wentmore, from £5 to 40s.; at Shelve, from 36s. to 26s. 6d.; at Harleigh, from £4 to 10s.; at Wyley, from 20s. to 12s. All these reductions were specifically attributed to the pestilence. In 1364 the nearby churches of Whyle and Pudlestone were united on the basis of a petition that the plague had depopulated the area. Subsequently plague was endemic throughout England and there were further major outbreaks in 1360–61, 1369 and 1379. The second of these, known as the Children's Plague, appears to have had a particularly severe impact. There is little evidence to suggest that the Marches suffered any worse than the remainder of England and Wales, but it is fairly clear that the population of the country as a whole fell by as much as 50% between the 1340s and the 1440s.

There is relatively little evidence to show how far the unstable political situation and periodic attacks from across the Welsh border had any permanent effect on settlement in the Marches, although it seems certain that a number of western manors were gradually abandoned because of such attrition. At Westbury, for instance, Thomas Corbet of Caus was engaged in constant warfare with his relative Gruffydd ap Gwenwynwyn throughout the thirteenth century. In 1406, following Owen Glendower's rebellion, a large number of western manors were excused taxation as they had been burnt down. One such, Burfield, today an isolated farmstead, was originally a township in the manor of Tempsitur near to Offa's Dyke. Allegedly the township and chapel were laid waste by Owen Glendower in about 1400 and thereafter it was known as the 'decayed township of Burfield'.

On the whole, however, village abandonment seems to have been a gradual reaction to changing economic, social and possibly climatic conditions. One of the abandoned Border settlements is appropriately named Cold Weston. The reason for the abandonment simply seems to lie in a poor site having been chosen in the first instance, lying as it does at 800 feet above sea level on a north-facing slope. The village was in decline before the Black Death. In 1341 it was stated that 'there had once been an abundance of cattle here, but they had decreased because of the murrain which had hit the region', and the account concludes that 'the chapel is in a waste place and the living has been presented to four parsons within the year, but none of them would stay and there are only two tenants living by great labour and in want and others have absconded'. Today the sad and now redundant little church of St Mary sits by itself in a thicket of trees, as if it were still sheltering from the cold and wind after all these centuries. Near by lies the deserted village of Heath which is far more complete than the average Marcher deserted village and has more the appearance of a classic Midlands deserted village. The almost perfect Norman chapel is the centrepiece of the site, and in the surrounding fields there are extensive earthworks of the old village representing the roads, houses and even the stone-lined well of the former medieval community. In addition close by there are the broken dams of two extensive fish ponds, remnants of the open field system and the boundary of a medieval deer park.

At Abdon, three miles away, the earthworks are even more spectacular. In the field to the east of St Catherine's parish church there are a number of distinct house platforms with an intersecting pattern of hollow ways, on one side of which the village earthworks are bounded by ridge and furrow. Fragmentary documentary evidence suggests that Abdon, like Heath, declined slowly during the later Middle Ages. The site was partly reoccupied in the sixteenth and seventeenth centuries when its inhabitants were employed in quarrying on Brown Clee hill. During the later eighteenth century, however, Abdon was deserted once more, for with the decline of the Clee hill industries the villagers moved away. After a visit to Abdon in 1793 Archdeacon Plymley observed that 'some houses had been taken down and several seem to have fallen down' and excavations undertaken at Abdon seem to confirm this. A longhouse found next to the church appears to have been abandoned about 1300 and there is no evidence of any subsequent occupation of that part of the old village. Lower down the field the base

Fig. 10a Plan of the deserted medieval and post-medieval village at Abdon

Fig. 10b Plan of excavated thirteenth-century longhouse, adjacent to St Catherine's church at Abdon

of a sixteenth- or seventeenth-century dwelling was located, but there too there was no evidence of any subsequent reoccupation.

Excavation has revealed that not all settlement desertion was so early. At Braggington in Alberbury parish, investigations were carried out before the site was levelled in the 1960s. The earthworks of Braggington lay at 400 feet, a quarter of a mile north-east of Braggington Hall on a north-facing slope at the foothills of the Breidden. A small stream which demarcates the Welsh border here runs eastwards at the foot of the slope, and banks and leats suggest that a mill once stood on it. Braggington is first recorded in 1255; its place name, however, with its 'ington' ending clearly indicates an earlier Saxon settlement here. It is therefore possible that this particular site is not that of the original community, especially as the site appears to be sitting on top of ridge and furrow. This means that the medieval settlement was planted on ancient arable land, a sign that there was a break in the continuity of settlement. There was a population of sixteen Welsh tenants living at Braggington in 1301 and it appears to have been occupied by Welsh families throughout the Middle Ages. The excavations show that there was a longhouse here which contains evidence of metal working in the form of iron slag and the bellows of a furnace, and that this building was occupied from the fourteenth to the seventeenth centuries. The village was abandoned before 1650 when work started on Braggington Hall, and the kink in the road to the north-east of Little Braggington suggests that the road which originally ran to the village was diverted at about the same time.

Such road diversions around newly emparked areas are a common feature in the Marches. An abrupt turn in the road on the outside of a park boundary is nearly always an indication of a deserted or moved village whose presence was considered unsightly by the country-house owner. Frequently, as at Braggington, the country houses which were erected were not necessarily particularly large. An excellent example of this process can also be seen at Morville where the church of St Gregory, initially a Saxon collegiate church of great significance, now stands isolated in a field in front of Morville Hall, which was originally constructed in the latter part of the sixteenth century. The village now lies strung along a road well to the north of both house and former village, which was clearly diverted there when Morville Hall and its surrounding landscape was being created. Evidence of former houses and some medieval pottery has been found in the vicinity of the church.

Many villages, however, do appear to have shrunk considerably during the fourteenth century. At Hampton Wafer in north-east Herefordshire there is today only a single farm, but in the early nineteenth century the ruins of a chapel survived nearby. Deeply eroded hollow ways and house platforms, together with a pond which proved to be the flooded stock yard of a farm, mark the site of a former settlement. The excavation of several house sites revealed that occupation went back to at least the eleventh century and finished perhaps around 1300. In 1330 it was recorded that the manor passed to the Fitz Allens who held Hampton Court by the river Lugg. We know that most of their resources went into that manor and that consequently they neglected upland Hampton Wafer, thereby perhaps encouraging enclosure and the consequent transfer of the population to newly established outlying farms.

These high up and somewhat inaccessible sites have survived as recognizable earthworks precisely because of their isolated locations. Others, particularly in the lower parts of Herefordshire, have suffered more severely. The irregular and often unidentified earthworks of deserted villages which contain the archaeological record of medieval rural communities are extremely vulnerable. A recent survey of sites in Herefordshire suggests that a considerable number have been ploughed up or severely damaged by agricultural activity over the past twenty years. Now the only surviving record of many of them is in the form of the aerial photographs which were taken before their destruction.

The Wool Industry

Despite the arable recession and the high level of settlement abandonment during the later Middle Ages, certain areas of the Borderland prospered. The wool trade is not one which is immediately associated with the Marches but Hereford, Leominster, Ludlow, Shrewsbury and Oswestry all fared well as a result of wool and the textile industry. Many of the fine half-timbered merchants' houses and market halls that grace small towns such as Ledbury and Pembridge were built, in part at least, on the proceeds of wool. The historian William Camden writing of Herefordshire at the end of the sixteenth century reported that 'for the three w's, of Wheat, Wool and Water it yieldeth to no shire of England'. At Leominster the local breed of sheep, the Ryeland, produced wool known as Leominster Ore. In Hereford the success of the wool trade in the fourteenth century was reflected in the almost continuous work on the fabric of the cathedral, in the restoration and beautification of the city churches and in the foundation of a grammar school in 1384. The city's ability to loan the King £100 in 1399 resulted in the acquisition of an important new charter.

If anything, Shropshire's wool industry was even more prosperous than that of Herefordshire. In 1273 English merchants exported nearly 1200 sacks of wool and of those 660 were provided by Shropshire merchants, the largest total of any inland county. In 1294 it was recorded that 'certain English merchants, licensed by the King, crossed the sea with their wool; these ought to have been led by Lawrence of Ludlow ...', but Lawrence, a powerful Shropshire woolman, had been drowned at sea. Draper's Row in Ludlow commemorates the wool trade and still contains some houses which were bought by Lawrence in the late thirteenth century. There are other monuments to the importance of Ludlow as a wool town, the most notable of which is the parish church of St Lawrence, the largest parish church in Shropshire and certainly one of the finest, built in the fourteenth and fifteenth centuries on the proceeds of the wool trade. The church, which is sometimes missed by visitors because it is hidden at ground level by infilling of the medieval market place, is best appreciated from the northern approach to Ludlow. Another monument to the wool trade lies a little to the north of Ludlow in the form of Stokesay Castle, probably the best known fortified medieval manor house in England. Its great hall, whose substantial windows make it scarcely defensible, was probably built in the 1270s. Stokesay, too, was built by Lawrence of Ludlow, who received a licence to crenellate the house in 1291, when he also probably added another tower.

56 Stokesay Castle and church; the former, which is the best known fortified manor house in the country, was built out of the proceeds of the south Shropshire woollen industry in the thirteenth century

The fashion for building fortified manor houses appears to have followed on from Edward I's conquest of Wales. Robert Burnell, Bishop of Bath and Wells and Chancellor of England, rebuilt the castle at Holdgate in 1280. He was well aware of the castles being built in north Wales by Edward I and the surviving tower of this remarkable structure sitting behind a sixteenth-century farmhouse indicates the extent of his wealth and importance. But perhaps more representative of this movement is the castle at

Acton Burnell, which was built after the conclusion of the conquest in 1284. It is a large rectangular house with round towers projecting at each corner; it is moatless and the doorways are at ground level. Despite its outward appearance, Acton Burnell Castle had a thoroughly domestic function. The castle sits next to the ruins of a structure which carries the grand title of Parliament Barn, supposedly as a result of the first representative parliament being held here during a visit from Edward I.

Shrewsbury was perhaps the most important of the Border wool towns, and by the thirteenth century at least a quarter of the population was involved in the manufacture and sale of cloth. It was during this time that the great wool families that were to dominate Shrewsbury until the seventeenth century began to emerge: the Colles, the Rowleys, the Prides and the Vaughans. Such merchants constructed large town houses which incorporated storage space for cloth. Vaughan's Mansion lies at the bottom of Pride Hill, its medieval street frontage having been successfully incorporated into Collier's, the men's clothing retailers.

In 1326 Shrewsbury, along with Cardiff and Carmarthen, became a staple town for wool and leather for the whole of Wales, and thereafter enjoyed a virtual monopoly of trade in north and central Wales. Goods from central Wales came up the river Dovey to Welshpool and then down the Severn to Shrewsbury and the town appears to have had effective control of the wool trade in the Marches as far south as Hereford. After a drop in wool production in the early fifteenth century, trade seems to have revived by the middle of the sixteenth century. Many of the Tudor and Jacobean houses for which Shrewsbury is justly noted were built as a result of this trade revival, when Shrewsbury enjoyed its most prosperous period. Ireland's Mansion, one of the best surviving examples of Tudor architecture in the town, was built by Robert Ireland in about 1575 and characterises the prosperity and confidence of the Marcher wool merchants. Owen's Mansion (1592), a slightly less ostentatious merchant's house, stands nearby, facing the square. The Owens lived in another fine Elizabethan hall at Condover and also built the Council House gateway in Castle Street which was used by the Council of the Welsh Marches.

By 1620 Shrewsbury drapers were paying over £2000 a week for Welsh cloth, which was brought by packhorse from as far away as Dolgelly and Mawddy. Soon afterwards the drapers moved their market from Oswestry to Shrewsbury, completing Shrewsbury's textile monopoly. The Merioneth clothiers had to travel the extra twenty miles and they were so late in arriving back home on Saturdays (the cloth was brought on Fridays) that in 1648 the rector of Dolgelly requested that the market be put back to Wednesdays. The Shrewsbury drapers compromised and agreed to buy the cloth on Thursdays. Such was the importance of the Welsh trade that Defoe on his visit to Shrewsbury noted, 'They speak all English in the town, but on market days you would think you were in Wales.'

As well as building themselves fine town houses the Shrewsbury merchants financed public buildings. Typical of these is Drapers' Hall (*c.* 1580) in St Mary's Place, the guildhall of the powerful Drapers' Guild whose religious meeting place was the south chancel of the church of St Mary's a few yards away. A little later the Old Market House was built by the master mason Walter Hancock in 1596. Merchants were responsible for other municipal benefactions, the foremost of which was Shrewsbury School in Castlegates, founded in 1551. The old school building which now houses the town library and has recently been splendidly restored, dates from the 1590s and 1630. The present Shrewsbury School, which occupies a dominating position overlooking the river and the town, moved in 1882, when it took over a building which had been erected as Captain Coram's Shrewsbury Foundling Hospital in 1765.

The Dissolution of the Monasteries

At the beginning of 1536 there were more than 800 religious houses, monasteries, nunneries and friaries in England and Wales. Four years later, by the middle of 1540, there were none. Their buildings and properties had been taken over by the Crown and leased or sold to new lay occupants. In 1536 an Act of Suppression of the lesser monasteries was passed which was presented by Henry VIII as a measure primarily of reform rather than expropriation. It seems reasonably clear, however, that the King was really interested in the financial rewards of suppression rather than reforming a corrupt monastic system. Under the 1536 Act only those monasteries worth less than £200 a year were affected, and this covered some 243 houses which were actually suppressed. Although considerable care was taken to prepare the case against smaller abbeys and to present the dissolution as a measure of reform, the work of the suppression commissioners in carrying off church furnishings and other treasures for the King's use aroused considerable hostility towards the government. This was particularly true in northern England and the suppression of the smaller houses prompted the great rebellion of October 1536, generally known as the Pilgrimage of Grace. The rebellion failed, but not before some of the larger monasteries had become involved with helping their smaller brethren, the result of which was that once the rebellion was crushed the Crown's attention then turned to the larger abbeys. Almost all the greater abbeys and the smaller ones which had escaped suppression in 1536 were eventually to come into the Crown's possession as a consequence of 'acts of voluntary surrender'. The movement gathered momentum and very soon what had started out as a limited exercise in raising revenue had been elevated to a political movement against all the monasteries.

The dissolution of the monasteries had a major impact on the Marcher landscape, bringing about as it did the largest exchange of property owner-ship since the Norman Conquest. Often it involved land passing to owners who lived far away from the Marches, and who in any case did not earn their living off the land that came into their possession. One of the results of this was to create conditions by which large new country houses and parks could be made. The new owners did not need to cultivate their estates and were thus able to put the land to an aesthetic use. For the most part the monastic buildings were sold off and demolished. In a few cases, such as Abbey Dore, Leominster, Chirbury and Shrewsbury, the church was saved for parochial use. Abbey Dore was suppressed in 1535, and the last Abbot Redman was granted a pension of £13. The site and its buildings, which soon fell into ruins, were granted to John Scudamore of Holme Lacy. It was not until 1632 that his great grandson, 'the good Lord Scudamore', under-took the repair of the church, but by this time its condition was so bad that it was used as a cattle shelter and there are references to prayers being read under a sheltering arch. Restoration began with the blocking of the great arch leading to the nave and the side arches to the nave aisles. The roof was rebuilt in Herefordshire oak, 204 tons of which was used at 5s. per ton and the famous 'architector' John Abel was contracted to undertake the work. A new, rather incongruous, tower was built and the whole still has the appearance of being half finished. Following a service of reconsecra-tion which took place on Palm Sunday, 26 March 1634, Abbey Dore has been one of the very few former Cistercian churches in England still used regularly for worship.

When in 1539 the monastery at Reading and its cell at Leominster were dissolved, the work of destruction began almost at once and the whole of the eastern end of the priory, together with the central church tower, was razed to the ground. The damaged church, however, was saved for the com-munity and today, standing in open ground, this magnificent glowing red church gives some impression of the original scale of the Benedictine build-ing that once stood there. Chirbury was a house of Augustinian canons and throughout the Middle Ages it had enjoyed a turbulent history with constant conflict with the Welsh. In 1423 commissioners found the house to be 'in a state of spiritual and material collapse'. Throughout the fifteenth century the priory was suffering from constant incursions from marauders and was regularly among the houses exempted from paying taxes on the grounds of poverty. It was, however, a double church where the nave acted as the parish church and the chancel served the canons. Following the sup-pression of the house in 1536 the chancel and other conventual buildings were dismantled while the nave, aisles and western tower, which formed the parish church, survived to serve the community.

Shrewsbury Abbey was dissolved in 1540 when the Abbot received a generous pension of £80 and the seventeen other resident monks received smaller pensions. Various uses were sought for the abbey. It was considered as one of the seats for a possible new bishopric; it was also proposed as a possible residence for the Council of the Marches, or that it should be turned into a college or free school, but finally it suffered the fate of other Marcher houses. However, the western part of the church was preserved as the parish church of Holy Cross serving the now fairly extensive suburb of Abbey Foregate, while the remaining buildings were either adapted to secular use or dismantled. Considerable portions of the conventual buildings were, however, still standing in 1743 but most have since been demolished by one means or another. In particular, the diversion of the London/Holyhead road from the north to the south of the church by Thomas Telford in 1836 removed much of the remaining medieval buildings. Even the abbey church suffered in the post-Reformation period and much fine Norman architecture including the clerestory was dismantled.

57 Holy Cross church, Shrewsbury, the remaining portion of Earl Roger de Montgomery's Benedictine abbey, founded c. 1080. In 1094 Roger entered the monastery as a monk and died there three days later. Most of the surviving abbey buildings were destroyed when Telford's London to Holyhead road was driven through them in 1836. However, the refectory pulpit can still be seen sitting incongruously in a builder's yard on the other side of the road

In most cases, however, all the buildings of the dissolved monasteries, including their churches, were destroyed, as the Borderland was already well, if not over, provided with churches. At Much Wenlock an attempt to create a new joint bishopric with Chester came to nothing and the priory complex, with the exception of the prior's lodging, was reduced to a ruin. The prior's lodgings and part of the infirmary which date mainly from the fifteenth century have served as a private house since the dissolution and has been described by Nicholas Pevsner as 'one of the finest examples of domestic architecture in England'.

The rural establishments at Llanthony, Buildwas, Lilleshall and Haughmond were largely dismantled, although the latter was converted into a private house and occupied for some years after the dissolution. Today these ruins provide tranquil and often beautiful sites to visit, a fitting tribute to the role they played in the making of the Marches. Other rural monastic sites have disappeared almost without trace at places such as Wigmore and Kilpeck, often leaving no more than a farm name as a legacy.

Within the towns the impact of the dissolution on the small institutions was just as dramatic. In Hereford the monastic buildings soon became ruinous, but in the case of Blackfriar's Priory the stone was used to build Sir Thomas Coningsby's Hospital. Henry VIII also authorised the destruction of two corn and two fulling mills belonging to the dean and chapter of Hereford cathedral and as a consequence there followed the decline of the former extensive trade in bread with Wales and the demise of the cloth industry. The petition to restore the mills by Thomas Kerry a few years later talks of the cloth industry having 'utterly ceased' and of the city being in a state of 'extreme ruin and decay'. The houses of canons and the mendicant orders were similarly dealt with in Shrewsbury, Bridgnorth, Ludlow and Leominster, leaving little behind except their names and fragments of wall.

Places to Visit

Battlefield Church
In 1406, just three years after the battle of Shrewsbury, a memorial chapel, now the parish church of Battlefield, was founded supposedly on the field of the battle by Richard Husse. He obtained a royal licence to convey to Roger Yve, rector of 'Albrygton Husee', two acres of land on which a chapel would be built. Its foundation charter made the rector and his successors masters or wardens of the chapel with the right to nominate five chaplains. Their duties were to celebrate divine office for the King during his life and after his death for his soul and those of his ancestors, and also for the souls of Richard Husse and his wife Isolda and those who died in the battle of Shrewsbury. The site was described in a document of 1410 as being sur-

rounded by a ditch with two twenty-foot entrances to the north and south, inside which many of the dead from the battle were buried. Although Battlefield began as a simple chantry chapel it evolved into an important college of priests and had the right to appoint clergy to certain parishes, thus allowing it to appropriate much of the income of those parishes to support the chancery. In its later years the college included a school. When in 1548 all collegiate chanceries were granted to Edward VI by parliament, Battlefield College was suppressed. Its last master was John Hussy, a member of the family which had founded the college. Its property was sold and the site was bought by the Hussy family.

Most of Battlefield church was built by 1409, except the tower which was added about a century later by Adam Grafton, then master of the college. After the Reformation, the chapel became a parish church while the other college buildings, which stood to the south of the churchyard, were demolished for the value of their materials. By the mid eighteenth century the church had lost its roof but this was restored in the middle of the nineteenth century when shields depicting the coats of arms of some of those who fought at the battle of Shrewsbury were added. The church is now redundant, but has recently been restored once more.

Heath Chapel and Deserted Village

Heath was a part of the great parish of Stoke St Milborough which in turn was originally part of the Prior of Wenlock's estate. Heath formed an upland settlement, almost certainly colonised from Wenlock in the later Anglo-Saxon period. Such dependent chapelries had the right of infant baptism, because of the very high rate of infant mortality during the Middle Ages which meant that a sick child would often die before it was baptised if it had to be taken to the mother church many miles away over inhospitable territory. The rites of marriage and burial however were retained by the mother church and Heath did not have its own graveyard until the late nineteenth century.

The process which created the settlement at Heath pushed the margin of cultivation well up the slopes of former wasteland, but as the height at which arable cultivation was possible dropped quite dramatically in the later Middle Ages so it was left stranded because open field agriculture was no longer feasible. In 1268 the manor was leased by John Fitz Allen from Wenlock Priory, when rents were said to be valued at 49s. 3d.; the same valuation noted that there was a mill here. In 1327 there were seven taxable families at Heath. If this represented the total population it is a much smaller number than suggested by the extensive earthworks here. A series of fifteenth-century rentals indicate that the village was slowly being depopulated. By 1407 the value of rents had fallen to 34s. 9d. and in the mid sixteenth century there were only five farms in the township, all of them dispersed within a now primarily pastoral landscape. In many respects

Heath is typical of settlement abandonment in the Marches; there was no sudden desertion, but rather a gradual shift to pastoral farming reflected in the slow shrinkage of the settlement.

58 Heath Chapel, Shropshire. A near perfect example of a twelfth-century Norman chapel sitting in the foothills of the Brown Clee hill. In the surrounding fields are extensive earthworks of a deserted medieval village

Stokesay Castle

The father of the great wool merchant Lawrence of Ludlow bought the manor of Stokesay in 1281, and nine years later Lawrence obtained a licence to crenellate (fortify) his manor from Edward I. He lived only a few more years, but before his death in 1296 he had built a strong high tower at the south end of the west front. The north tower had been built by an earlier owner in 1240, and is the oldest surviving structure in Stokesay; to this Lawrence added a top storey with fine projecting timber-work. Being a man of considerable wealth, he could afford to pull down the earlier hall and set up what must have been a most splendid new building 31 feet wide and 52 feet long with glazing in the upper windows – a sure sign of opulence, for this was a period when glass was so expensive that families with several houses tended to take their window-panes with them from one manor to another. Though some of the timber-work may have been modified in the nineteenth century, much of it is original, and the great blackened crucks which support the roof show how it functioned as an open hall with a central fireplace. Lawrence surrounded this elegant complex of buildings with a moat and curtain wall of stone as his outer system of defence.

The Ludlows subsequently held Stokesay for more than 300 years. Afterwards it was sold and resold, but suffered only minor reverses. During the Civil War it was garrisoned for the King as an outpost of the crucial neighbouring stronghold of Ludlow Castle, but surrendered promptly in 1645 to the Parliamentarians, thereby avoiding a siege. The subsequent damage was nominal and left the north tower intact, but without its battlements. Before this at the beginning of the seventeenth century the impressive timber-framed gate house was added to replace the original thirteenth-century entrance. This gate house incorporates some fine wooden carving comparable with that on the Council House in Shrewsbury and the Reader's House in Ludlow. During the late Tudor and Jacobean period there was a renaissance in wooden carving, both on the exterior and interior of buildings. Like the Romanesque sculptors before them, these seventeenth-century artists working in timber used a wide range of designs, including some which may have been borrowed from the Norman churches, and some which still clearly show a strong Celtic influence. The carvings are almost exclusively secular, using figures such as mermaids, serpents and grotesque heads.

Stokesay Castle's gradual decline was less damaging than it might have been. It became rundown rather than ruined and was put to various uses, as a granary and a cooper's workshop among others, but since the nineteenth century it has been well cared for. The adjacent church of St John the Baptist incorporates a Norman door, a gallery and, most unusually, a nave which was rebuilt in 1654 during the time of the Commonwealth.

Wigmore

For almost a thousand years the administrative centre of the extreme northern part of Herefordshire was Wigmore. The Romans had a fort here, east of the present Bury Farm, though nothing can be seen on the ground today. In the Anglo-Saxon Chronicle, it is recorded that in 921 King Edward had a fortress built at Wigingamere, which was unsuccessfully attacked by the Danes in the same year. Legend records that Eadric the Wild was lord of Wigmore, but this is not confirmed by the Domesday Book (1086) when Wigmore is recorded as follows: 'Ralph de Mortemer holds Wigmore Castle. Earl William erected it on the wasted land which is called *Merestun*, which Gunuert held in 1066.'

The Norman castle was probably the small motte and bailey just to the west of the church, and closely linked to the streets of the borough, not the great mound and ruins which can be seen today further west. The earliest part of this later fortress appears to be the twelfth-century shell-keep on top of the great mound. Much of the curtain and its wall towers and gateway date from the fourteenth century. To this centre of Mortimer power came, among others, Llewellyn, Prince of Wales, Queen Isabella, Edward I, Edward III, and 'dark-eyed' Gladys, daughter of Llewellyn, who became the wife of Ralph de Mortimer. The King's Council met here and great tournaments were held, perhaps the greatest being the one held in 1330. These contests may have been the reason for the great enclosure north-east of the castle which ran down across what is now the main road and can still be traced as a cropmark today.

The male line of the Mortimers died out early in the fifteenth century, but a great-grandson, Edward, Duke of York, became King Edward IV.

The parish church, with its late eleventh-century herringbone masonry, predates the main castle and must have been a large Norman building. Apart from the fine roofs there are two other notable pieces of woodwork in the church – the early sixteenth-century decagonal pulpit and the stalls.

59 View of Wigmore medieval borough, church and castle (centre left). A tranquil place today which belies its turbulent history and association with the Mortimer family during the Middle Ages

Wigmore was to retain its borough status for almost 800 years although it never had parliamentary representation. The timber-framed market hall, open on the ground floor and with a meeting room above, stood at the head of the market place or 'pavement' looking down the village street until the middle of the last century. Like so many of these Marcher markets the 'pavement' was triangular in shape, the main street running out at an apex and the hall standing at the base.

Holdgate

One south Shropshire site of particular interest which falls between the category of deserted village and deserted town is at Holdgate, which sits in the very heart of the Corve Dale, the wide valley which lies between Wenlock and Ludlow, and which, in the early Middle Ages, formed a major line of communication between the Welsh frontier and the Midlands. Holdgate stands on a marl ridge at the narrowest point of the Corve Dale and during the Middle Ages it enjoyed effective control of the two major routeways running to the north and south of the ridge. All that is left of this once considerable settlement is a Norman church which contains a doorway and font executed by the Herefordshire School, a large motte and a sixteenth-century farmhouse which incorporates the tower and northern wall of a thirteenth-century stone castle. To the rear of the farm are some castle ramparts and in a field to the south is an area of recognisable house platforms, sunken ways and ridge and furrow.

In 1086 the manor was assessed at five hides, with fourteen tenants; it was also unusually recorded as having both a church and a priest, and furthermore there was a castle recorded there. It was clearly a place of some substance in the early Middle Ages when it was held by the Knights Templar. In 1115 three royal courts were held at Holdgate and various licences for markets and fairs were granted. In 1292 the manor was highly valued at £22 9s. 8d., and it is probable that the Bishop of Bath and Wells rebuilt the castle here about 1280. This was at the same time as he was building his mock fortified castle at Acton Burnell and the remarkable fortified house at Cheney Longville not far away. As the theatre of conflict moved further westwards during the Middle Ages the settlement lost its strategic importance and it reverted to being a normal south Shropshire rural settlement. Following the pattern of many Marcher villages it gradually disintegrated in the later medieval period. Today it is a splendid, haunting place to visit with an anachronistic icehouse dug into the side of the overgrown motte and close by the gently decaying church with its quite magnificent Norman font.

CHAPTER TEN

The Post-Medieval Landscape

The Rise of the Country House

During the late Middle Ages a considerable number of castles fell into disrepair and were eventually abandoned. However, a minority continued to be occupied and their buildings were renovated from time to time to bring them up to the standards of the day. Some of these, such as Broncoft Castle in the Corvedale which Leland described in 1540 as 'a very good place like a castle', consist of a largely nineteenth-century mock castle built on to the core of an original fourteenth-century fortification. In Herefordshire the Croft family have inhabited Croft Castle since the Norman Conquest, apart from the century after the reign of George III when it was inhabited by a member of the Knight family. The rugged stone castle dates from the fifteenth century and now nearly surrounds two courtyards, with sixteenth-century and later additions. It was much modified about 1765 when it was given a new internal structure with Gothic features. Beside the castle stands a small late medieval church containing the impressive tomb of Sir Richard Croft (died 1509), whose wife was governess to the sons of Edward IV at Ludlow. The grounds are particularly known for their oak, beech, lime and Spanish chestnut avenues, the last dating back to perhaps as early as 1588.

Just over the Welsh border lies Chirk Castle, in Clwyd. This massive border fortress was completed in 1310 by Roger Mortimer, to whom Edward I had given the Chirk estates in 1282. The estate was bought by the merchant adventurer Sir Thomas Myddelton (Lord Mayor of London) in 1614 and the Myddelton family still inhabit the house. The design is a square around a courtyard. The south wing had become a house by Tudor times and the outline of the Tudor gables can be traced in the infilling carried out during the eighteenth century. The park, which is crossed by Offa's Dyke, is entered from the little town of Chirk through some superb iron gates completed in 1721, the work of the Davis brothers. On the Welsh side of the border also sits one of the greatest castles that evolved into a country house, Powys, which is still inhabited after some 700 years. The castle dates from the late thirteenth century when Edward I granted Gruffydd ap Gwenwynwyn the baronetcy of Delapole. In 1587 the castle was bought by Sir Edward Herbert who added the Long Gallery and did much internal remodelling. There was further reconstruction in the seventeenth and nineteenth centuries, and again at the beginning of this century. The late seventeenth-century terraced formal gardens are reputed to be the work of William Winde and are generally recognised as some of the finest gardens in Britain.

Generally speaking, however, it was not the castle but the fortified manor house which represented the forerunner of the great post-medieval country houses that abound in the region. The undulating Border landscape with its dramatic vistas and abundant running water provides ideal settings for country parks and houses. When Celia Fiennes visited Herefordshire at the end of the seventeenth century she described it from the 'Pirramidy' top of the Malverns as appearing 'like a Country of Gardens and Orchards'. The great age of Marcher country houses starts somewhere in the middle of the sixteenth century, partly as a result of wealthy town merchants building themselves fashionable rural residences. Pitchford Hall was built for Adam Otley, a Shrewsbury merchant, in the 1560s, and Condover Hall for Thomas Owen in the 1590s, while the Newports built a vast mansion at Eyton-on-Severn of which only one small tower and a few small fragments incorporated into a farmhouse still survive.

There were a considerable number of interesting smaller houses and parks created in the sixteenth century. A fine, but sadly neglected, early brick house still stands at Upton Cressett, not far from Bridgnorth. This house is dated 1580, and the turreted gate house is earlier (*c.* 1540); the truly remarkable feature of the house, however, is its splendid medieval wooden hall encased in Tudor brickwork. The first reference to Upton Cressett Park was in Wolsey's Inquisition of Enclosures (1517) when it was alleged that Thomas Cressett had emparked 40 acres of arable land at Upton. The village of Upton was deserted then, or possibly slightly later in the mid sixteenth century, when the house was rebuilt and the park extended. The road running south-west from Bridgnorth was stopped and there was some landscaping done. Later the park was broken up and Upton Park Farm and Upton Lodge are the only reminders of its former existence. The decaying gate house still stands near the Norman church, surrounded by scrub and the earthworks of the former village. Together they create a nostalgic and striking picture of earlier prosperity and grandeur.

Another ruined house of about the same period which has managed to maintain some of its former dignity is at Moreton Corbet, near Shawbury. Moreton Corbet Castle incorporates a medieval keep, but has extensive Elizabethan additions dated 1579. The exterior has a facade of Tuscan columns which provides an impression of real splendour rarely seen in Shropshire houses. Around the castle are the earthworks of the medieval defences and village of Moreton Corbet. In 1503 there were still thirteen 'messuages in Moreton towne' but the village appears to have been deserted at about the same time as the rebuilding of the castle, when a park was created and the road diverted.

60 The sixteenth-century brick gate house at Upton Cressett (Salop)

The other major stimulus to the spread of country houses was provided by the dissolution of the monasteries. The consequences of the dispersal of former monastic land in the Border were profound, either directly after the dissolution or gradually during the subsequent decades, when large areas of land came into new hands, often those of London lawyers anxious for a country estate. The estates of Lilleshall Abbey, for instance, passed to James Levisan whose family was later actively involved in attempts to drain the

Weald Moors and whose successors eventually became the Dukes of Sutherland. A particularly interesting group of country houses and associated parks was carved out of land along the back of Wenlock Edge which had for many centuries belonged to Wenlock Abbey. The dissolution resulted in the establishment of a series of smaller-scale country houses here with parks, at Shipton Hall (1587), Lutwyche Hall (1587), and Larden Hall (1607).

The creation of landscaped parks introduced a completely new element into the Border landscape: for the first time land was being used principally for aesthetic rather than purely economic purposes. In some cases land that had previously been farmed was enclosed into new parks, as at Longnor, which was first recorded as a park in the early sixteenth century, and where ridge and furrow within the park pale shows that it had once been arable. At Berrington in northern Herefordshire the earthworks of a deserted village and a complete medieval field system can be seen within the park close to Berrington Hall. Even so, many early parks still had a strictly functional side to them, and a 1682 plan of Longford Hall, for example, to the southwest of Newport, shows that landscaping there was limited to a small area of formal gardens in front of the house. There were avenues of trees leading from the house, although these did not interfere with the enclosed paddocks, and some medieval fishponds reused as ornamental pools. Aldenham, near Morville, has a similar history, where the park appears to have been laid out at about the same time as the hall was rebuilt in 1691. The driveway, which is almost half a mile in length, gives a grand but deceptive impression of the extent of the park, a device employed in many other Border houses.

61 Aerial view of Berrington Hall and park. In close vicinity to the house are the earthworks of a deserted village and extensive remains of ridge and furrow

In Aldenham Park there were coppices for the iron industry as well as normal arable fields.

Many parks were used for improving breeds of sheep, cattle and pigs and at Attingham Hall, for example, Lord Berwick bred Alderney, Hereford and West Highland cattle. The house at Attingham was built on to an existing building, Tern Hall, for Noel Hill, the First Lord Berwick, in the late eighteenth century. The massive entrance front, the colonnades and pavilions and the stable block were designed by George Steuart whose other major buildings, with the exception of the unusual circular church of St Chad's, Shrewsbury, have all been demolished. Humphrey Repton (1752–1818) was responsible for the landscaping at Attingham and his views on the park are expressed in his *Red Book* (1787/8) which is still kept in Attingham Hall. Repton also did some landscaping at Ferney Hall (1789), Condover (1803), Hopton Court (1803) and Longnor Hall (1804).

Humphrey Repton became a professional landscape gardener in 1788, continuing the work of the first major landscape designer to work in the Border, Lancelot (Capability) Brown. Capability Brown improved Tong Castle (1765) and Oakley Park (1772–5), but one of his most ambitious projects in the Borderland was at Berrington Hall, the ancient home of the Cornewall family, built for Thomas Harley by Henry Holland. Holland began work in 1778 and built a relatively simple house of local pinkish sandstone which fits well into the Herefordshire landscape – today the hall is in the capable hands of the National Trust. The park as we see it now is a splendid example of Brown's work, being a composition of grassy slopes broken up by belts and clumps of trees with openings which provide wide views of the hills in the near and far distance, and diversified by the glint of water from the pool and artificial lake made out of the previously swampy ground. Brown also worked at Moccas Court, producing a park which contrasts strikingly with the nearby deer park.

Herefordshire has particular significance in the history of landscape thought. The county produced two of the greatest landscape designers ever in Richard Payne Knight and Uvedale Price, and in the Wye valley had the sort of scenery which particularly appealed to devotees of the picturesque who followed Gilpin on the Wye Tour like ancient pilgrims. William Gilpin was a Hampshire clergyman who in 1782 published the first of many 'observations' he made on undertaking tours to different parts of the country, the first of which was to the Wye valley. His observations were 'chiefly relative to picturesque beauty'. Gilpin was particularly partial to such objects as ruined castles and rugged rocks, especially when seen alongside the picturesque with a trace of the Gothic, which he admired not only for its pictorial quality but because it aroused an emotional response to the romance of history and the melancholy of the past. Out of that feeling grew the Gothic revival, with its attendant restoration of old buildings and the construction of 'new' buildings using medieval designs. Gilpin looked upon

Fig. 11 Plan of Moccas Court Park in 1778 after it had been landscaped by Lancelot Brown. Robert Adam designed Moccas Court itself (1775–80) in a severe classical style for the Cornewall family

scenery according to a list of rules – 'the principles of picturesque beauty'.

Capability Brown in his sketches and hints on landscape gardening published in 1794 outlined the principles on which he worked. These were controlled by what he called the character of the scene, which in turn determined its potential or 'capabilities' for improvement, and by his search for unity in the composition of the whole scene. In the late eighteenth century there arose a school of thought opposed to Brown's now rather stereotyped manner. It was led by two Herefordshire squires, Uvedale Price (1747–1829) of Foxley and Richard Payne Knight (1750–1825) of Downton, both of whom were responsible for executing ambitious landscaping schemes in their own parks. Both were travelled, scholarly and distinguished dilettantes of the arts and a controversy was launched in 1794 when Price published an *Essay on the Picturesque* and Knight a didactic poem called *The Landscape*. Repton joined the argument and a wordy yet extremely courteous battle followed.

Price wrote when Brown embarked upon landscaping a scene:

Adieu to all the painter admires – to all intricacies – to all beautiful varieties of form, tint, and light and shade; every deep recess – every bold projection – the fantastic roots of trees – the winding paths of sheep – all must go; in a few hours the rash hand of false taste completely demolishes what time only and a thousand lucky accidents can mature, so as to make it become the admiration and study of our Ruysdael or a Gainsborough and reduces it to such a thing as an oilman in Thames Street may at any time contract for by the yard at Islington or Mile-End ... A good landscape is that in which all the parts are free and unconstrained, but in which, though some are prominent and highly illuminated and others in shade and retirement, some roughly and others more smooth and polished, all are necessary to the beauty, energy, effect, harmony of the whole.

Price felt that it was with this end in mind that the landscape designer should work. Knight in particular was enthusiastic about the introduction of more exotic and flowering trees into the landscape. His aims were to be achieved in Victorian times when many newly discovered trees were used, particularly conifers from the Pacific coast of North America. Indeed many of these trees were subsequently planted out at Price's gardens at Foxley, giving them their present luxurious appearance.

The influence of these two amateurs of taste on the English landscape was considerable. They undoubtedly forced Repton to introduce greater variety into his work, while Price influenced Sir Walter Scott both in his writing on landscape gardening and in the design and planting of Abbots Wood, which in turn had a considerable effect on the Victorian garden. J. C. Loudon, in his *Encyclopaedia of Gardening* (1827), wrote of Herefordshire, 'The county will hereafter be celebrated in gardening history as being the birth place or residence of Uvedale Price and R. P. Knight.'

To the north of Shrewsbury, at Hawkstone, the natural landscape of rugged sandstone cliffs fitted Price's theories admirably. When the improvements began here there was already a ruined medieval castle, perched on its rock presenting an ideal setting for the landscape designer with the new concepts. The improvers at Hawkstone were Sir Rowland Hill (*d.* 1783) and Sir Richard Hill who succeeded him. There are descriptions of the whole scheme as it was originally conceived, including over ten miles of walks, rocks compared with the ruins of Palmyra, an effigy of the ancestor of a neighbour in the grotto, a hermitage complete with hermit 'generally found in a sitting position', a vineyard laid out with fortifications and turrets, walls and bastions and an Elysian hill, an 'Awful Precipice', a menagerie, a Gothic greenhouse and so on. An obelisk with a statue of Sir Rowland Hill (Lord Mayor of London in 1759) on top was added in 1795. Dr Johnson visited Hawkstone and pronounced it to be a place of 'terrific grandeur' but rather pompously concluded that 'the house was magnificent compared with the rank of the owner'.

The building of country houses often had an impact on the landscape outside the immediate emparked area. In some instances this resulted in the complete rebuilding of the village to fit into the new landscape. When Celia Fiennes visited Herefordshire about 1696 she described Stoke Edith as a 'very good old house of timber work, but old-fashioned, but good room for gardens, but all in an old form and mode, and Mr Foley intends to make both a new house and gardens'. The new gardens were staked out and 'a fine bowling green walled in and a summer house in it all new' already made. Above the house were fine woods and a 'delicate park'.

In the 1790s alterations on a much larger scale were made by Repton, who drew up designs for the complete replanning of the park at Stoke Edith. On his advice the line of the turnpike road from Hereford to Ledbury was moved from its course along the hill almost immediately behind the mansion to the line of the present road and the line of this road was incorporated into a ha-ha which divided the garden area from the remainder of the park. So deeply engraved was the road that the ha-ha still stands some 20 feet high in places and requires a bridge to cross it. A new village was planned to lie around an oval green, skirted by a new road. Schools, a cider mill and a blacksmith's shop as well as cottages were planned in 1792 by William Wilkins, a landscape designer who frequently worked with Repton. The project was, however, not fully implemented. Repton himself advised against moving the whole village to the new site: the smoke, he said, arising from the chimneys of the cottages in the dell west of the mansion made a pleasing prospect against the wooded hills. Regrettably Stoke Edith Mansion was gutted by fire in 1927. Today only the walled garden and bowling green survive along with a few village houses and the lodges; otherwise Stoke Edith provides a notable example of a model village only partially completed and now abandoned.

A particularly good example of a surviving model village is to be found at Eastnor in eastern Herefordshire. It is a complete village of picturesque cottages built by the Somers family (founders of Somerstown in north London) to complement the house, Eastnor Castle, built in its present form in 1808 by Sir Robert Smirke in a Baronial (not Gothic) style but with neo-classical symmetry. The church and rectory here (1849–50) were by

G. E. Scott; there is a drinking fountain with decorative terracotta panels standing in the centre of the village green. In addition, the school and stores were built to fit in with the overall scheme and there are a set of picturesque cottages, including a thatched post office. However, there had been a park at Eastnor since at least the early fifteenth century when it is recorded that Henry VI gave permission for a stone tower to be built within the park and for deer leaps to be constructed there. Eastnor Park is still stocked with deer, but unusually not fallow but red deer.

62 The neo-baronial country house at Eastnor

*63 Part of the model village of Eastnor created in the mid nineteenth century to comple-
ment Eastnor Castle and deer park*

At Brampton Bryan there is also an ancient park still stocked with deer, a castle, country house and estate village. The Harley family have been there since 1309 when Sir Robert de Harley of Harley in Shropshire married Margaret Brampton. It was he who built the great gate house of the castle which still remains, and one of his descendants was a later Sir Robert Harley, the Puritan leader. Lady Brilliana Harley defended the castle against the Royalists in 1643 for seven weeks. She died that October and in the following April, after a three-week siege, Colonel Wright was forced to capitulate. A few weeks later the castle, the library, its works of art and manuscripts were all destroyed. A new brick house was built close to the ruins of the castle in 1663 and it was this which was incorporated into the present Georgian house in 1748.

To the south of Bridgnorth there are two interesting model villages, at Quatford, sited beneath a mock castle in the vicinity of the putative late Saxon 'burh' (all the cottages have barge boards and lattice-work porches), and its neighbour, Quat, which has a number of stone and half-timbered cottages situated along the roadside – even the bus-stop is designed to match!

An extremely interesting piece of late landscaping was carried out at Brockhampton by Ross. Brockhampton Court was built on the core of an eighteenth-century rectory that lay close to the medieval church. It was rebuilt in a neo-Tudor style in the late nineteenth century, and the medieval church, which is now an ivy-covered ruin within the grounds, was abandoned. The creation of a small park and the building of the new church of All Saints (1901–2) designed by W. R. Lethaby followed. Lethaby was a follower of William Morris and this fine little early twentieth-century church contains furnishings by Burne-Jones and William Morris. The parish was also extensively landscaped, traces of former open field agriculture suppressed and roads realigned as part of the overall scheme.

Fig. 12 Brockhampton by Ross in 1840 and 1964. Note the dramatic landscape changes which were associated with the creation of a small park and the building of a new church

New Churches

During the later Middle Ages, although there was a modest amount of church building and restoration, increasingly surplus finance went into public buildings and country houses. It would, however, be a grave mistake to believe that church building in the Marches ceased entirely by the sixteenth century. There are many churches of the different denominations scattered throughout the region. Herefordshire in particular can boast a very wide range of parish churches. Bampton Bryan church, for instance, was destroyed during the Civil War at the siege of the castle in 1653, and was rebuilt in the old Gothic tradition in 1656. The medieval Gothic influence is also to be seen at Monnington on Wye, which, with the exception of the tower, was completely rebuilt by Uvedale and Mary Tomkyns in 1679. The church which now lies at the end of a cul de sac close to the remains of a deserted village is worthy of a visit, not least because of its splendid isolation on the banks of the river Wye. The whole of How Capel church, rebuilt with the exception of the medieval chancel between 1693 and 1695, is also medieval Gothic in mood.

Many landscaping schemes involved the country house 'capturing' the parish church, but increasingly such schemes also led to the restoration and rebuilding of the church. The pleasant church at Tyberton was built in part by the elder John Wood of Bath in the early eighteenth century to accompany his now demolished Tyberton Court, erected for the Brydges family. The church is brick built with an attractive tower surmounted by a stone cornice, pediments and urns.

At Shobdon, the important Norman church, with the exception of the west tower, was pulled down and rebuilt by John the Second Viscount Bateman in 1752. He was a friend of Horace Walpole and had been converted to neo-Gothicism by Walpole's house at Strawberry Hill. Despite the immeasurable damage done in the destruction of the Norman architecture of the Herefordshire School here, Shobdon church is a fascinating example of rococo Gothic and is one of the most important survivals of its kind. The design was influenced by Horace Walpole's house: it has shallow transepts, the south was for the Bateman pew complete with fireplace, and the north was for the servants. The interior decoration of the church is pure rococo, including an elaborate three-level pulpit and a striking blue and white colour scheme. All that remains of the early church is the Kilpeck-type font and the arches on the hill to the north, magnificently carved but now unfortunately badly weathered after two centuries of exposure to wind, rain and frost.

Not all new churches were associated with parks and houses. Throughout the Borderland in the nineteenth century medieval churches were ruthlessly renovated or completely rebuilt. Herefordshire has a particular abundance of these. At Grendon Bishop the completely isolated church of St John the Baptist, which is inaccessible by road, was entirely rebuilt in 1797–8, incorporating just a few features of the earlier medieval church. Interestingly enough, the church marks the site of a deserted medieval village which can be traced in the form of adjacent earthworks representing a moated manor house and other building plots. At Bishops Frome the church retains its medieval tower and impressive Norman chancel arch; otherwise it was completely rebuilt in a mock Romanesque style in the late eighteenth century. At Stretton Sugwas the medieval church was demolished and a new church built on a new site in 1877–80. The chief characteristics of this building are the half-timbered west tower and the remarkable reset Norman tympanum depicting Samson and the lion. Among the most unusual of this new generation of churches is the Italianate Romanesque building of St Catherine's, Hoarwithy. This building, which was personally paid for by the vicar, the Revd William Pool, adds a totally unexpected exotic element to an otherwise modest riverside hamlet. Hoarwithy was built (1880–85) by J. P. Seddon, encasing and embellishing an earlier church of 1843 described as a 'neat brick building'. Seddon, who practised mainly in south Wales and the West Country, was a diligent student of medieval architecture and developed a style of his own which was influenced by his love and study of the Venetian Gothic style.

64 *The Italianate church of St Catherine at Hoarwithy, built by J. P. Seddon in the late nineteenth century*

Even in its isolation, with the coming of the railroad new ideas and new material were brought to Herefordshire and numerous churches had their interiors and exteriors dramatically altered. In particular there were two local architects who between them built at least sixteen new churches in the county: F. R. Kempson and Thomas Nicholson, who was commonly known as 'The Destroyer'. Opinions on their work still differ. In 1883 Kempson built the nave and aisles of Holy Trinity, Hereford, which was described by one observer as 'the dullest design I have ever seen – not worth describing'.

It is perhaps too easy to dismiss the energetic works of the Victorian restorers, and a visit to the sad little church of St Andrew's in Leinthall Earls reminds us that nineteenth-century restoration must have saved many churches from ruin. St Andrew's was not restored and, although it is pleasant to see a parish church with many of its medieval and sixteenth-century features intact, the fabric has suffered severely because of lack of attention. Many isolated churches like St Andrew's, which lies hidden on the edge of a farmyard, are in a similar condition, and some, such as the little medieval church at Wacton, are already ruined, representing nineteenth- and twentieth-century casualties which have died partly because of the absence of attention during the Victorian era.

The story of parish church building really comes to an end at the beginning of this century with W. R. Lethaby's church of All Saints at Brockhampton by Ross, which I have already mentioned. Throughout the Marches there are of course numerous churches of other denominations.

65 *All Saints church at Brockhampton by Ross, built (1901–2) by W. R. Lethaby. The church formed part of a fundamental landscape redesign in the parish*

In scattered rural hamlets, particularly where there used to be some industrial activity, brick Nonconformist chapels are common, but these, like their older relatives the parish churches, are finding times hard in the late twentieth century. Much of the energetic work of restoration carried out a century ago is now beginning to require attention and both parish and Nonconformist churches are becoming redundant at a depressing rate. It is only a matter of time before perhaps as many as half of the Marcher churches close their doors to their congregations for good. In most cases alternative uses have been found for them, but it would be a tragedy if this great reservoir of historical architecture were allowed to decay by default, without a conscientious attempt being made to rescue them from total or partial destruction.

Enclosure – The Making of the Rural Landscape

Open field agriculture, which was so much a feature of the English rural scene from the Norman period until about the eighteenth century, appears to have enjoyed a short life in the Borderland. The evidence of ridge and furrow and cropmarkings together with the documentary records shows that two- and three-field farming was operating extensively in the Marches by about 1300. However, the Marcher arable open fields on the whole seem to have been much smaller than their Midland counterparts, and to have formed only part of the agricultural regime. Over much of the region they appear to have operated alongside pastoral farming, which remained dominant in many upland areas. The process of enclosure of the open field strips seems to have started in the fourteenth century as gradually the open fields were broken up and enclosed by hedges, walls and fences. Sometimes, as at Clee St Margaret in south Shropshire, it is still possible to see how bunches of strips were gathered together and hedged at this early date.

Although a few open field systems survived into the eighteenth century and vestiges of open field agriculture are common, the majority of the Borderland appears to have been enclosed as early as 1600. In 1597, for instance, Shropshire was exempted from an Enclosure Act which encouraged the growth of corn because 'it was best treated as a pastoral county'. During the seventeenth century some enclosed parts of Shropshire, particularly around Oswestry and Ellesmere, began to specialise in dairy produce. Out of eighteen livestock markets in Shropshire at this date no fewer than seven specialised in cattle and some of this pastoral farming took place on land newly cleared of woodland in the north-west of Shropshire.

Enclosure enabled other specialisations to occur, in particular in Herefordshire where the growing of cider apples and hops became important. Hop growing seems to have started in Herefordshire as early as the thirteenth

century and constant references to hop kilns and hop poles appear in medieval documents. In 1657 John Beale was able to claim that around
Bromyard 'we make haste to be the chief hopmasters in England'. Herefordshire is still a major hop growing region, with production concentrated in
the triangle between Hereford, Bromyard and Ledbury. In this triangle hopfields and kilns are common; the permanent hop poles are twentieth-century
– previously the constant demand for new poles was met by numerous ash
plantations scattered over the county. Similarly, since the eighteenth century brick kilns have replaced wattle and daub structures.

Records of Herefordshire fruit production start in the fourteenth century
and Beale in his book *Herefordshire Orchards: A Pattern for All England* (1657)
notes, 'This county is reputed the Orchard of England.' He goes on to claim
that fruit trees were grown by people of all stations, and even the hedges
were 'enriched with rows of fruit trees, pears or apples'. By the late
eighteenth century there were fifteen varieties of cider apple and six of pear
grown within the county and a century later Herefordshire was surpassing
Devon as the premier orcharding county with a total area in excess of
27,000 acres. It is estimated that in a good season 20,000 hogsheads of
cider were produced in Herefordshire, of which a considerable proportion
was shipped to Bristol and London. Today the county is the fourth largest
fruit producer in Britain, but in some areas such as the lower Teme valley,
up to 75% of land is still given over to orchards which together with the
hopfields give the modern landscape a highly distinctive appearance.

Until the 1930s farm cider was common, but now it is only produced
commercially, largely by the firm of Bulmers, a family who first made cider
at Credenhill Rectory in 1887. Winemaking, too, is beginning to creep back
into the Borderland – another tradition which began in the Middle Ages,
when there were at least thirty-five vineyards in Herefordshire. In 1287
it is recorded that the Bishop of Hereford's vineyard to the south of Wall
hills yielded seven types of good white wine. For the most part, however,
farming remained small-scale and mixed. A survey of the demesne farm at
King's Pyon of 1623 sums up the character of most Border farming; it consisted of 'a dairyhouse, kiln house, storehouse, six lofts well boarded for malt-
ing and other uses, a fair stable with chambers over, a new tiled barn, and
one other large barn, a large beast house, a large sheep cot, a swinehouse
and a good pigeon house of stone and a hopyard with 6000 poles'.

Although early enclosures enabled some of this specialisation to take
place, large-scale agricultural improvements had to wait until the
eighteenth and nineteenth centuries. There were, however, some early pion-
eer attempts at agricultural development. The most notable of these was
Rowland Vaughan's waterwork scheme in the Golden Valley, where an
elaborate system of channels and sluices was proposed and in part built
between 1585 and 1610 in order to irrigate the land and to provide water
transport. Vaughan proposed to 'raise a golden world in the Golden Valley,

being the pride of all that country with trees bordering on Wales'. He described the valley as 'the Lombardy of Herefordshire' and set out his plans for his utopia in a book called *Most Proved and Long Experienced Water Works*. His scheme depended upon a series of irrigation works from Peterchurch to Bacton, part of which can still be identified on the ground today, including the remains of his first channel known as the Trench Royal. The Golden Valley works seem to have been the first of a series, as other irrigation works can be identified at the great Vaughan mansion at Hergest, near Kington, Hampton Court, Kingsland, Risbury and elsewhere. An extensive system of water meadows was constructed at Stanton on Arrow between 1660 and 1710 and another system of water meadows was dug on Lord Scudamore's estate at Holme Lacy in 1709.

66 *Parliamentary enclosure in the hill country of western Shropshire has left an erratic pattern of regular fields reaching up the hill slopes*

Throughout the Marches the main stimulus to agricultural improvement came from the great estates such as those of the Dukes of Sutherland based at Lilleshall. In 1812 James Loch was appointed estate steward and he supervised a radical rationalisation of farming and land reclamation in eastern Shropshire. Roads and field boundaries were altered, new farmhouses were constructed, distinctive estate-style cottages were built for agricultural labourers, and logically planned groups of barns, cow stalls and wagon sheds were designed, becoming models of their kind and remaining such throughout the nineteenth century.

Although the Borderland was largely unaffected by the parliamentary enclosure of open fields, the enclosure of the surviving stretches of moor and marsh was achieved by legislation in the eighteenth and nineteenth centuries. There were over seventy acts dealing with open common land in Shropshire alone. It is significant that thirty-seven of these acts were brought forward during a period when the margin of cultivation was pushed much higher as a consequence of food requirements during the Napoleonic wars. The first act related to Newport Marsh and was passed in 1764; the final act, concerning upland common in Llanfair Waterdine, was not passed until July 1891.

During the French wars open common land was viewed unfavourably by agricultural commentators. The prevalent attitude towards the commons is reflected in this extract from Bishton's *Report on Shropshire* (1794):

> The idea of leaving them the commons, in their unimproved state to bear chiefly gorse bushes and fern is now completely scouted except by a few who have falsely conceived that the enclosing of them is an injury to the poor; but if these persons had seen as much of the contrary effects in that respect as I have, I am fully persuaded their opposition would at once cease. Let those who doubt go round the commons now open, and view the miserable huts and poor, ill-cultivated, impoverished spots erected or rather thrown together and enclosed by themselves . . .

The process of enclosure is best observed by examining an omnibus award. In 1795 an act was passed to enclose 2550 acres of land in north Shropshire, waste and common land in the townships of Prees, Darleston, Faulsgreen, Mickley, Willaston, Moreton Say, Longford, and Stanton upon Hine Heath. Three commissioners, Henry Bowman, Valentine Vickers and Arthur Davies, were appointed and were on oath to carry out their duties 'faithfully, impartially and honestly . . . without favour or affection to any person whatsoever'. Public notice was given in church of the meetings, and all claims made were scrutinised and could be objected to.

A surveyor was appointed to 'form roads which had to be at least forty feet wide' and which had to be completed within two years of enclosure. Such enclosure roads in Shropshire were largely limited to heathy upland and lowland moor, particularly in the north and east of the county. The old tracks were closed and new wide, straight roads constructed in the enclosed area. The enclosure roads did not follow geographical features, but were systematically and often geometrically laid down by the commissioners. Consequently, short stretches of enclosure road contrast strikingly with the older roads; often the meeting place of the two types of road is marked by an awkward turn. Enclosure roads were of a statutory width, normally 40 feet, but varying with the status of the communities they were linking. Rural depopulation in some areas has meant that some of these roads now run between isolated farms. Accordingly, the metalled area of the small road that is all that is necessary occupies only about half of the available area, so that many enclosure roads in remote rural areas are characterised by wide grass verges.

The expenses of enclosure, except for fencing, were met by selling part of the commons. In all, the enclosure cost just over £3000 – £1 3s. 6d. an acre – on top of which fencing for the new allotments had to be paid for by individual allotment holders.

The commissioners then divided the lands among the freeholders. They gave Sir Richard Hill and his brother John 'one full fourteenth part and also all pools and fisheries thereon', in lieu of their joint manorial rights over the common. The poor and the squatters were hardly considered.

Despite a series of acts passed to enclose the Clee hills, much open common remains there today. In 1809 an act was passed to enclose the common land in Abdon and Stoke St Milborough on Brown Clee. To meet the expenses of enclosure, something like a third of the allotments were put up for public auction and realised £3803. Most plots were bought by local farmers; one exception to these was Samuel Childs, a squatter coalminer who bought a small allotment next to his encroachment. It appears from contemporary accounts, however, that the Clee miners were generally impoverished and dependent upon their harvest earnings to supplement their wages.

The effects of parliamentary enclosure on the landscape can be seen on the ground today. The lots sold by auction were hedged with quickset bushes, frequently interspersed with small trees and a few with dry stone walls; in the late nineteenth century most of the remaining open allotments were fenced and the grazing land improved. This has resulted in a striking contrast along the parish boundary between Stoke St Milborough, which has improved pasture up to 1300 feet, and Clee St Margaret, which was never enclosed. Further awards for enclosing on Brown Clee appeared in 1813 and 1841.

Despite the theoretical extinction of common rights of grazing arising from enclosure, the summit of the Brown Clee remains one of the largest areas of open common in Shropshire. Freeholders are supposed to graze their animals in certain specified areas, but the wild nature of the country makes this impossible in practice. One positive result of enclosure was to push the frontier of farming up the slopes of the hills, where it has remained to this day.

In the middle of the nineteenth century considerable areas of upland common in the old Clun Forest were enclosed by acts of parliament. Between 1845 and 1891 some 20,000 acres were affected. These acts covered some of the remotest country in Shropshire: for instance, in 1847 'a tract of unenclosed Common Land in the Honour or Lordship and Forest of Clun' amounting to 8600 acres was enclosed, and in 1858 a further 3580 acres was the subject of an enclosure award. As a result of acts passed in 1852, 1865 and 1880, over 2000 acres in the parish of Llanfair Waterdine alone were enclosed, and the final act passed concerning Shropshire completed the enclosure of the parish in 1891. This area, still forming part of the wildest and most exciting countryside in Shropshire, is now traversed by fences, hedges and stone walls dating from enclosure. Over the past decades the Forestry Commission has been particularly active in this area of south-west Shropshire and many hillslopes in the Clun region carry a covering of coniferous woodland.

Townscapes

Hereford

The lack of good communication within the Marches was a major reason why its towns, generally speaking, did not flourish in the eighteenth and nineteenth centuries. Writing of Hereford in 1724, John Beale ascribed the basic cause of the city's poverty to 'lack of transportation'. On her visit to Herefordshire in the 1690s Celia Fiennes talked about 'pretty long miles', and a century later Marshall reported that the roads were 'such as one might expect to meet with in the marshes of Holland or the mountains of Switzerland'. It was recorded that a Scottish army advancing to besiege Hereford in 1645 was able to march only eight miles a day when nearing the city because the roads were so bad.

The episode during the Civil War which led to this comment about the roads had some curious repercussions. In the summer of 1645 the Scots under Lord Leven laid siege to Hereford on behalf of the Parliamentarians. Hereford, a Royalist city, was defended by Barnabas Scudamore. The Scots succeeded in destroying the powder mill on which the garrison depended for ammunition, but the local architect, John Abel, was said then to have responded by making hand mills which saved the day. In September the King himself raised the siege by riding into the city and granting John Abel the honorary title of King's Carpenter. In October of the same year the Governor of Hereford planned to lead a force out of the city to try and capture the castle of Canon Frome, then in Parliamentarian hands. In order to do this he sent for John Abel and asked him to make a moveable siege engine which would be capable of being taken right up to the castle walls. The machine which John Abel designed is described as follows in a contemporary document:

> It was called a Sow and was carried upon great wheels to be drawn by oxen. It was made with room lofts over one another musket proof, and very strong out of which were holes to play and shoot out . . . It was so high that it could discharge it over all the works at Canon Frome, beside which a door open to bring them into the works, out of which a bridge could be drawn for entrance . . .

This strange war engine left Hereford for Canon Frome with 400 men. The remainder of the story is, however, an anticlimax, for when the soldiers reached a position only a mile and a half away from their destination, they halted and rested and a few of them went off to inns in Ledbury. The Parliamentary forces discovered the Sow and carried it off to Canon Frome and in the words of Webb, the chronicler of the Civil War in Herefordshire: 'Their shout of triumph made the valleys ring.'

Herefordshire was exceptionally fertile and with its cider, hops, sheep and cattle, Hereford, as the market town, should have benefited greatly. However, at a time of national growth on an unprecedented scale in the eighteenth century, it was unable to make itself much more than a local market. The Wye was an erratic means of transport and during the eighteenth century there were complaints that 'in plentifull yeares it choaketh up the commodities of corne and fruite'. The main causes for this were the difficulty of improving the navigation of the Wye and the fact that the cost of maintaining proper roads and bridges was too high. Although the turnpike roads did something to improve communications, Hereford at the end of the eighteenth century was still a remote county town with no good connections with the ports or with the expanding industrial towns. The main market for hops was Worcester, while Ledbury and Upton upon Severn took most of the cider, perry and fruit; Ross took the wool, while Leominster, as always, remained a rival general market. Another reason for Hereford's stagnation was its lack of any substantial manufacture of its own. In 1700 gloves were the town's principal manufacture, but, as Cox observed, that is 'too poor a trade to make a place to flourish', and the industry was in any case declining by the end of the eighteenth century.

Hereford's weak economic position was radically altered, however, in the first half of the nineteenth century by the completion of neighbouring canals, and by the coming of the railways. The city's population in 1757 was 5592 of which 3878 were within the walls and 1714 outside; by 1801 it was no more than 6828, but by 1851 it had nearly doubled. The coming of the railway provided an additional stimulus to the city, which was then able to trade much more effectively with the rest of the country. Nevertheless, at the time of the compilation of the first edition of the 25-inch Ordnance Survey Map of Hereford in the 1880s it was still a town largely confined within its medieval walls. During the late nineteenth century and early twentieth century, with the coming of municipal services such as gas and local public transport, the city burst its ancient limits and rapidly spread outwards, including a substantial suburb to the south of the river Wye. Today the city has expanded to the point where it has swallowed up the ancient village centres of Holmer and Lower Bullingham, and a considerable number of surrounding villages act as dormitory settlements for the shire capital that has lost its county, but not its character or prosperity.

Leominster

Today Leominster is a thriving market town with a new industrial estate and has continued its long tradition of providing a centre for the commercial and social life of northern Herefordshire. Perhaps if its rivers, the Lugg and the Pinsley, had been faster flowing it would have become a major eighteenth- and nineteenth-century centre of wool manufacture like Stroud.

67 *The Old Market Hall (the Grange) in Leominster, built by the famous local architect John Abel in the early seventeenth century*

However, here on the plain instead of on a steep-sided valley, the water wheels did not have the power to drive the big textile mills. The fame of Leominster wool was such that it prompted the poet Michael Drayton to write of 'Lemster ore. That the silkworm's web for fineness doth compare.' Despite the red stone of the great church, Leominster is a black and white town. A short distance from the churchyard the Grange (the Old Market Hall), now the offices of the District Council, is one of Herefordshire's best timber-framed buildings, built in 1633 by John Abel of Sarnesfield as a town hall to stand at the top of Broad Street. It was offered for sale in 1853, bought by John Arkwright of Hampton Court, and re-erected on its present site. Originally it had an open ground floor which was used as a butter market in the same way as Ross and Ledbury market halls still have their open ground floors today. When it was sold for £95 and was re-erected on its present site, the ground floor was filled in with masonry. It is one of the loveliest timber-framed houses in Herefordshire, two-storeyed, with fine bays and adorned with elegant carvings. The windows of the upper storey project and have carvings of male and female busts. John Abel's original inscription can still be read on the frieze, in which he says his columns support the fabric as 'noble gentry . . . support the honour of a Kingdom'.

This market hall is the finest remaining example of the work of John Abel (1577–1674), who was the leading Herefordshire craftsman of the seventeenth century. In addition to the hall at Leominster he built those at Brecon (1624) and Kington (1654), the stone grammar school at Kington (1625) and the ceiling of Abbey Dore church (1633). Abel worked in a number of other places and his name is associated with a considerable number of Borderland buildings, in many cases perhaps spuriously so.

Shrewsbury

The other major Marcher town, Shrewsbury, fared somewhat better than Hereford, continuing to benefit from its position as unofficial 'capital' of north Wales as well as Shropshire's county town. Shrewsbury benefited greatly from the wool trade. The wool from the Welsh borderland was of poor quality, but great fortunes were made by some merchants engaged in collecting and selling it for cheap clothing. One rich wool family were called the Prides, possibly as a nickname indicating their prosperity. The Great Plague caused a decline in population, and a disastrous trading recession followed in the fifteenth century. But fortunes revived, the population doubling from about 3000 to 6000 between 1560 and 1660. This was a period of great rebuilding in Shrewsbury, and many of the best timber-framed houses, such as the mansions of Owen, Ireland and Perche, were constructed at this time. The wealth of the town was also expressed in the continuing power of one of the medieval guilds, the Fellowship of the Drapers, with the founding of a new institution, Shrewsbury School, and the building of the market hall. 'This is indeed a beautiful, large, pleasant, populous and rich town,' wrote Defoe in the 1720s. Following the disruption caused by the Civil War, during which the castle was dramatically taken by the Parliamentarians, Shrewsbury emerged as a fashionable county town. The gentry built or rented houses in the town for the social season and so that they could influence both the county and borough elections. These developments are reflected in the Georgian flavour of Belmont, Claremont Hill and other elegant streets laid out within the town walls.

68 *A photograph taken at the end of the nineteenth century of Butcher Row, Shrewsbury. The house in the foreground is known as the Abbot's House, because it was wrongly believed to have been the town house of the Abbot of Lilleshall. The house dates from c. 1500 and the ground floor consists of original shop fronts; the half-timbering and jettying is typical of sixteenth-century town (and country) houses in the Marches*

In the last years of the eighteenth century the town finally lost control over the Welsh wool trade. However, improvements and the arrival of the canal and the railway promoted food marketing and new industry. Though Shropshire was so much at the heart of the early Industrial Revolution, Shrewsbury was never very heavily industrialised. The saw mills, tanneries, various iron foundries and the notorious lead works all remained on a relatively minor scale. The population increase was correspondingly modest in comparison to other towns, but even so it doubled during the nineteenth century. Several public buildings were provided such as the infirmary, the music hall, and a new market hall, but local political conflict tended to restrict the scale of such schemes. The main feature of the last two centuries has been the progressive expansion of residential areas outside the loop of the river, with a new limit of expansion being set by the by-pass built in the 1930s. This road has not, however, prevented an increasing amount of traffic passing through the centre, partly drawn by Shrewsbury's modern role as a shopping centre. Fortunately the post-war road improvers, intent on building an inner ring road, have been largely defeated by the local geography and tortuous medieval street plan which, though still congested, for the most part survives with all its closeness and intricacy.

Shrewsbury's position was considerably strengthened first by Thomas Telford's improvements to the London to Holyhead road and later by the coming of the railways. For over fifty years Shrewsbury was one of the principal railway junctions in Britain. New railway towns were also created at places such as Gobowen, to the north of Oswestry, and Craven Arms, where the town streets were laid out along the lines of former medieval open field strips.

Ross-on-Wye

Ross occupies a prominent hill on the eastern side of the river Wye and has all the characteristics of a Marcher market town, except that much of it, in particular its public buildings, are constructed in sandstone. The centre of town around the church is open and known as the Prospect, which was given to the town by John Kyrle (1637–1724), known as the 'man of Ross'. The market hall, built between 1660 and 1674, is of red sandstone and is built on the normal pattern of open arcaded ground floor with hall above. From here the triangular-shaped market place falls away steeply down the hill to become Broad Street.

In 1770 the Revd William Gilpin took a boat down the Wye as a result of which in 1782 he published *Observations on the River Wye*. Thomas Gray and Samuel Ireland also wrote about the Wye and its natural beauty and the cult of the picturesque had a considerable effect on Ross and the Wye below it. By the end of the century there were eight boats taking the wealthy to Monmouth for one and a half guineas or as far as Chepstow for three guineas. In 1799 Charles Heath brought out the first edition of his *Excursion Down the Wye* – the Wye tourist industry had been born.

The cult of the picturesque affected not only Ross but the Goodrich area to the south, where there is one of the best preserved castles in the Marchlands in a magnificent situation overlooking the Wye. In 1828 Goodrich Court was begun, a vast and fantastic turreted and castellated building, only half a mile from the castle. For 120 years it dominated the scene looking down the Wye – Wordsworth called it an 'impertinent structure' and wished for the power to blow it away. In fact it has now gone, with the exception of the east gate house on the dual carriageway from Ross to Monmouth.

Round red sandstone gate towers with conical roofs and crenellation give us some idea of the appearance of the original building. Goodrich village itself, however, still has a number of romantic buildings inspired by Ross and the Wye tourist industry.

Ludlow

The Palmers' Guild was a dominant institution in late medieval Ludlow. This was a religious guild founded in the mid thirteenth century which originally endowed three chaplains to pray for the dead and in honour of the Cross. It prospered considerably, and came to employ as many as eight priests, to attract members from all over the southern part of Britain, and to own many properties in the town and elsewhere. It was responsible for much of the late medieval adornment of the parish church of St Lawrence, for the founding of such charitable institutions as almshouses, and from the early fifteenth century for the administration of a school. The guild was dissolved in 1551 when its property and many of its functions passed to the town corporation.

From the mid fifteenth century until 1689, Ludlow Castle was the main centre of administration for the Council of the Marches of Wales, a commission set up by the Crown to dispense justice in the turbulent Borderland region. Ludlow's role as an administrative centre generated trade and, together with the flourishing cloth trade, made it a prosperous town in the late medieval and Tudor periods. In the eighteenth century it became a town of fashion and resort, to which the moderately wealthy retired and where many landed families kept town houses. This is reflected in the many fine Georgian facades which can still be seen, most of which seem to be the work of local craftsmen. The fashionable social life of this period was paralleled by industrial prosperity arising from a variety of industries which used the water power provided by the Corve and the Teme, among them corn milling, paper making and the manufacture of woollen cloth, blankets, and leather dress. From the last of these arose the trade of glove making, which employed as many as a thousand people in the late eighteenth century.

In the early nineteenth century several of Ludlow's industries began to decline, and improved communications, first turnpike roads and then the railways, made the town less attractive to the wealthy as a resort as it became less exclusive, although new assembly rooms were constructed as late as 1840. However, Ludlow continued to flourish as a market centre and for the first time since the end of the Middle Ages began to expand its built-up area. The Victorian era was, nevertheless, a time of relative stagnation in the history of Ludlow; no large industrial enterprises were established and fortunately few of its fine buildings were destroyed.

Ludlow today flourishes as a centre of trade and administration for a wide area of the Borderland, but, as in the past, its prosperity also depends on industry and on attracting visitors. Clothing and agricultural machinery are now its chief manufactures. The Ludlow Festival, held in June and July, marks the zenith of the town's tourist season. We have seen that several planned medieval towns over the centuries withered away to become no more than agricultural villages or less, but in spite of some periods of relative stagnation, Ludlow has continued to thrive as a centre of trade and small-scale industry and as a tourist centre. Its continuous prosperity is reflected in its many fine houses and public buildings of all periods.

Places to Visit

There are a considerable number of country houses and parks open to the public in the Marches, which include a large number of properties owned by the National Trust. Among the most noteworthy are Benthall Hall, near Broseley, Berrington Hall, Chirk Castle, Croft Castle, Dudmaston Hall, Erddig (Clwyd), Lower Brockhampton (Bromyard), Morville, Powys Castle and Wilderhope Manor (Wenlock Edge). In this section just one house is dealt with in more detail.

Attingham Hall and Park

Attingham Hall and Park lie immediately to the east of the Severn about five miles south-east of Shrewsbury, adjacent to the village of Atcham. The present hall was built for the First Lord Berwick in 1783–5 to the design of George Steuart and was altered by John Nash at the beginning of the nineteenth century. It was the grandest house of its time in Shropshire and certainly one of the most representative Georgian buildings in the area. Nash also built the Italianate village at Cronkhill which was probably 'The Villa in Shropshire' exhibited at the Royal Academy in 1802.

It has been suggested that the original siting of Attingham Park was influenced by the presence of an earlier ironworks there. The Tern Forge stood from 1710 to 1757 on the river Tern in what is now Attingham Park. It is recorded in the 1717 list of ironworks compiled by Fuller as producing 300 tons of iron goods per annum; yet virtually no trace of it remains beyond a few lumps of slag on the bed of the Tern at its original site. This is all the more surprising in view of the scale of the works. A letter of 1713 records how, within three years of the start of operations, there was already 'a mill for Rowling of Brass plates and Iron hoops and Slitting of bar iron into Rods for making of nails . . . a Wire Mill, forge and a furnace for Converting of Iron into steel'. In addition, workshops and housing had been built for forty men and their dependants. Following the closing of the works, however, in 1757, the housing and workshops were demolished to remove squatters who had quickly moved into the vacant premises.

69 *Attingham Hall, built 1783–5, with the river Tern on the right. Thought by many to be the most elegant country house in the whole of the Welsh Marches*

It seems probable that Humphrey Repton used some of the ponds and pools here for his landscaping in the late eighteenth century. Repton, who was employed to improve the park in 1789, expresses the aspirations of the Georgian landscape gardeners in his *Red Book* (1797–8), which is still kept at Attingham Hall. In his criticism of Attingham Park prior to the alterations, he complains that there were no trees to assist perspective and divert the eye towards the house and that barns and other outbuildings which were visible detracted from the hall. Among his suggestions for improvement were the plantation of trees to hide the park pale, the diversion of water, the construction of bridges and the setting of hedges. His general idea was to contrast wide natural views, using the Wrekin and the Welsh mountains as a backcloth, against the beautiful miniatures or set-pieces. Some, but not all, of Repton's improvements were carried out; but the importance of the *Red Book* lies in its concept of landscaping.

The present approach to the house from Atcham dates from soon after 1807. About this time a number of cottages on the north side of Watling Street were demolished and the line of the Uffington road altered so that the park could be extended. Before this the main entrance was midway between Atcham and Tern bridges, but it did not meet with Repton's approval when he worked on his *Red Book* for Attingham. He was concerned about the proximity of the house to Tern bridge and suggested extending the park across the road and building a pair of lodges, one on each side of the road, at the eastern extremity of the park 'so that we shall induce the stranger to conceive that he passes thro' the park and not on the outside of it'. This idea was inspired by the existence of a turnpike cottage which Repton visualised as being remodelled as a classical building worthy of a nobleman's park. Only one of these lodges survives, that on the north side, which served as the entrance to the former east drive to the house. It was presumably designed by Nash.

Apart from reinforcing the planting in the park and introducing shelter-belts round it, Repton's main contribution was to make the river Tern play a greater part in the landscape. He suggested the building of a weir to the south-east of the house to maintain the water level in the upper reaches of the river and a cascade which should be visible from the house. This still exists, but not situated as Repton recommended. He also constructed another weir below Tern bridge so as to create above it a much wider river that would be visible from the house. However, his idea of making the bridge more monumental in its design was not adopted, and nor was his suggestion that a spire should be added to the tower of Wroxeter church some two miles to the south-east of the house!

CHAPTER ELEVEN

Industrial Landscapes

THE WELSH Marches are still essentially rural and even the relics of early industry are largely preserved within a rural setting. It is difficult today to appreciate that in the Roman period *Ariconium*, in south-eastern Hereford-shire, was an industrial town based on iron manufacture and that during the eighteenth century Shropshire was the premier iron-producing county in the kingdom. The Industrial Revolution, if not born, was certainly nurtured in a small valley in central Shropshire – Coalbrookdale. For it was here in 1708–9 that Abraham Darby first successfully smelted iron ore, sub-stituting coke for charcoal, thereby heralding the introduction of the second Iron Age. Today Ironbridge and the Coalbrookdale have largely reverted to rural tranquillity, although aspects of the Industrial Revolution are being excitingly re-established through the Ironbridge Gorge Museum.

The wealth of mineral deposits in the Marches, usually lying in reasonably accessible places near to running water and timber, has meant a long history of extractive and manufacturing industry in the region. These extractive industries can be traced back to before the Roman Conquest, when much of the industry was of an itinerant nature, leaving little permanent impres-sion on the landscape. Excavations at *Ariconium* have revealed rock-cut depressions containing remains of Roman iron-smelting furnaces and asso-ciated slag heaps; furthermore there is clear evidence to show that some of these slag heaps were reworked during the seventeenth century. Both the Roman and later iron workings are overgrown and indistinguishable without judicious exploration. Elsewhere only the occasional isolated row of cottages, derelict railway track, disturbed hillside, or unexpected non-conformist chapel tells of the intense industrial activity in the past. The real impact on the landscape did not come until the sixteenth century and later. Even then, most industry was transient and short-lived and evidence even of eighteenth- and nineteenth-century industrial activity has, in some instances, merged back into the rural countryside. Today, apart from stone quarrying, there is little extractive or primary industry in the Marches.

There are basically two types of Marcher industrial landscape. Firstly, there are the open upland areas where lead, ironstone, limestone or coal have been quarried for centuries. Such activities have left a scarred countryside of hollows and mounds, now overgrown and given over to rough grazing with scattered stone cottages straggling along the roads. Because of the comparatively small scale of activity in these areas, miners tended to follow industry, often building squatter cottages on common land. The miners were frequently part-time farmers and a tradition of smallhold-ings grew up in these parts of the Marches. The landscape they left behind is confined largely to the foothill areas in such places as the Tanat valley, the Stiperstones, the Clee hills, Bringewood Chase, the Malvern hills and around the edge of the Forest of Dean. Industry in these areas was largely unplanned, working on a piecemeal basis to the capacity of the primitive mining equipment employed, and often a seam or deposit was abandoned long before it was exhausted. The mines were normally not served by any specialist communication system and as the work was constantly moving, there was little time for large-scale settlements to develop.

The second landscape type, found mainly in eastern central Shropshire on the Shropshire coalfield, where the rural outlook has been completely devastated by industry, was associated with the extraction of coal, iron and clay on a large scale and also with the manufacture of a wide variety of goods, principally ceramics and iron products. Industrial activity here declined during the latter part of the nineteenth and the early twentieth century, as new centres of manufacture were established in places such as the Black Country to the east. Since the late 1960s the main area of ancient industry, the Coalbrookdale coalfield, has been incorporated into Telford New Town. Prior to the building of the new town, open-cast mining was undertaken to clear up the coal seams, during the course of which many old shafts were uncovered. Before tracing the imprint of the iron industry, let us first examine two redundant industrial areas, where the scars of early industry have not yet completely healed.

The Shropshire Lead Mines

There are deposits of lead located in a relatively small area between the Stiperstones and Corndon. The lead is all to be found within a three-mile radius of the hamlet of Shelve, yet in the early 1870s, the ten Shelve mines produced over 10% of the country's lead ore. However, the seams have been exhausted now or are so fragmented that mining is barely profitable. The activities of the lead miners have left a stark landscape of derelict engine houses, decaying chimney stacks, stagnant engine pools, and a maze of abandoned pits and shafts. The huge quantity of lead that was mined here is indicated by the white tips of waste spar, which until very recently could be seen for considerable distances in central Shropshire. The Romans began lead working here and pigs of lead stamped with the name of the Emperor Hadrian (AD 117–38) were found near Linley in 1767. Other Roman remains found in the old workings include mining tools, notably wooden shovels and candles with wicks of hemp, as well as coins and pottery. Professor Barrie Jones has suggested recently that extensive earthworks in the vicinity of Linley Hall may have been caused by Roman lead working, which used a system of artificial streams to wash out the ore. In north-western Shropshire, near Brompton, traces of lead and possibly silver working have been found in a number of early Roman military camps, perhaps suggesting one reason for Roman involvement in the region in the first instance. During the early Middle Ages, Shelve appears to have been an important lead-producing area for Henry II laid down conditions governing the mining of lead in the Forest of Stiperstones and in 1180, the mines here were leased for £55. Lead was transported considerable distances to places as far away as Gloucester, Builth Wells and Wiltshire.

70a (left) A nineteenth-century photograph of lead mining in the Shelve district of Shropshire. 70b (right) A disused lead mining landscape at the Gravels

The lead mines belonged to the ground landlords, principally the Earls of Tankerville and the More family. The former owned most of the northern and eastern parts of the orefield, which included the Tankerville, Pennerley, East Roman Gravels, Batholes and Roundhill mines. The latter owned most of the southern and eastern part of the orefield, including Roman Gravels,

Ladywell and the Grit mines. Snailbeach, the richest mine in the orefield, was owned by the Marquis of Bath, and Bog mine, in the south, by the Lister family, lords of Rowton. The chief ore, galena or lead sulphide, was originally smelted at Snailbeach and Pontesford, where tall chimney shafts with hundreds of yards of flues were erected to recover by-products such as arsenic. Later on, much of the ore was carried out of the region by way of the railway which ran from Minsterley to be smelted in Wales, Deeside and Bristol.

The first large-scale attempts at mining began in the mid eighteenth century on the Grit sett (the term sett was used commonly in Shropshire to describe a mining property). John Lawrence, a local man, became a leading figure in large-scale mining in the area and by the end of the century had become so successful that he had gained a controlling influence over every major mine in the orefield, with the exception of Snailbeach. As the mines were not very deep, adits or tunnels dug into the hillside were used to extract the ore, although horse-powered winding engines or gins were used to raise water to the surface in barrels. John Lawrence was one of the first in the region to experiment with steam engines, and bought several from Boulton and Watt in Birmingham, but he did not keep them in use for long and sold them to mines in other parts of the country.

At this time John Lawrence also operated smeltworks on the coalfield, as did the Snailbeach Company, and with the high mineral prices enjoyed during the Napoleonic wars, it was a period of prosperity. In the 1820s, however, Lawrence lost possession of most of his mines which were leased by the surface landlords to companies from northern England. By 1835 the Lawrence possessions had all been lost, but his successors did not fare particularly well, for lead prices fell steeply and by the mid-1840s all the new companies had also abandoned their ventures.

In the 1850s the area experienced another substantial boom in which several new companies were established to work existing mines and sink new ones. The new companies brought Cornish engineers to the area, who erected the characteristic Cornish engine houses with their prominent chimneys wherever necessary. However, prices fell yet again and these ventures also failed eventually. The mines passed back into local hands during the 1860s, and despite relatively low lead prices it was again a time of prosperity, for two very rich deposits were discovered at Tankerville and Roman Gravels. Towards the ends of their working lives, many of the mines showed an increased output of zinc ore, first recorded in 1858, and of barytes, first recorded in 1860.

The middle years of the 1870s were the ones of maximum output from the Shropshire orefield, and the buildings erected during this period are the ones which remain as ruins today. In 1873 Shropshire produced 7600 tons of lead ore, but by the end of the decade lead ore prices had started to fall once more, and this time they continued to fall and did not recover until the twentieth century. One by one the mines closed as they could no longer cover their operating costs, and by 1895 there was only one left, at Snailbeach. This mine, one of the richest in Europe, continued working until 1911, by which time it was almost completely exhausted.

Much of the lead mining in Shropshire was always piecemeal, and even at its height miners built cottages on the edge of commonland with small attached pastures in order to supplement their incomes. The Earls of Tankerville encouraged miners to settle on the edge of the commons in the northern portion of Stiperstones. By the middle of the nineteenth century about 250 acres of common had been taken up by some ninety-three small-holdings who created the communities of Pennerley and Perkins Beach. The hamlet of More had appeared by 1881, but by 1902 some cottages had already been abandoned in response to the decline of the mines. The demise of the lead industry meant that the area was heavily overpopulated, and the subsequent story of the region has largely been one of painful adjustment to marginal pastoral farming. The wealth made in the lead mines did not find its way back into the area; cottages, churches and chapels are uniformly simple, roads are still only just adequate and the single-track railway which served the region has long since been taken up. Until about 1960 the story of abandonment continued, but since then these roughly built dwellings and the plots of land attached to them have been increasingly in demand, and today they are eagerly sought after as retirement, commuter and holiday cottages!

Lead is no longer mined in Shropshire, but for a century and a half the county was one of Britain's premier production areas. Working conditions must have been poisonous, but the industrial remains left behind have a strange attraction and mystery.

The Clee Hill Industries

It is perhaps surprising that the highest of the Marcher hills on the English side of the border, the Clee hills, are the least well known and the least visited. They consist of the Brown Clee, Titterstone Clee and Catherton Clee. Geologically they are made up of sandstone deposits, rich in minerals, but capped by a hard layer of basalt which gives them their curious flat-topped appearance. The Clee hills contain a wealth of minerals – coal, iron, limestone, basalt and copper are all found there. The industrial activity associated with these rocks comes to a fairly abrupt halt in the Teme valley, where the county boundaries of Shropshire, Herefordshire and Worcestershire converge and where the deposits of Old Red Sandstone begin to dominate. The relics of past industrial activity on the Clees merge with a landscape of pastoral farming; for this too was a region inhabited by cottagers. The open heathland used for common grazing and the work in the collieries and quarries on top of the hill have been constant attractions over the centuries for men seeking work. As early as 1745 there were forty-nine squatter cottages on the wastes of the township of Smitton alone. According to the geologist Sir Roderick Murchison, writing in the nineteenth century, 'Some cottagers [kept] horses to carry lime and coal and were able to earn two or three shillings a day.' Other sources suggest that the miners were impoverished and were obliged to take on several occupations including farming, as well as carrying lime and mining coal. Even today, when there is no longer and industrial work on Brown Clee and quarrying on Titterstone Clee is limited to the supply of roadstone, the Clee Hill Commoners Association still thrives.

71 A squatter cottage on the edge of the Clee hills in the nineteenth century. Many of the miners lived in such dwellings and farmed a few acres of rough grazing

The Clees sit immediately to the south of Wenlock Edge, and the Corve Dale and the Brown Clee form an hour-glass shape in plan with two distinct summits, Clee Burf which rises to 1650 feet, and Abdon Burf which rises to 1790 feet – the highest point in Midland England. Such is their prominence that they are the only hills in England to feature on an early map of the world, the *Mappa Mundi* (c. 1300), kept in Hereford cathedral. Titterstone Clee has a distinctive face in profile, rather like a high peaked cap. Reaching up to just below 1750 feet above sea level, it can be clearly identified for many miles from every point of the compass.

Today the landscapes of the two Clees are rather different from one another, although both have been deeply affected by man's activities. The hills boasted four major prehistoric hillforts until the nineteenth century, when three of them were severely damaged during a frenzy of mining activity. The fort which crowns the Titterstone Clee is both one of the largest and highest in England and is unusual because it has no ditch, although the ruins of a massive stone wall which once surrounded it can still be seen. It has been quarried away extensively on the south side and now houses a radar station. On Brown Clee the hillforts at Abdon Burf and Clee Burf are inextricably bound into the remnants of nineteenth-century industry. The third fort on the Brown Clee, however, at Nordy Bank, is both easily accessible and clearly identifiable on the ground with a single bank and ditch.

After the end of the Iron Age the Clees seem to have been left alone, perhaps until the late Anglo-Saxon and early Norman period, when, as noted in Chapter Eight, the Brown Clee hill formed the centrepiece of a Royal Forest which appears to have covered much of the Corve Dale and part of the Titterstone Clee as well. In the middle of the twelfth century the forest was handed over to the Clifford family of Corfham Castle in the Corve Dale, who operated the area as a private hunting chase. Corfham was a substantial castle in the Corve Dale where Fair Rosamund, Henry II's mistress, was born ; today it has been reduced to a field of irregular earthworks. During the later Middle Ages the sole rights of hunting claimed by the lords of Corfham over the old Clee Forest gradually decayed; however, some interesting common rights survived until recent times as a consequence of the area having once been under strict seigneurial control.

The inhabitants of all the settlements that originally lay within the chase were allowed certain general rights of commoning on the summit of Brown Clee hill and in particular within an area known as Earnstrey Park. The commoners who lived in settlements some way distant from the Brown Clee were known as strakers and moved their animals by way of cattle drifts known as straker routes across the lands of other parishes until they reached common land. These old ways are still deeply engraved into the modern landscape, having cut their way down into the sandstone and are now often followed for short distances by local streams. The outcommoners, as they were known, held only restricted rights on the hilltop, compared to the inhabitants of townships immediately adjacent to the upland commons, who enjoyed a wider range of rights. Similar rights were to be had on a number of other common land areas in England, notably Cranborne Chase, where the two different types of commoners were known as inbounders and outbounders, and the outskirts of Galtres Forest, Yorkshire, and Duffield Frith, Derbyshire, where the commoners were called bounders. The Veneille tenants of Dartmoor, as they were known, seem to have exercised customs very similar to those on the Brown Clee: those tenants living within the old Devon Forest (later Dartmoor Chase) had the right to take anything from Dartmoor except green oak and venison. The method by which the Veneille tenants were able to claim their animals and by which stray animals were impounded was called 'the drift'. According to this custom, the tenants were not informed until the morning of the rounding up that the drift was about to take place, so that interlopers would have no opportunity for removing their animals. Similarly, on the Brown Clee, the Clee chase keepers annually informed every township within the old forest area that there was to be a drift the following day by blowing horns one hour before sunset. Every household was obliged to send a man to the meeting at Botterell's Cross, an ancient stone high up on Brown Clee, within an hour of sunrise, and if they failed to report they were fined twelve pence. The old straker rights operated on a restricted basis right up until the time of parliamentary enclosure, when they appear to have been effectively extinguished. This did not stop, however, a latter-day pretender to the lordship of the Clee Chase, Thomas Mytton, claiming the right to impound strays throughout the Clee hills as late as 1809!

By the early nineteenth century industrial activities of various sorts had begun to make a major impact on the Clee hills, but as early as the thirteenth century Wigmore Abbey was recorded as having taken coal from Titterstone Clee and in 1260 the lord of Corfham granted land with a licence 'to dig coals within the forest of Clee or to sell or give it away'. Piecemeal mining continued on the Clees for centuries and the summits of the hills where the coal is most readily accessible are dotted with bell-pit mines. Some of these are medieval, but as the bell-pit techniques continued until at least the eighteenth century, it is difficult to distinguish the earlier workings from the later. Bell-pit mines takes their names from the profile of the workings: the coal is reached from a central shaft which is dug into the seam from the surface, so that eventually a small underground bell-shaped pit is created. The coal which was produced was brought to the surface by the use of a simple windlass and bucket. When abandoned, the mines collapsed and filled up leaving a circular mound with a central hollow around the old mine entrance. These mounds have the appearance of Bronze Age burial barrows and areas which have been intensely worked over, such as that lying immediately to the west of Abdon Burf and on Catherton Clee, appear 'pockmarked' when seen from the air.

The antiquarian Leland, writing in the early sixteenth century, noted 'a blo shope on Titterstone Clee', perhaps a reference to a wind furnace. These consisted of piled-up stones which were arranged to enable the dominant westerly winds which sweep across the Clees to fire the wood and smelt the iron ore. He also recorded that the Brown Clee 'is exceedyng good for lyme, whereof there they make much and serve the countrie about'. Although ironstone quarrying for local furnaces continued, coal mining gradually became far more important and as early as 1727 coal produced on Titterstone Clee was valued at £1500; however, mining was still carried out in an erratic manner. The nineteenth-century geologist Murchison commented, 'Coal has been wrought from these hills for time immemorial, and numerous old shafts attest the extent of the operations . . . as the ground, however, has never been allotted, each speculator having begun his work where he pleased, abandoned it when he saw a difficulty, it is impossible to say how much mineral has been wasted and what quantity remain in uncollected and broken masses.' Murchison's words are still valid today, as a recent survey of mineral deposits on the Clees has recommended that mining should recommence once more.

One of the perennial problems of mining and quarrying on the summit of the Clees was the transport of the raw materials down the steep slopes of the hills. The coal and ironstone were carried down by pack-horse or even on the backs of cottagers' wives, and Richard Jones of Ashford who was attending the Titterstone Wake in 1846 recalled the young women 'fine and handsome upstanding wenches they were, and well dressed too; but you wouldn' not know t'em the next day with a bag of coal strapped to their backs, for in them days coal from the Clee Hill pits were carried down the hill on women's shoulders'. Close to one of the tracks leading to the summit of Titterstone Clee it is recorded that there used to be a large flat slab known as the resting stone. Here the women were able to rest without removing their loads from their backs. They then continued down to a mud track road where their burdens were lifted into horsedrawn carts and transported to places as far afield as Hereford. The Clee coal was of a good quality and as the nineteenth-century writer Plymley noted, such was the demand that 'the inhabitants [of south Shropshire and north Herefordshire] purchase at great expense the land carriage coal from the Clee Hills'. In the nineteenth century regular roads were constructed and later inclined planes were built from Bitterley to the summit of Titterstone Clee and from Ditton Priors to the summit of Brown Clee. Though long since abandoned, remnants of the steep access slopes used by these railways can still be clearly identified.

The caps of the two Clees are made of basalt, known locally as dhu-stone (which means 'black' in Welsh), and there is a small industrial settlement on Titterstone Clee with the same name. This stone was much prized for both building and road construction in the past; Thomas Telford spoke highly of its qualities and used it extensively. Ironically, the very strength and resistivity of the dhu-stone has made it less attractive as a road covering in recent years. Poorer stones are preferred today as they break a little as they wear and provide a better surface for modern tyres, so now the use of Clee hill stone is restricted to minor and estate roads. Some local villages, including the churches, are built almost exclusively of dhu-stone. When weathered, the stone turns a grey-brown colour, giving the villages and walled fields a rather sombre appearance, but like most local stone it blends harmoniously into the landscape.

The Clee hill industries were relatively short lived, but during the late nineteenth century men came to work here from various parts of England, Wales, Ireland and Scotland and it is estimated that there was a working population of between fifteen hundred and two thousand. Once they arrived they were isolated, because of the poor roads and a journey to Ludlow and back, only ten miles away, would have taken a full day. As a result, a particular Clee hill dialect developed which was a conglomeration of dialects from various regions in Britain. Alfred Jenkins has recently produced a book recording the dialect, at its richest between 1890 and 1939, but which has now all but disappeared.

The Early Iron Industry

The iron industry in the Shropshire coalfield began during the Middle Ages. However, coal was the first of the mineral resources of east Shropshire to be exploited on a large scale. The Cistercian monks of Buildwas Abbey were granted rights to mine coal by Philip de Benthall in 1250, while the Cluniacs of Much Wenlock in 1322 allowed Walter de Caldbrook to mine coal at the Brockholes in Madeley parish. At the time of the dissolution of the monasteries the monks of Wombridge had an income of £5 a year from their mines. Later in the sixteenth century Leland noted, 'Coles be digged hard by Wombridge where the Priory was', and Camden regarded Oakengates as 'a small village of some note for the pit cole'. In Donnington township in Lilleshall parish there was a 'Colpytt Way' as early as 1592. By the late sixteenth century in the Severn gorge, and particularly in the parishes south of the river, the coal industry had developed into a highly organised and well capitalised enterprise.

It is recorded in 1397 that James 'Mynor' of Derbyshire obtained Crown permission to work a mine of copper and silver within the lordship (Wenlock Edge) of Wenlock Priory. In 1540 Wenlock was working two iron foundries as well as the ironstone quarries in Shirlett Forest. An early record of iron working dates from 1559 when a man was killed digging in the Shirlett mines. Wenlock Priory also had coal mines in Little Wenlock by the early sixteenth century. Most significant of all, the Buildwas monks had a small iron forge on their demesne in the sixteenth century, possibly representing the beginnings of the Coalbrookdale iron industry. At the dissolution these iron works were taken over and developed by families such as the Reynolds, the Baldwins and later the Darbys, all names closely linked with the Industrial Revolution.

During the sixteenth century there was a burst of industrial activity in the Marches, starting near the river Severn and spreading westwards. This industry was based on charcoal blast furnaces, generally sponsored by local landowners. The blast furnace first appeared in England at the end of the fifteenth century, but it was almost a century before it completely replaced the ancient and unreliable bloomery process in the Marches, thus making way for the later developments in the iron industry. Like most early industry, iron making was to be found on rivers and streams, generally close to the sources of raw material and power to work the bellows. Accordingly, we find the iron industry developing in comparatively remote places during the sixteenth and seventeenth centuries.

The first Shropshire blast furnace was built on Shirlett Common in the 1540s, another was built by the Earl of Shrewsbury on the edge of the coalfield near Shifnal in 1564, and a third at Cleobury Mortimer was built by the Earl of Dudley, at about the same time. Others were built at Lilleshall (1591) and Bringewood (1601). The old blast furnace at Coalbrookdale, which may justly be considered the most famous in the world, was originally built by Sir Basil Brooke, lord of Madeley Manor, in 1638. Later furnaces were built at Bouldon (1644) and Willey (1658). The Shropshire iron works formed part of a network which extended from the Lake District down to South Wales.

The development of the iron industry rapidly led to the exhaustion of the remaining supplies of local timber. As early as 1561 a licence was granted to Sir William Acton to fell trees necessary for making iron and to sell timber from Shirlett for his 'lately buylded and set up iron mills in Morveld [Morville]'. Because of the shortage of timber, Crown authority was required to clear woodland within fourteen miles of the river Severn at this time. Supplies of accessible timber required for the emerging iron and glass industries were largely provided from newly planted coppices. With the widespread creation of iron furnaces between Willey Park to the east and Bringewood in the west, the first attempts at controlled coppicing for industrial purposes were made. In 1550 Richard Minton and Richard Stokes coppiced an area of pasture in Shirlett Forest valued at £7. In 1583 a coppice in the Earl's Wood, Shirlett, 'was enclosed and fenced . . . and contained 1000 trees then standing and growing'; within ten years the coppice had doubled in size. In the early seventeenth century the inhabitants of Ludlow complained bitterly about the clearance of wood on Bringewood Chase for use in the Bringewood furnace, since they claimed it was common land. By 1650 there were regular coppices throughout south Shropshire and northern Herefordshire, found mainly on the valley slopes and escarpments.

From the mid seventeenth century onwards charcoal, which was made from wood of up to twenty years' growth, was obtained from coppices where young trees were grown as a crop. There is an interesting description of coppicing at Gilbert's Wood, Abbey Dore, during the late seventeenth century, where it is recorded that it took three cords of wood to make a load of 'coal', and that the purchases of the wood must have 'reasonable and convenient wayes allowed . . . for the cariadge of the cole ariseinge of the woode . . . with libertie to take turf, buyld cabbeines, make coal pittes and such other necessaries for cutting of the said wood and makeinge of the said cole'.

As late as 1728 a survey of his lands by the lord of Ditton Priors was undertaken to determine how much coppice wood could be grown for the local iron furnaces, and during the mid eighteenth century some 12% of the parish was coppiced. Once established, the coppices became important, not only for the iron furnaces, but also for other industrial processes, as well as for that perennial consumer, the building industry. An enquiry into the state of Shropshire woodlands in 1791 clearly demonstrated the exhaustion of other forms of woodland, even hedgerow trees, which led to an ever-increasing dependence on coppice wood. One remedy that seems to have been applied was to plant a number of different tree species in newly created enclosure hedges. Much of Shropshire's surviving woodland was originally planted for the iron industry, and ironically some of the most densely wooded parts of the county, such as the area to the south of Wellington, owe their tree cover to the requirements of the charcoal blast furnace.

Many charcoal furnaces enjoyed only short lives, leaving few visible traces of their activity. The site of a small remotely sited seventeenth-century furnace at Abdon is represented today by overgrown trackways and a wooded dingle with a slag floor. However, the furnace footings are still there to be sought out, the furnace pond and weir can still be identified, and there is an abandoned road between the site and the deserted village of Abdon, which lies half a mile to the east. Abdon furnace was operating in 1654 when Sir Humphrey Briggs had 'liberty of getting and carrying away all mines of ironstone off the Brown Clee hill', but by the end of the seventeenth century the furnace had ceased to function. There were other furnaces in the region, at Bouldon, Charlcotte, and Bringewood, the latter lying on the river Teme a few miles west of Ludlow. During the eighteenth century these furnaces were all operated by the Knight family of Downton. Some of the iron was treated in local forges such as those at Wrickton, Prescott and Cleobury Mortimer, but a considerable quantity was carried by cart to Bridgnorth and afterwards by barge to Stourbridge.

At its height, the Charlcotte furnace produced over 400 tons of iron annually, while Bringewood was making considerably more. Charlcotte is the best preserved of the three furnaces. The site, occupying a typical valley setting on the Clee Brook, consists of a fine stone-built furnace approximately twenty feet square and twenty-four feet high, with the foundations of an ore house to the north. Although the hearth has gone, the interior of the furnace is in good condition. Huge tree-covered mounds of charcoal furnace slag surround the site and give the farm its modern name of Cinder Hill. In the second half of the eighteenth century Charlcotte, however, drew upon coppice wood from increasingly distant parts and, being unable to compete with the coalfield furnaces, finally closed at the end of the eighteenth century. Bouldon furnace appears to have stopped iron production at about the same time, when it was converted into a papermill. Today there is little legacy of the iron works at Bouldon. Only the formidable mill wheel from Coalbrookdale and the tree-covered slag heap behind the mill bear testimony to the former ironworks here.

The same cannot be said of Bringewood, for although the furnace and

72 Forge Bridge over the river Teme at Bringewood in Herefordshire. Built in 1772 for the Knight family's industrial activities in the vicinity, it was designed by an accomplished local surveyor, Thomas Farnold Pritchard

its buildings are now largely gone, there remains a magnificent eighteenth-century bridge across the Teme as a monument to the early ironmasters. In this remote spot the Knight family developed as major ironmasters, making cannons during the Civil War and incidentally producing cast-iron tomb slabs, several of which are to be found outside the little church at nearby Burrington. This collection, the earliest of which dates back to 1619, is the finest of its kind outside the Kentish Weald. Elsewhere other subtle reminders of the early iron industry litter the banks of the Teme. Originally, the Knights lived at Bringewood Hall, but later moved to Downton, where Richard Payne Knight, virtuoso, archaeologist and poet, whose ideas on parkland landscapes we have already come across, designed and built Downton Castle (1772–8), one of the first castellated romantic buildings in England. Later an imposing church was built in the castle grounds and the northern banks of the Teme were extensively landscaped. Two bridges were built across the gorge to link the house with the iron works, one of which used to carry the Ludlow to Leintwardine road until it was diverted to avoid the castle. This fine, absolutely isolated bridge is one of the marvels of the Borderland.

Close by, the school, chapel, houses and iron works are also deserted and are gradually sinking into the tranquil wooded landscape. Below the bridge there is a small wharf and a little further downstream there are the remains of a tin-plating works; both are now completely overgrown and forgotten and large numbers of exotic flowers and shrubs grow on both sides of the Teme. This part of the park was now run wild, and it is one of the most delightful and completely rural spots in the whole of the Welsh Marches.

73 Downton Castle at Downton-on-the-Rock, which was built by Richard Payne Knight on the proceeds of the Knight iron furnaces, sits at the centre of an area of extensive exotic landscaping

Ironbridge, Coalbrookdale and the Shropshire Coalfield

In his *History of Salop*, published in 1837, Charles Hulbert described Coalbrookdale as 'the most extraordinary district in the world'. Coalbrookdale and the Ironbridge still have a charisma which is derived from their striking geography and their unique industrial history. The Ironbridge gorge was formed by the river Severn cutting through the southern extension of Wenlock Edge, revealing seams of coal, ironstone, clay and limestone in the process. The close juxtaposition of these resources, together with the potential for transport provided by the river, gave the area all the characteristics required for the industrial explosion which occurred during the eighteenth century. Such was the speed of industrial development on the Shropshire coalfield that by the late eighteenth century it was the premier iron-producing region in Great Britain.

74 The Ironbridge, which was opened on New Year's Day 1781, is Britain's outstanding industrial monument. It now forms the centrepiece of the Ironbridge Gorge Museum

To begin with, in the seventeenth and early eighteenth centuries, industrial activity concentrated on the Coalbrookdale, a narrow valley which runs north from the gorge, where the first Abraham Darby set up his furnace in 1708. The frenzy of activity that followed led to the area attracting numerous visitors both from home and abroad. In a very full description of Coalbrookdale written in 1801 by an unknown author, the Dale is described thus:

> The works and the vicinity are frequently visited by numbers of people, of most ranks and stations in life, who seem much astonished at the extensiveness of the Manufactory, and the regularity with which it is conducted, oft expressing their surprise that a situation so passing excellent, should be fix'd upon for the seat of so large a Manufactory, but these ideas generally vanish, when they are inform'd that they are situated amidst ev'ry requisite for the purpose of carrying them on, viz. Coals, Ironstone, Limestone and Water. Also the beautiful River Severn washing the bottom for the beneficial purpose of conveying the Goods to Market.

It was indeed the river Severn which provided the economic lifeline for the coalfield industries. For, despite the erratic and sometimes dangerous nature of the Severn, the Shropshire coalfield was essentially part of a riverside economy until the coming of the railways. The Severn provided easy and direct access to markets as far away as Bristol, more than eighty miles from Coalbrookdale. The river carried Shropshire coal downstream to Tewkesbury and upstream to Shrewsbury and mid-Wales and was the principal means of communication between the many iron works of the Borderland.

75 *The Coalbrookdale warehouses linking Severn barges with a tramway from the Coalbrookdale ironworks*

From the ports of the upper Severn, Uffington, Shrewsbury, Montford, Landrinio, Pool Quay and Clawdd Coch, road links extended into Wales, Cheshire and the north-west. To Bridgnorth and Bewdley, the ports of the mid-Severn, came pack-horses and wagons with textiles from Manchester and earthenware from north Staffordshire. Goods such as tobacco pipes from Broseley were distributed throughout the Midlands by barge and mugs from Jackfield ceramic works gave their name to a number of inns along the length of the river. Often, however, cargoes could not be brought directly to or from the Severn gorge itself because road access was so bad; indeed, iron from Coalbrookdale bound for Stafford, to the north-east, was sometimes sent by road several miles south to Bridgnorth before being offloaded on to barges to travel upriver to its final destination, passing through the Severn gorge on the way! The carriage of wine, tea, spirits and tobacco also created important commercial ties between Shropshire and Bristol. The Severn's tributaries extended the communication network, the Avon took Shropshire coal to Pershore and iron goods to Stratford, while the Wye conveyed a variety of cargoes to iron works near their mouths and the Vyrnwy took barges as far as Llanymynech.

The Coalbrookdale blast furnace which stood in ruins after an explosion was leased by Abraham Darby I in 1708. Darby had been born in the Black Country, but had moved to Coalbrookdale from an iron foundry in Bristol. He rebuilt the furnace and began to smelt iron using locally made coke rather than the traditional charcoal. Although the Coalbrookdale iron was suitable for making castings it did not produce good wrought iron; however, before he died in 1717, Darby had built a second furnace at Coalbrookdale and within a decade the Dale was producing a wide range of products which were distributed throughout the Midlands. Darby's successors continued to refine the iron-making process and the Shropshire iron industry was given a particular boost in 1756 with the outbreak of the Seven Years War. By 1760 there were nine furnaces operating in the region and Shropshire was well on its way to being the principal iron-producing area in the country.

Although the Darby family acted as a catalyst for industrial innovation in Coalbrookdale and the Shropshire coalfield, there had been important developments before their arrival. Wooden rails seem to have been used as early as 1605 at Broseley, when they were the objects of 'riotous behaviour', and in 1711 the Revd Francis Brokesby was able to write about a sophisticated railway system at Madeley where 'small carriages with four wheels' were 'thrust by men . . . along long underground passages to the boats on the Severn'. In the mid eighteenth century a plan for a wagonway between Little Wenlock and Coalbrookdale was proposed in order that 'coals may be conveyed in the easiest and best manner, to make a wagonway and lay rails on sleepers in such a manner as is commonly used, and with coal wagons and horses and oxen to draw the same on or along the said railway to Coalbrookdale'. It was Abraham Darby II, son of the original Abraham Darby, who extended the railway system, dramatically cutting transport costs in the Dale as a consequence. A little later Richard Reynolds began to replace the wooden rails with iron rails and between 1768 and 1771 it is reported that Reynolds was responsible for the laying of some 800 tons of cast-iron rails in the Shropshire coalfield. The new rails linked the iron-ore fields at Dawley with the coalfield and the furnaces, and by 1785 there were twenty miles of rail in Coalbrookdale.

Among other innovations, John Wilkinson launched the first iron boat called *The Trial* in 1787 and in 1802 Richard Trevithick built a steam railway locomotive. A little earlier, in 1784, Lord Dundonald made coke using enclosed ovens; this had the effect of condensing the gases which were given off and could then be used to produce tar and varnish. By the end of the eighteenth century there were proposals to diversify industrial activity on the coalfields by producing soda, glass, fertilisers, dye stuffs and soap. The first porcelain manufacture was established at Caughley in 1772 by Thomas Turner.

In 1773 Thomas Farnolls Pritchard, a Shrewsbury architect, approached the ironmaster John Wilkinson suggesting the building of an iron bridge in the Severn gorge. Pritchard (born 1723) had been responsible for a variety of important buildings in Shropshire and neighbouring counties. He was surveyor in 1772 for the fine bridge over the river Teme at Bringewood Forge, and in 1773–5 he designed a bridge over the Severn at Stourport which appears to have used iron as a foundation for the masonry spans.

An act of parliament was passed in February 1776 to enable the building of the first iron bridge. Because of the various delays in implementing the act there is some confusion about precisely what role Pritchard played in the bridge that finally emerged. It does seem probable, however, that he contributed substantially to the design of the bridge as it was finally built, but that the iron founder Abraham Darby III, who actually made the bridge, was also deeply involved in its design. It appears that at least part of the bridge was fired in a modified version of the old furnace at Coalbrookdale. The Ironbridge was eventually opened on New Year's Day 1781, at a cost of £2737 4s. 4d. which compared most unfavourably with the estimate of £550 put forward just five years earlier. The bridge rapidly became an attraction to sightseers. In October 1781 a regular stagecoach service, 'The Diligence', began to cross the Ironbridge on its way to Shrewsbury from London via Broseley and in the nineteenth century several other stagecoach services including one from Liverpool to Bath used the bridge. One proprietor in the 1790s advertised his service by extolling 'that striking specimen of art and so much admired object of travellers', the Ironbridge across which his coaches passed.

76 A nineteenth-century photograph of the Coalport inclined plane, taken when it was still working

77 St Michael's Church, Madeley, built by Thomas Telford in 1796. Madeley now forms part of Telford New Town

The little town of Ironbridge grew up on the eastern banks of the Severn by the new bridge and a little further down stream another new town developed at Coalport. Coalport was the creation of William Reynolds, one of the most influential eighteenth-century Shropshire ironmasters. The town developed at the junction between the Shropshire Canal and the river Severn and it was to this point that Reynolds brought china manufacturing, chain making and boat building. At Coalport there is another wonder of the coalfield, the Coalport inclined plane. This was the means by which canal boats were raised and lowered through a vertical height of 207 feet between the end of the Shropshire Canal and the Coalport basin on the banks of the Severn. Tug boats were floated on to cradles on wheels which were carried up and down the incline on rails. At the top of the incline a steam engine pulled the cradles and boats out of the water. Generally the heavier load from the top was used to draw up the lighter load from the bottom. In cases where the load from the bottom was the heavier, the steam engine was used. An incline was able to pass a pair of five- or six-ton boats in three and a half minutes compared with three or four hours that would have been required if conventional locks had been used. The incline was fully operational by 1793 and in use for about a hundred years.

At the foot of this incline, and driven under it, is the famous Tar Tunnel, begun by William Reynolds, who, unaware of the presence of tar, hoped to connect up with the lower workings of some pits at Blists hill and so obtain easy loading into river boats on the Severn. The walls of this tunnel discharged a tarry petroleum substance for a number of years which was 'exported in large quantities to all parts of Europe'. The Tar Tunnel appears to have been constructed about 1787 and when the tar spring was first located the flow averaged about a thousand gallons a week, although within a few years it had considerably diminished.

78 Pontcysyllte aqueduct, which carries the Shropshire Union Canal over the river Dee. The aqueduct was one of Thomas Telford's great achievements in the Welsh Marches

However, the flame that had been ignited in rural Shropshire rapidly moved on to areas with richer deposits and better communications, where increasingly specialised industries could be better served. In 1805 the area was producing some 50,000 tons of iron a year, representing 20 per cent of the national output, but by 1869, the coalfield's peak year of production, its 200,000 tons of iron accounted for only 2 per cent the national output. This relative decline was followed by an absolute one, and although industries continued to diversify within a century, iron production in the area had virtually ceased. The last iron was smelted in Shropshire in 1959 and in the 1960s the coalfield presented a sorry sight: waste and slag tips, the unkempt ruins of furnaces and kilns, delapidated industrial housing, the ceramic manufacturing settlement of Jackfield gradually sliding into the Severn and the Ironbridge itself breaking up. However, over the past fifteen years, a second miracle has occurred. As part of Telford New Town, the Ironbridge Gorge Museum Trust has energetically set about restoring the industrial monuments and buildings and has in the process again made this region one of the most interesting and exciting in Europe.

Places to Visit

Ironbridge and the Ironbridge Gorge Museum Trust

Ironbridge grew up at the eastern end of Abraham Darby's first cast-iron bridge which was opened on New Year's Day 1781. It was a small industrial new town which profited greatly from the Coalbrookdale and Ironbridge gorge industries. During the twentieth century, however, the little town, along with its associated industries, fell into a deep decline and was in a state of considerable depression until the late 1960s. It was at this stage that work began on Telford New Town with the intention of creating a completely new industrial community on the ruins of the old. Since then the town of Ironbridge has revived considerably as a tourist and educational centre, and the area around it has rapidly been transformed into one of the most impressive open-air museums anywhere in the world.

The core of the museum is at Blists hill which was at the top of the major inclined plane carrying barges from the river Severn to the Shropshire coalfield. Here a considerable number of major industrial attractions have either been restored or reconstructed, including the Blists hill iron furnaces and the Hay inclined plane. Also incorporated within the museum now are Abraham Darby's original Coalbrookdale works and the furnace where he first successfully smelted iron ore, using coke instead of charcoal. In addition there are numerous other attractions dating from the Industrial Revolution including the Coalport china works, the Jackfield ceramic works and tile museum, the Severn wharf and warehouses and the world's first iron bridge. The Ironbridge Gorge Museum provides a welcome success story against the background of a new town valiantly trying to survive in difficult circumstances during the late twentieth century.

CHAPTER TWELVE

Twentieth-century Postscript

Agriculture and the Landscape

Despite many changes, the Borderland remains essentially rural and agriculture is still the dominant economic activity, although agricultural depression of the late nineteenth and early twentieth centuries affected the Marches as it did the rest of the country. One of the results of this rural depopulation has been a feature of the more remote parts of the region until very recently. The rural population of Herefordshire dropped by 22% between 1871 and 1931, and in the moorland areas of the Black Mountains this figure reached just below 50%. Some upland farms were abandoned as the height at which profitable agricultural activity could take place dropped, just as it had done during the later Middle Ages, and the result was that moorland which had been enthusiastically enclosed during the nineteenth century was now left to revert to waste in many marginal areas.

The mechanisation of agriculture since the First World War accelerated the process and the 'ploughing up' campaign of the Second World War only partially halted the drift. After about 1960, however, the pattern began to change. A number of factors combined to make the rural Marches more attractive and to reverse the trend of depopulation. Improved communications through better metalled roads and universal motor transport meant that even the most remote parts of the Marches were within one hour's drive of a market town. The provision of piped water throughout the region led to an immediate improvement in living conditions; added to which the quality of the Marcher landscape has recently begun to be better appreciated. Many former agricultural and industrial labourers cottages have been taken over as retirement or holiday homes. Around the larger towns of Hereford, Chester, Shrewsbury and Telford many villages now act as dormitory settlements for commuters, although in a number of cases this had led to insensitive house building programmes which have effectively ruined the visual attraction of some villages. On the Clee hills former squatter cottages are now occupied by people who travel to work in the West Midland conurbation just twenty miles to the east. These developments in the rural landscape may be viewed as a mixed blessing, but they are bringing life, money and interest back to many parts of the Marches which were in danger of dying.

79 *The detached medieval bell tower of St Mary's church, Pembridge. Such bell towers are a curiosity of the Herefordshire landscape – there are six more in the county*

The face of agriculture, too, has been changing. The Marches remain predominantly an area of mixed farming with an emphasis on dairy and sheep farming in the upland areas, but new crops and techniques have been introduced. Between the wars sugar beet was developed as a major cash crop and more recently the unpleasant yellow oil-seed rape has made a spirited entrance. Neither has the Borderland been immune from other worrying agricultural developments. The removal of hedgerows is common, and some parts of the Herefordshire plain and eastern Shropshire now have areas of prairie farming reminiscent of East Anglia. The EEC farming policy has meant that large areas of permanent pasture have been ploughed up and planted with cereal crops and wheat now grows at altitudes unheard of since the early Middle Ages. Because of its gentle aspect, Herefordshire has been particularly badly affected, but even in upland areas of Shropshire such as the Clun Forest, valley sides with slopes that previously seemed quite impossible to plough are now contributing to the European surplus. Policies designed to help poor European peasant farmers improve their land and yields are also being ruthlessly applied to precious and dwindling areas of marsh and moor. Since the Second World War, pressure on the upland areas has also come from the Forestry Commission, who have created dark coniferous deserts in areas of former moorland and mixed woodland.

Quarrying and Mining

Quarrying, which has been a feature of the Borderlands over the centuries, also presents a threat to the landscape, primarily because of the scale of contemporary operations. The eastern section of Wenlock Edge is being systematically removed, as are a number of other hills such as the Breiddens and the summit of Titterstone Clee hill, while in Herefordshire the destruction of the interior of the massive hillfort at Sutton Walls by quarrying is a disgraceful story that has recently been emulated in some other places. The extraction of sand and gravel from the river terraces of the Severn and Wye has so far been only on a relatively modest scale, but needs careful monitoring if the errors committed elsewhere in the country are not to be sadly repeated.

The picture, however, is not completely bleak. Areas of former quarrying and mining activity, such as the coalmines of eastern Shropshire and the scarred lead mining district around Minsterley, are being either landscaped or allowed to heal themselves peacefully.

Towns in the Late Twentieth Century

The fate of the Border towns during this century mirrors that of the countryside on which they have depended so much. Until 1939 there was a general picture of stagnation or even decline, a decline that continued after the war in small western market towns such as Bishop's Castle and Kington, and which has only recently been reversed. In the 1960s ambitious schemes for redeveloping the two county towns began. In Shrewsbury the cumbersome, but not unlovely, Victorian market hall was demolished and replaced by an equally cumbersome but very unlovely edifice. There were other casualties, though, including some fine half-timbered buildings which were demolished in order to provide 'improved' shopping facilities and to make motoring in the centre of town easier. Fortunately the complexity of the medieval road system, together with the virtually insurmountable problems posed by the geography of the site on which Shrewsbury sits, have thwarted all attempts to bring more cars rapidly into the town centre by way of an inner ring road. At the time of writing, an uneasy truce prevails, with a pedestrian precinct occupying the historic core of the town.

Hereford has not fared so well. Not only has it lost more historical buildings, but its geography has not proved to be a match against the penetrative power of the motor car. An inner ring road following the line of the city's medieval walls creates a *cordon sanitaire* between the much mutilated historic centre and the suburbs. Despite this the city centre is not without charm and, like Shrewsbury, possesses a traffic-free area.

The process of redevelopment has not permeated far enough down the urban hierarchy to have done much serious damage to the smaller Marcher towns. However, despite strenuous efforts to achieve the impossible and damage Ludlow's matchless townscape, it has survived largely intact. Even further down the scale there are some of the finest small towns or large villages to be found anywhere in Britain. High on the list must come Weobley, where not only has the town's medieval layout been preserved, but many fine half-timbered houses survive. Nearby Pembridge, with its detached belltower (one of seven in Hereforshire), runs it a close second.

The most dramatic urban development in the region has been the creation of a completely new city based on the debris of the Shropshire coalfield. Telford, which is now the most populous settlement in the Marches, was created in order to relieve urban congestion from around Birmingham and Wolverhampton and provide an alternative industrial base to the Black Country. The old centres of Dawley, Madely, Oakengates and Wellington were to be welded together with their surrounding largely derelict industrial landscapes to make Britain's twenty-first post-war new town with a population of just under a quarter of a million. Since work started on the scheme in the mid sixties, however, the economic climate has changed greatly, and not only is the West Midlands conurbation no longer seeking to accommodate its overspill, it is actually fighting for its own economic life. Industrial Telford has therefore suffered with the rest of industrial Britain, and has a very high level of unemployment. Telford's predicted population has now been revised to 150,000 by the mid nineties.

Telford has also suffered from the traditional Marchland malaise of isolation – the M54 linking the town with the national motorway system was not opened until 1984. The only other stretch of motorway in the region, the M50, runs irrelevantly, as far as the Marches is concerned, across southern Herefordshire, joining the M5 to south Wales. Visually Telford suffers from the same problem experienced by similar developments elsewhere, and some of the early housing schemes were particularly unfortunate as they used cheap materials which have rapidly deteriorated. But if Telford cannot be judged an unqualified success neither is it an unqualified failure. The grain of the landscape on which the new town sits is being used to good effect to create spacious tree-covered vistas which are as pleasant as any to be found in a modern town anywhere in the country. Ironbridge and the Severn gorge which form Telford's southern boundary, are now as healthy as at any time since the nineteenth century, and certainly more attractive. Much of this improvement can be attributed to the work of the Ironbridge Gorge Museum Trust, which is conserving monuments of the Industrial Revolution many of which would have been discarded as worthless until very recently. This has resulted in the influx of tens of thousands of visitors to the area, justly making it one of the most popular tourist centres in the whole of the Marches.

Conservation and Tourism

Attitudes to the Border landscape and its past have changed markedly over the past twenty years. This is particularly true in the towns, where a number of factors have combined to promote the preservation of historic buildings. Large-scale redevelopment has become too costly and many have come to question its desirability. The steady growth of tourism as a major source of income and employment has also encouraged preservation rather than destruction. Added to which the changing national attitude expressed through legislation has worked towards the preservation of our historic heritage.

In Shrewsbury, for example, the restoration of the Bear Steps in the heart of the historic town in 1972 set the pattern for the adaptive reuse of historic buildings. Subsequently, new and profitable uses have been found for a variety of buildings, including the medieval timber houses in Barracks Passage, the medieval church of St Julian and more recently the Victorian edifice which dominates the town's river view, the Royal Salop Infirmary. Rowley's Mansion (1618), the first brick building in the borough, and the adjoining Tudor building known as Rowley's House have recently been restored to accommodate the town museum. Finally, the restoration of the Shrewsbury Library, formerly Shrewsbury School, has been the largest, most ambitious, most expensive, and most successful conservation scheme ever undertaken in the town. Throughout the Marches similar, if more modest, schemes have been enacted. Another development which reflects the changed attitude to the past has been the creation of several new museums to add to those founded in the nineteenth century. Apart from the Ironbridge Gorge Museum, a section of the Severn Valley Railway has been reopened: some thirteen miles of track between Bridgnorth and Bewdley carry steam trains through magnificent countryside down the Severn valley. A farm museum has opened at Acton Scott and a museum of cider in Hereford. Along the western length of the Marches runs the Offa's Dyke Path which was opened as a long-distance footpath in 1971 and provides access to some of the wildest and most dramatic scenery in England.

The story of landscape preservation in the Marches is, perhaps inevitably, not such a happy one. Pressures on the countryside continue to take their toll on historic features and natural habitats. Nevertheless the Marches do have their share of Sites of Special Scientific Interest, which are part of an attempt to preserve a representative example of environments rich in both historical sites and flora and fauna. One of these is Moccas Deer Park to the west of Hereford, where a management agreement is working to maintain the balance between modern estate management techniques and the conservation of rare trees and insects within the context of a surviving medieval deer park.

80 Tranquil village scene at Eardisley, Herefordshire

Conscious conservation can only go so far; economic reality will ensure that the Marches do not become one massive museum. It is up to all of us to make sure that any changes respect the integrity of the unique Border landscape. There has always been change and change there will always be.

On Wenlock Edge the wood's in trouble;
His forest fleece the Wrekin heaves;
The gale, it plies the saplings double,
And thick on Severn snow the leaves.

'Twould blow like this through holt and hanger
When Uricon the city stood:
'Tis the old wind in the old anger,
But then it threshed another wood.

Then, 'twas before my time, the Roman
At yonder heaving hill would stare:
The blood that warms on English yeoman,
The thoughts that hurt him, they were there.

There, like the wind through woods in riot,
Through him the gale of life blew high;
The tree of man was never quiet:
Then 'twas the Roman, now 'tis I.

The gale, it plies the saplings double,
It blows so hard, 'twill soon be gone:
To-day the Roman and his trouble
Are ashes under Uricon.

(from *A Shropshire Lad* – A. E. Housman)

Further Reading

Brook, Fred, *Industrial Archaeology of Britain: West Midlands* (Batsford, 1977)

Davies, Wendy, *Wales in the Early Middle Ages* (Leicester University Press, 1982)

Finberg, H. P. R., *The Early Charters of the West Midlands* (Leicester University Press, 1961)

Fox, Sir Cyril, *Offa's Dyke* (Oxford University Press, 1955)

Gelling, Margaret, *Signposts to the Past* (J. M. Dent, 1978)

Houlder, Christopher, *Wales: An Archaeological Guide* (Faber & Faber, 1974)

Millward, Roy & Robinson, Adrian, *Welsh Borders* (Eyre Methuen, 1978)

Pevsner, N., *The Buildings of England: Herefordshire* (Penguin, 1963)

Pevsner, N., *The Buildings of England: Shropshire* (Penguin, 1958)

Plomer, William (Ed)., *Kilvert's Diary* (Penguin, 1977)

Rees, William, *An Historical Atlas of Wales* (Faber & Faber, 1959)

Rowley, Trevor, *The Shropshire Landscape*, (Hodder & Stoughton, 1972)

Stanford, S. C., *Welsh Marches* (Collins, 1980)

Tonkin, Jim W., *Herefordshire* (Batsford, 1977)

Trinder, Barrie S., *Industrial Revolution in Shropshire* (Phillimore, 1973)

Trinder, Barrie S., *History of Shropshire* (Phillimore, 1983)

Index

94